IN BLOOD

BETRAYAL IN BLOOD

THE MURDER OF TABATHA BRYANT

MICHAEL BENSON

PINNACLE BOOKS
Kensington Publishing Corp.
http://www.kensingtonbooks.com

PINNACLE BOOKS are published by

Kensington Publishing Corp.
850 Third Avenue
New York, NY 10022

Copyright © 2006 by Michael Benson

All Kensington Titles, Imprints, and Distributed Lines are available at special quantity discounts for bulk purchases for sales promotions, premiums, fund-raising, and educational or institutional use. Special book excerpts or customized printings can also be created to fit specific needs. For details, write or phone the office of the Kensington special sales manager: Kensington Publishing Corp., 850 Third Avenue, New York, NY 10022, attn: Special Sales Department, Phone: 1-800-221-2647.

Pinnacle and the P logo Reg. U.S. Pat. & TM Off.

First Printing: May 2006

10 9 8 7 6 5 4 3

Printed in the United States of America

Author's Note

This is a story of a small group of people—related by blood, marriage, and lust—who built their own prisons, bar by bar. Some built theirs out of misguided restlessness, others from drug dependency and jealousy. With their self-made cages complete, their lives spiraled out of control in a tragic maelstrom of betrayal. Today one is dead, two others are in prison until they die, and the other is caged for a long time, now by literal—rather than figurative—bars.

And it is the story of a woman who, in the wake of losing her youngest son in a horrible accident, had to deal with the fact that her oldest son had murdered her youngest daughter. The toll on her children over a five-year span had been horrible. Out of four, two dead, one behind bars.

This book hopes to tell the story of the murder of Tabatha Bryant as a cautionary tale, one that will influence its readers in a positive way. It includes details of the happenings of July 13 and 14, in Penfield, New York, that cannot be found anywhere else, not in the daily reports of the local newspapers or in the sound bites of Rochester's electronic media.

It is based on the recollections of the eyewitnesses I interviewed, on the records of the Monroe County Sheriff's Office of New York, on court transcripts, and other documents acquired during research.

Although this is a true story, some names have been changed to protect the privacy of the innocent. Pseudonyms will be marked as such upon first usage.

When possible, the spoken word has been quoted verbatim. However, when that is not possible, conversations have been reconstructed as closely as possible to reality, based on the recollections of those who spoke and heard those words. In places, there has been slight editing of spoken words, but only to improve readability. The denotations and connotations of the words remain unaltered.

Acknowledgments

The author wishes to acknowledge the cooperation and assistance of the following individuals and groups, without whom the writing of this book would have been impossible: my investigative associate Amy Cavalier, of the Messenger Post Newspapers, agent extraordinaire Jake Elwell, of Wieser and Elwell, my editor Gary Goldstein, the Honorable Patricia D. Marks, Monroe County district attorney Michael Green, court reporters Anthony DiMartino and Judy Ging, Essie Bassett, Leroy Bassett, Cleo and Ginny Winebrenner, Patty Winebrenner and "Little One," Becky Hentges, Samantha Bassett (Tabatha's sister), Tabatha's uncle Terry J. Smith, minister to young adults and families in the Grove City (Ohio) Community of Christ, Michael Zeigler, crime reporter for the Rochester *Democrat and Chronicle*, Corporal John Helfer, public information officer at the Monroe County Sheriff's Office, attorney Charles Testa, Philip Semrau, and Tekla Benson and Bridget Agosta for their help with the photos.

PART I

CHAPTER 1

Penfield

The story takes place in and around Rochester, New York, along the south shore of Lake Ontario, about fifty miles east of Buffalo. Rochester is what's called a medium-sized city, with a population of approximately 250,000. It is the third largest city in the state, behind only New York City and Buffalo.

Rochester grew where it did because it was a prime location. That's where the Genesee River flows into Lake Ontario. Later, it became the spot where the Genesee River crossed the Erie Canal. Rochester was a hub of water transportation. The land that was to become the city of Rochester was first settled in 1803 when Colonel Nathaniel Rochester, Colonel William Fitzhugh, and Major Charles Carroll purchased a one-hundred-acre tract on the west side of the Genesee River. The original settlement was near the falls that now marks the city's downtown area. It was only a few hundred yards from the courthouse where the trial in this case was held. The location was not immediately popular; it was largely swamp with dense forest, and swamp fever, later known as malaria. But the swamp was cleared and buildings were erected. The city took root and grew outward.

The Erie Canal was moved to a new route south of the city, and its name was changed to the Barge Canal. Rochester was no longer there because of water transportation. It found a new raison d'être in cutting-edge technology. Eastman Kodak, Xerox, Bausch & Lomb all made their homes in Rochester. In addition, Wegmans, one of the country's top grocery-store chains, was headquartered in Rochester.

Like many cities in America, during the middle of the twentieth century, suburbs surrounded Rochester as old-time Rochesterians moved out and were replaced by newcomers, often poor minorities, who took their place in the city proper.

Though the city itself had shrunk in population, from 350,000 to 250,000, the metro Rochester area (which included most of Monroe County) had grown by 2003 to a population of close to 1 million. The crime rate in the suburbs was only a fraction of that which law enforcement had to battle in the city. There were, however, lower-middle-class suburbs and middle-class suburbs where the county sheriff's office was kept busy. While crime within the city limits of Rochester was under the jurisdiction of the Rochester Police Department, crimes in Monroe County, but outside the city, were investigated by the Monroe County Sheriff's Office. Despite the boundaries of jurisdiction, the sheriff's headquarters and the Monroe County Hall of Justice, the courthouse, were in Downtown Rochester.

On the other hand, there were sections of Monroe County where crime was practically nonexistent. One town that rarely experienced violent crime was upscale Penfield. The murder profiled here made large headlines, in the beginning, not because of the fascinating tale behind the crime, but because of its location. There hadn't been a murder in Penfield in years.

The biggest problems facing town officials were more commonly: where to install new sidewalks?

The murder occurred in the jurisdiction of the Monroe County Sheriff's Office. That year, the sheriff's office would handle 12,080 crimes, about thirty-five crimes a day. That's not bad when you consider the office patrols thirteen towns, and a population of greater than five hundred thousand. Penfield was not contributing its fair share of those twelve thousand crimes. The murder happened in the unlikeliest of spots: on the main floor of a beautiful two-story home not far from Penfield's country clubs, Shadow Lake and Shadow Pines.

CHAPTER 2

Night of the Full Moon

July 13, 2003, a quiet and hot Sunday night. Eleven o'clock news was over, but it was still hot enough for fans to be on. Sky clear. Moon brighter than the streetlights. Full moon—and the sky speckled with stars. To the east, the sky was black. To the west, the sky above the horizon only darkened to a dusky blue because of the lights from the city, so the stars were harder to see on that side. There was some light traffic on the nearby main thoroughfare, Five Mile Line Road. But things were quiet on Pennicott Circle. Although some of the residents of the street were still up watching television, most had retired for the night. After a summer weekend, folks were going to bed early, getting ready to return to work the following day. Some neighbors were away all together during July and August, living in summer homes.

The street of Pennicott Circle started and ended on the main road, forming a semicircle. All the action that night was in front of the two-story colonial-style white-with-black-trim clapboard house at the corner of Pennicott and Five Mile Line.

The front of the house faced north, toward the entrance to the tract. The east side faced Five Mile Line Road. The west side consisted of the garage and the driveway, which led to the road where Pennicott Circle had just about completed its lap. Behind the house was a large lawn with a well-tended garden. Since the backyard was at basement level, a wooden deck and stairs had been built so that one could get directly from the yard to the main floor through a set of sliding glass doors. On the other side of those doors was the kitchen. The backyard was enclosed on all sides by a six-foot-tall wooden-plank fence, contoured into a wavy curve at the top.

The front door had a small concrete stoop in front of it, but there was no sidewalk leading to that door. In times of mud or snow, it was bothersome to enter the house that way, so the garage functioned as the front door for much of the year—although not so much in July. There were pine trees along the front of the house for privacy. On either side of the front stoop was a row of flowers to decorate the base of the house.

It looked like an idyllic spot. From the outside there were small indications of neglect, however. The outside glass front door was still decorated with sprayed-on artificial snow left over from Christmas. There were finger smears going through it.

Neighbors had heard a commotion on the street earlier in the evening, a lot of yelling, but no one could really be sure from which house it had come. That commotion had died down hours before. Everything was quiet now.

Sometime between eleven and twelve o'clock that night, a deep pink Monte Carlo pulled off the main road onto the circle and pulled into the driveway of number 2. Driving the car was a tiny young female, eighty pounds tops, in her early twenties. She had dirty-blond hair pulled back into a ponytail. She was disheveled, not a relaxed muscle in her body, a rubber band stretched and ready to snap. Her eyes were wide and her face was bruised. The guy sitting next to her in the "shotgun seat" had recently smacked her around. He was in his early twenties. Recently out of the service on a medical discharge, he still had closely cropped hair. He was wearing a black T-shirt with a decal of a dragon ironed onto it under a leather jacket. Across his lap was a .22 Marlin-Glenfield rifle, with the initials *CG* burned into the stock with a wood-burning set. The rifle belonged to the young woman behind the wheel, a gift from her father.

All indications were that things were quiet inside the house. The children, two small boys, were upstairs in bed, asleep. The wife, as was her habit of late, had unfolded the downstairs couch and had gone to sleep in the living room. The husband was awake in bed, reading a Tom Clancy thriller.

Only seconds after midnight, 911 operator Jacqueline Sanabria took her first call of Monday, July 14. She said, "Nine-one-one center."

Kevin Bryant: "Nine-one-one, there's been a shooting and someone is, uh, been shot, been, my wife has been shot. I heard someone screaming. Jesus Christ, there's blood all over the place."

"Your wife has been shot?"

"Yes."

"Who shot your wife?" Sanabria asked.

"I don't know. I didn't see anybody . . . ," Kevin replied.

Jacqueline shifted gears. Enough with who-did-it for the moment, establish the condition of the victim.

"Where is she shot?" she asked.

"It looks like the throat."

"Does she have a pulse?" Sanabria asked.

"No, let me see. I do not feel one. Nope."

There had been less-than-a-second pause between "Let me see" and "Nope," as though there had not been time for the man to check anything.

Sanabria knew it was important to keep the man on the phone for as long as possible, so she kept asking questions. The man identified himself as Kevin C. Bryant. He was forty-five years old. The victim was his wife, Tabatha. The 911 operator was used to dealing with hysterics when reports of dead loved ones came in, but Jacqueline wasn't having that problem with this caller. The husband was not hysterical. In fact, she thought, Kevin Bryant spoke in a strangely calm voice as he explained that he had been reading a Tom Clancy thriller upstairs when he heard noises coming from the living room.

His wife had shouted, "Oh, my God!"

Then, Bryant said, he heard gunshots, screaming, and a car outside pulling away. One of his sons was startled by the sounds and alerted his father that something was wrong. Bryant said he immediately went downstairs and found his wife dead on the pullout couch in the living room, where she had been sleeping.

"Is there anyone who might have wanted to hurt your wife?" Sanabria asked.

Kevin replied, "She has a boyfriend and a friend and we have been having some difficulty and trying to resolve the situation, and, I don't know, she may have had a—"

Jacqueline Sanabria: "She had a boyfriend?"

Kevin: "Well, a friend. I don't, I don't . . ."

"Your wife had a friend?"

"Yes."

"Was she having a problem with him?"

"I do not know. I didn't inquire. I wanted to try to—"

"How old is your wife?"

"Twenty-six."

"Where are you now?"

"I'm sitting right on the bed. She was asleep on the couch. I was sleeping upstairs. Can you send an ambulance?"

At one point during the conversation, Sanabria thought she heard the man on the other end yawn.

"Were there any weapons in the house?" she asked.

"Not that I know of," Kevin answered.

"Stay on the line until emergency personnel arrive," she instructed.

In other words, *don't run away.*

CHAPTER 3

Three Gas Stations

The young woman with the dirty-blond ponytail had stayed behind the driver's wheel while her boyfriend went into the house. She heard a sound— had it been the rifle, the same rifle that had always hurt her ears when she went target shooting?

The sound had not been loud, muffled by the thick walls of the big house, probably not loud enough to cause the neighbors to call the police. Shoot a gun off inside a mobile home and the whole court wakes up, although in some lots it is unlikely that anyone will call the cops.

She would say later that the sharp sound reminded her a bit of a champagne cork popping out of a bottle. Looking at her, you wouldn't figure her for an expert in champagne corks—except for maybe those she had heard popping on TV.

Only a few minutes after she heard the sound, her boyfriend came out of the house. He had the gun and, surprisingly, had picked up a new weapon as well. He had a big kitchen knife and she could see in the blue light of the full moon that he was wet, shiny with blood.

The young man threw her gun into the backseat of the car and climbed in. She hit the gas and they high-tailed it for home. From Pennicott Circle, she turned right onto Five Mile Line Road and headed south.

She navigated toward the expressway to take the quickest route home, but she was not thinking clearly. Later, she would almost laugh when she thought about it. Trying so hard to be cool, and they had gotten lost. She got on the expressway going north rather than south, which she didn't realize until she saw signs announcing upcoming exits in the town of Irondequoit, a heavily populated middle-class suburb northeast of Rochester.

She got off the expressway and retraced her path on back roads, back to Penfield. After fifteen minutes of getaway driving, the woman had the car to within a mile of the crime scene. She was freaking out. That blood. They needed to stop.

They needed to clean up. They needed cigarettes. They needed beer. The woman pulled into the parking lot of what would turn out to be a series of gas stations, but they never got out of the car.

"You go," the man said.

The woman, who was very young and appeared even younger, said, "I can't."

"Why not?"

"No ID."

Because of her youthful appearance and size, she knew that she wouldn't be able to buy cigarettes without the kind of photo identification that gas stations demanded. She didn't say if "no ID" meant she was driving without her license.

"I can't go," the man said. He didn't have to say why. He just looked down at himself. He had blood on his clothes. They left the first gas station and drove around.

The woman told the man that she had brought along a spare pair of clothes for him, so he could change, if he wanted to. This, he did, while she drove around Penfield. The truth was that the woman had brought along a change of clothes for herself, too. That wasn't unusual. Her lifestyle was such that she was often away from home overnight. But she had made it through the tough part of the night without soiling her clothes and didn't need to change.

Once he was changed, she pulled into another gas station and the man got out to buy the beer and the cigarettes. The man cracked open the bottle of beer and they shared it. They had cigarettes, and felt a little better.

She pulled out of the gas station parking lot and back onto the road. They had planned to do lines after they got home, but they couldn't hold out that long. They needed a boost bad. The third stop—to sniff coke—they made only one gas station down the road from the second.

Refreshed by the blast, they again headed south. When the woman got to Old Penfield Road, also known as Route 441, she turned right and headed west for a time. This took her to Route 65, also known as Clover Road, where a left-hand turn took her on a southerly route, headed toward Bloomfield.

On Clover Road, they passed a county park known as Mendon Ponds. There, the man rolled his window all the way down, pulled out the big bloody knife, and tossed it out the window. It would never be found.

Again there was blood on his hands from the knife. It was not the blood of a stranger. The woman who had died at the end of that knife and the man with the bloody hands had shared the same mother. She was his half sister.

CHAPTER 4

Blood Was Splattered
Everywhere

By 12:02 A.M., Monroe County sheriff's deputies were on their way to 2 Pennicott Circle in Penfield in response to Kevin Bryant's 911 call. Jacqueline Sanabria kept Kevin talking on his cordless phone until sheriff's deputies arrived at the Bryant home. Only then did she allow the strangely calm man to break the connection. It was approximately 12:08 A.M.

Deputies, noting that there was no walk, crossed the lawn and came into the house through the front door. Straight ahead was a hallway that led to the kitchen. Looking to the left, they saw the minimally decorated living room. The living-room rug was whorehouse red, a strange choice, some of the deputies thought. There, they discovered Tabatha on the foldout couch. She was dead—both shot and stabbed. First job: get the family out of the house.

Kevin called his parents, who came over immediately to pick up the two Bryant boys. Sheriff's deputies sealed the house. Crime scene investigators (CSI) arrived and began the long process of going over every square inch of the home. Within minutes the quiet semicircle street was lined on both sides by official vehicles, some with lights flashing. By this time all of the other residents of Pennicott Circle were out on their lawns. Something had happened at the lawyer's house. No one had heard the popping of the champagne cork.

Kevin wanted to leave with his dad and the boys, but he had to remain behind. Leaving was out of the question. He was going to need to answer just a few questions. Kevin followed a sheriff's deputy out of the house through the garage. Barefoot and still in his blue T-shirt and plaid shorts, Kevin stood out in the driveway. Two deputies accompanied him, one on either side. One of them was Deputy Bridget Davis, a six-year patrol deputy. A systematic grilling of the husband began. The neighbors could see him clearly, the little guy—clear as day out there, with the full moon. Although there were no streetlights on the tract, additional light came from the streetlights and headlights on the nearby main road.

Kevin must have felt like he was in a spotlight. He answered the deputies patiently, but from time to time, he would have to excuse himself in the middle of a question or an answer so he could fold over at the waist and convulse with dry heaves. For three hours he stood there, answering question after question.

In the meantime, inside the house, there was also the occasional sound of retching. Even the hardened members of law enforcement, used to seeing the more unpleasant manifestations of society's underbelly, were shocked by what they saw in the living room of the Bryant house.

The young blonde was still on the bed—actually

the couch that had been pulled out into a bed. She was on her back, her face now a ghastly mask of blood. She had been stabbed repeatedly, including, most noticeably, in the neck, where there was a gaping, and still frothing, wound.

There was also a wound to Tabatha's right eye. As it turned out, her largest wound was in the back of her head, the exit wound, but that wasn't apparent at first.

The attack had been horrifically violent. Blood had splattered in all directions, onto the lamp shade of a nearby table lamp, on the walls—in particular, the north wall—on the ceiling, and onto the blades of a ceiling fan overhead. The splatter, experts surmised, was probably caused mostly by the knife attack. The throat wound looked like it might have severed the jugular. That would have caused a rhythmically squirting wound. The killer had been frenzied and had stabbed the victim many times in a short period of time. The violent pulling out of the knife after each stab and the raising of the knife for the next stab was what sent blood flying onto the ceiling fan.

The medical examiner would later determine that Tabatha had been shot once in the eye and stabbed fourteen times in the neck and upper body. Semen was found on her body.

Crime scene investigators went over the entire home, square inch by square inch. To the right after entering the front door, you went into a small room. Deputies could tell by the scattering of toys that this was a playroom for the kids. Connected to that was the dining room, which went along that side of the house on the bottom. Also, to the right of the living room was another hallway that led to a small bathroom and to a door that led to the garage. Behind the living room was the kitchen, which provided access to the backyard deck through the sliding glass door. Just inside the front door, a little bit to the left, was the flight of stairs that led to the house's upper level. At the head of the stairs, a right-hand turn took you into the master bedroom, where Kevin said he had been reading. Pretty much straight across from the head of the stairs was the upstairs bathroom. To the left was the kids' bedroom, a spare bedroom, and a third bedroom, which had been converted into an office. Once the house was cleared of the Bryants, the deputies checked every room for evidence.

The crime scene investigators who arrived at the murder scene knew one axiom to be true: the truth can often be found in the blood. And that didn't just mean determining how much blood there was, or to whom a drop of blood evidence originally belonged. The matter of where the blood was, and how it was arranged, tended to paint an accurate picture as well.

It was true, killers frenzied enough to cause this kind of mess were often careless enough to cut themselves, leaving their own blood evidence at crime scenes. But puzzles were also solved by analyzing the manner in which the blood had splashed. The splatter patterns told a story.

In addition to the mess in the living room, the only obvious blood were the droplets that led down the hall and across the kitchen. It appeared the killer had been dripping blood as he or she made an immediate exit from the house.

The CSI personnel were used to searching carpets for bloodstains, but that was going to be harder than usual in this case because of the crimson rug.

Each speck of blood had to be identified by location and tested for type. If a second type of blood was found, there was a chance it could be matched later with an accused killer's. Investigators checked to see if there was evidence of ejaculation elsewhere, first in the living room, and then in the rest of the house. They looked carefully for specks of blood elsewhere in the house. A quick scan of the house told them that most of the blood was in the living room, although there were several drops on the flowered linoleum floor of the kitchen, which turned out to belong to the victim.

Those scientists of the county sheriff's office paid particular attention to locations near the house's several sources of running water—bathroom sink and tub, both upstairs and downstairs, kitchen sink, and the outlet for the garden hose at the back of the house. Blood in these areas would indicate that the killer or killers had made an attempt to wash themselves up before fleeing. At this early stage, investigators knew that the husband had called the crime in, and that he claimed the killer or killers had fled before he could get down the stairs to see who they were.

If blood had been found on or near the house's drains and faucets, it would have been an indication that more time had passed between the crime and the phone call than had been indicated by the husband's statements.

Of course, from a police mind-set, just the fact that the victim's husband had reported the crime was suspicious. Add to that the fact that he was offering a seemingly unlikely scenario—attempted burglary, or was it a breaking-and-entering boyfriend? Whatever, it turned—just like that—into savage homicide, on an ultraquiet suburban street.

Deputies doubted right off that Tabatha's killer was a stranger. Whoever did that to her *cared*. Maybe it was love, maybe hate, maybe a combo—but he or she *cared*. There were real feelings involved.

It was a hot-blooded crime. For experienced law enforcement, these things raised the red flag.

After three hours in his driveway, in his shorts, retching every now and again, Kevin Bryant was put into a sheriff's car and taken to the Monroe County Sheriff's Office headquarters in Downtown Rochester. There, his interrogation continued.

Back at Pennicott Circle, the fingerprint experts came in and did their thing, dusting all of the surfaces. Those who lived in the house, including the victim, would need to be fingerprinted so that those prints could be matched against those found by the investigators. They were interested in prints that didn't match the family members. No matter how sure the investigators might have felt at that early hour that the victim's husband had at least something to do with the death of his young and pretty wife, they knew that fingerprints were not going to help their case. Kevin Bryant's fingerprints could have been found on every surface of every room in the entire house and it would have been evidence of nothing. He lived there. Fingerprints could help exonerate Kevin; they couldn't convict him.

Of course, any blood found near the drains would have been evidence that Kevin's scenario wasn't true, but it might not have been evidence that he was the killer. It might have been simply a case of cowardice.

Kevin Bryant was a small man—indeed, one of the smaller men that the members of law enforcement at the scene had seen in some time. He was the sort of man who would have had a lifelong vulnerability to physical threats from men and verbal barbs from women—the sort of man who would compensate, try to achieve power in other ways. Because of his size, it was easy to imagine him as less than courageous in moments of danger—such as when there was an intruder in the house with a gun. Perhaps he had waited until the killer or killers had left the house before he went downstairs, waiting upstairs even as the killers cleaned up. And perhaps now Kevin was afraid to admit to that because he didn't want to expose his cowardice, a weakness theoretically displayed as the life of his wife and the mother of his children hung in the balance.

If the husband had killed his wife, apparently with both a gun and a knife, he would have gotten bloody. There was no indication that Kevin had blood on him at the time sheriff's deputies first responded to his 911 call.

If Kevin Bryant had done it, he'd had some major cleaning up to do. The search went on, in and around the house, for a pile or bag of bloody clothes that someone might have changed out of and dumped. Except for the mess in the living room—the victim's blood splattered outward from the point of attack—and the spot of blood on the kitchen floor, no blood was found in the house—not even near cleanup spots, the various sources of running water.

The only thing suspicious the crime scene investigators found was in a garbage can outside, there was a pair of latex surgical gloves, the kind that come out of a box—perfect for a murderer to wear if he or she didn't want to leave fingerprints. They found DNA evidence in the form of skin cells on those gloves.

Law enforcement gave the house the once-over and there was nothing immediately recognizable at the crime scene that would throw doubt onto Kevin's story— nothing except for the fact that it didn't quite make sense.

PART II

CHAPTER 5

Baby Girls

The story starts a generation before when the victim's mother, waitress Virginia "Ginny" Hentges, got together with the victim's dad, college student Carroll Leroy Bassett—and they were known to everyone as Ginny and Leroy.

Ginny grew up on a farm in Elk River, Minnesota, until she was thirteen. She was the sixth of eight kids. They were, oldest to youngest, Sharon, Roy, Jerry, Sue, Chuck, Ginny, Russ, and Denise. Her dad worked his whole life for the same company in industrial hard-facing.

"They built a new plant down in Iowa when I was thirteen, and that's when we moved," Ginny remembered years later.

Being a rather typical teenager, academics were not at the top of Ginny's priority list: "I went to the first semester of tenth grade, when I quit. I was young and stupid and bored out of my mind, so I didn't finish school then."

Instead, Ginny took a job waiting tables at a restaurant when she was fifteen. "I was a truckin' waitress," Ginny said.

"I worked at the same place as my sister Sue. She was living in Lamoni, Iowa, at the time and I was living there."

She met Leroy Bassett because her sister Sue married his roommate in college, Graceland University. The school was affiliated with the Community of Christ (C of C) Church. That was Sue's first marriage. Sue didn't go to Graceland, but her first husband did. Ginny met Leroy in 1974 and they got married in 1975.

Leroy was from the Southern Tier Region of New York State, south of Lake Ontario and north of the Pennsylvania border. He was the son of Essie and Carol Bassett, of Greenwood, New York, who were likewise affiliated with the Community of Christ Church. Carol had the same name as his son, but they spelled it differently. Essie and Carol had had five children—four girls and Leroy, their only son.

Ginny and Leroy had their first baby on March 20, 1975. The baby girl, whom they named Samantha, nicknamed Sammy, was born in Leon, Iowa, the county seat of Decatur County, which borders Missouri. It is about twenty miles south of Osceola.

A year later, Tabatha "Tabby" Marie Bassett was born in Mount Ayr (pronounced like *air*), Iowa.

Ginny chose the names Samantha and Tabatha for her daughters. Pretty names, but the fact that Ginny chose those two names in particular is revealing. Those names exist in combination in popular culture. They were the names of the mother-and-daughter witches in the 1960s TV comedy series *Bewitched*.

The show ran from 1964 through 1972. It was about a mortal man who married a witch. The husband didn't want his wife to use her magic because he hoped to live a normal suburban existence, but each week the comedic situation inevitably led to Samantha using her powers to resolve the plot. In the end, Darrin loved her anyway.

Actress Elizabeth Montgomery played Samantha Stephens. On January 13, 1966, during episode fifty-four, the Stephenses had a baby, to coincide with Montgomery's real-life pregnancy.

On the show the Stephenses had a daughter and named her Tabitha, with an *i*. But, on the credits that ran at the end of each episode, the baby's name was listed as Tabatha, with an *a*.

It was Montgomery's idea to name the character Tabitha. In an interview published in the February 1967 edition of *Screen Stories*, Montgomery said, "The name was my idea. I loved it, because it was so old-fashioned. I got it from one of the daughters of Edward Andrews, the actor. . . . But, somehow or other, her name came out 'Tabatha' on the credit roll, and that's the way it's been ever since. Honestly, I shudder every time I see it. It's like a squeaky piece of chalk scratching on my nerves."

After twenty-one episodes of mystery, it was revealed, to tremendous ratings, that the baby, like her mother, had supernatural powers. In 1967, at Montgomery's insistence, the spelling of the character's name was changed to "Tabitha" on the end credits—a correction that Ginny Bassett apparently did not notice.

When her second daughter was born, Ginny named her Tabatha, with an *a*. Ginny had named her daughters after TV witches, beautiful and benevolent witches, for sure, but witches nonetheless.

According to Ginny, "You know, I didn't watch *Bewitched* that much, but I loved the names. If I would have had another girl, she would have been Sabrina," Ginny said, referring to the name of a fictional witch, this one first appearing in the Archie comics, and later the subject of an ABC-TV show, *Sabrina the Teenage Witch*.

"It's probably a good thing that I didn't have four girls, because the only one left was Endora, and she would have killed me," Ginny added, referring to the character of Samantha's highly flamboyant and somewhat villainous mother. Endora, played by Agnes Moorehead, encouraged Samantha to act like a witch and could never get her son-in-law's name right, most frequently referring to him as "Durwood," instead of Darrin.

Ginny remembered those first few years with her baby girls. She remembered them clearly, because they were the only years she had.

"Sammy was first. She was—they were both wonderful babies. Neither one of them gave me problems. Sammy would get sick. She would catch a cold. When Sammy would teethe, she would get such a fever on the inside that, when it came out, she would just pass out on me. Scared me to death. But, as soon as the tooth came in, she was fine. There was nothing. It was just one big scare and that was it."

In the meantime, Leroy had left college and had taken a job that involved considerably more travel. He joined the army. With a baby to take care of, Ginny saw her husband rarely, but it was better than never. After one visit from Leroy, Ginny found herself expecting a second blessed event.

"Tabby was born small," Ginny said. "She weighed four pounds twelve ounces. The doctors told me she was two months premature, but trust me, she was born nine months to the day. And I know because I only saw my husband once during the time I got pregnant. He was in the service at the time. Even though she was small, there were no health problems. They had her on premature formula for a little while, but she didn't need it.

"We brought Tabby home in a boot box, if you can believe that. The hospital wouldn't let me take her home unless we had a warm blanket. Well, she was born in October and I didn't have a warm enough blanket that the hospital thought was appropriate, so we cut holes in a boot box and wrapped her in a little receiving blanket, and that was how we took her home.

"When we got Tabby home, Sammy took one look at the box and said, 'Present for me!' I opened the box and she goes, 'Mine!' Tabby was basically Sammy's from that point on. She helped me hold her. They were definitely close. Both girls were healthy, happy babies.

"Tabby was bubbly. Right from the moment she got up in the morning. She was disgustingly happy in the morning. I'm a grouch in the morning. It takes me an hour or so, a cup of coffee and a cigarette. When Tabby was just little, she would jump on me while I was still asleep and she would say, 'Up, Mommy! Up!' She wasn't just a morning person. She was an all-day person. Even when she was older and she would come to visit with the kids, she would wake them up in the morning by jumping at them.

"She would lay in bed with me, with her face about three inches away from mine, and she'd say, 'Good morning, sunshine. Time to get up.'

"I would say, 'It's morning, 'Tab,' there's nothing good about it.'

"And she'd say, 'Yes there is. I'm here.'

"Sammy is more like me, a little bit slower to get started in the morning—so you can imagine what a trial Tab was for us first thing in the morning.

"I do crafts and I made a sign that I hung in my dining room in Iowa when Tab would come to visit. The sign said, 'Cheerfulness in the morning is strictly forbidden. All violators will be shot!' In response, Tab sent me a T-shirt that said, 'Instant human, just add coffee.'"

But that was years later when mother and daughter tried desperately to make up for lost time; so much time had been lost. Baby Tabby went to stay with her paternal grandmother off and on from the time she was nine months old. Then Leroy was transferred to Germany and Ginny didn't want to make the trip with him, so they broke up.

Ginny was moving on with her life. In 1979, when Samantha was three and Tabby was two, they again went to live with the Bassetts. This time the move from Iowa to Greenwood, New York, was permanent.

According to Tabby's aunt Lorraine Warriner, Leroy Bassett's sister, "My mother raised her because my brother was in the service and traveled a lot."

Here's how Ginny remembered it: "My husband went to Germany and I was working two jobs at the time. I was working at an art store during the day and at a restaurant during the weekends. Leroy was going to New York to visit his parents and he asked if he could take the girls with him, and I said sure. Leroy and I were already having problems at that time. And, he didn't bring them back. By the time I got up enough money to go to New York and pick them up, I found that New York had a law that you can't take children out of a house that they've been in for longer than six weeks without a court order— or something along those lines—even if you are the children's mother. I was young and dumb. I was nineteen at the time, I believe. Leroy and I divorced soon after that. We just couldn't get along."

Hearing of Ginny's claims that she didn't give up the babies, but rather sort of lost them, Samantha huddled with Grandma Essie, and they said the claim was simply not true.

"Dad and Mom brought us to Grandma's and Mom was going to come back later after she got settled in her new home," Samantha said. "Dad was going to Germany in the army. Mom told Gram to get custody of us because she was going to be a trucker, and so Gram did. Then she was mad that Gram did. Mom asked to take us to her parents, but Gram wouldn't let her because she didn't know if she would get us back. Gram did not tell her to get a court order if she wanted us. She asked to take us to visit, but not to keep."

However they got there, the girls were at the Bassetts' to stay. They would be brought up in a strong religious atmosphere. The entire Bassett family was very involved with the local Community of Christ Church in Greenwood. Ginny was a Catholic girl.   .

After the girls moved to Greenwood to live with Grandma Essie and Grampa Carol, Ginny remembered: "Surprisingly, we all got along pretty good. The only time we had a problem was when Essie first started taking care of the girls. I got over my mad and we talked. She never stopped me from calling the girls or anything else. I always called the girls once a month, on the first Saturday after the first. I could only afford to call them once a month. We would talk for an hour. I also called on their birthday, on Christmas, you know. . . ."

Greenwood, New York, is a tiny village south of Hornell, located along a creek. When you come into Greenwood from the north, you cross a little bridge that goes over a small creek, with a pretty waterfall. The town is located at the junction of Route 248, the north-south thoroughfare, and Route 417, which runs east-west, in the western part of Steuben County. Although it was formed back in 1827, it remained so small that there were no restaurants, traffic lights, or gas stations. In 2000, the Greenwood population was 849 residents. That number has not changed much over the years.

Samantha referred to Greenwood as a "tiny little town where there wasn't much to do."

Said Tabatha's aunt Lorraine, "It's one of those little communities that if you blink as you go through it, you'll miss it."

The Bassett home was right on the main road, Route 248, a two-story wooden house on forty acres of land. It was located about halfway between Canisteo and Greenwood, but it was considered both in the Greenwood postal district and the Greenwood school district. It was a big house, but nonetheless it was often crowded.

Asked who lived there, Samantha recalled, "My grandma and grandpa. Tabby and I. My grandma had a couple of foster kids that lived with us for a while. My aunt Linda, my dad's sister, and her husband and their family. They lived with us off and on a couple of times. They had four kids."

Using recent statistics, the median household income is around $30,000 a year and the average house goes for $45,000. Like most of the town populations in that region, almost everyone is white. Of those, the heritage was split evenly between Irish, German, and English. Only sixteen residents of Greenwood listed their ethnicity as anything other than Caucasian, and eight of them were of Native American heritage. The remainder listed their race as a mixture of two or more races.

It was not a rich community. Three out of four adults in Greenwood had graduated from high school. Only one out of ten had earned a four-year college degree, well below the state average. Another one out of ten was out of work, about normal.

It was a family town. Although a quarter of the adults had never been married, only 8 percent were separated or divorced. Well over half were married.

The only noteworthy landmark, and it didn't exactly bring in the tourist trade, was a spot just west of town where the first gas well drilled on state land was located.

Spectacular, no—but pretty, yes. A lovelier spot you won't find anywhere in New York State's Southern Tier. About Greenwood, local Robert Huff (pseudonym) said, "I've lived here all my life, except when I was in the Air Force. I came back because this is where you raise your kids." Huff, who was an athletic coach for combined Canisteo-Greenwood sports teams, added, "They can go up to the school at ten o'clock at night and skateboard, and you won't worry about them."

The largest building in Greenwood was five miles down the road from the Bassett home. It was Greenwood Central School, which housed all students, from pre-K through seniors in high school. The total enrollment for all twelve grades was usually around three hundred. This was the only school Tabatha Bassett would ever attend.

In 2004, the Greenwood school district and the Canisteo district, to the north, merged for activities, such as sports and clubs—but back when the Bassett girls went there, that was not the case. Because of this, often there were not enough kids for certain activities to continue. That same year, testing results revealed that only 21 percent of Greenwood's eighth graders were meeting or exceeding grade-level standards in English Language Arts. More encouragingly, 57 percent were meeting or exceeding standards in math.

To get to the highest point in Greenwood, one climbed to the top of the New York State Highway System sign. It wasn't that the sign itself was so tall, it's just that it rested atop Greenwood Hill.

Canisteo, the larger town to the north of Greenwood, is best known for its "Living Sign"—an arrangement of pine trees on the side of a hill that spells out "Canisteo." When you enter Canisteo by car, you pass a road sign that says, "WELCOME TO CANISTEO, HOME OF THE WORLD FAMOUS LIVING SIGN." The living sign is pretty impressive, and everyone who has seen it remembers it, but to call it world-famous is a bit of a stretch. Most travelers figure it's truly famous only about as far as Elmira.

After moving in with their grandparents, Samantha and Tabatha didn't see much of their parents. The girls had switched homes, and visits from parents were infrequent, such as one might expect from a distant aunt.

"We saw my mom once when I was in seventh grade and Tabby was in sixth," Samantha recalled. "She would call every once in a while. She called once a month for a while, but then she didn't."

Visits from her dad were equally rare.

"We would see my dad about once every two or three years," said Sam. "He'd visit when he was on leave from the army. One time it was two years without seeing him, and another time it was three years."

Among the townfolk, Tabby was not known as a shy girl. She was the girl with the funny laugh. When she laughed, everyone laughed. She was effervescent, always on the move. She was the girl who brightened a room.

Greenwood locals remembered Tabatha as a girl who, no matter what she was doing, seemed to be having fun. History was her favorite subject. Her favorite teacher was Mike Bronson, who taught history.

Like many sisters who are close in age, Sam and Tabby did not always get along.

"We didn't always have the greatest relationship, and I really regret that now," Sam said in 2005. Samantha and Tabatha were both active in school, but they weren't drawn to the same activities.

"I was in the yearbook club, taking pictures. And I played a year of basketball, even though I wasn't very sporty. Tabby did other things. She was a cheerleader, and she played softball, although I don't remember what position she played."

These weren't intramural sports, either. The girls' basketball and softball teams played games against other schools. Because the talent pool in Greenwood was what it was—that is, tiny—it was not very hard to get on a team.

"There weren't any such thing as tryouts," Samantha remembered with a laugh. "If you showed up, you got to play." There was always a chance, before each game, that not enough would show up to play, so participation by all was highly desirable.

During the summers, Samantha and Tabatha always went to church camp. They spent several weeks each summer attending Community of Christ events held for children and teenagers.

"We would go for one week to a camp for our age group," Sam said, "and then later in the summer we would go for another week, Reunion Week, for the whole family. The camp was in Pennsylvania."

That was about a four- or five-hour drive, and those trips were often elongated by extreme tension.

"That's because Tabby always got car sick," Samantha remembered. The family learned the solution was in conking Tabby out. "One year they gave her a motion-sickness pill and she slept the whole way. It was better than throwing up."

Once, the church reunion was at Graceland University in Lamoni, Iowa—the same school that the girls' dad, Leroy Bassett, had attended—which put them within driving distance of their mother. Ginny remembered all of the times she had seen her daughters. Sadly, they were few and far between.

"When the girls went to Graceland, I would go see them or they would come over and visit me. I would go pick them up, we'd visit for a couple of hours, and then I'd take them back to the college. Tabby came here to visit for a week when she graduated. Sammy went to Graceland for a short time, so I had an opportunity to visit her then."

CHAPTER 6

Baby Boys

Ginny Hentges Bassett had lost her girls and her husband. It was a lonely time, but that loneliness was to a great extent relieved in 1980 when Cleo Winebrenner entered her life.

"I was living in Kentucky with a girlfriend of mine and he was a bouncer in a bar," she said. "If you met him, you would realize how funny that is. He stood maybe five feet eight and weighed one hundred forty pounds. But he was, as you can imagine, pretty tough. The toughness was mostly in his personality, though.

"Cleo and I were together for seven years before we got married. We got married in 1986—and we're still together. When I met Cleo, I was already pregnant with Cyril, but I didn't know it. I guess I was about two months along when I found out. I told Cleo that there was something about me he should know about. I was pregnant, I was still married, and the baby wasn't my husband's—since we hadn't been together in a long time. Cleo said, 'So?' That was his only response.

"Cyril was born in 1981 and Cleo raised him like he

was his own. When Cyril was thirteen or fourteen, Cleo adopted him. It wasn't just that Cleo wanted to adopt Cyril. Cyril wanted to be adopted.

Chris was born July 15, 1983. He was born in Bemidji, Minnesota. Bemidji is only about eighty miles from Canada; you're up in Indian Reservation territory. Chris was three when Cleo and I were married."

The 1986 wedding of Cleo and Ginny was, according to her, a "good old-fashioned shotgun wedding—literally." Everyone got dressed up in older clothes. Reverend Sparks, the neighborhood minister, performed the ceremony. They lived out in the country and the minister came out to the house. With a wedding decor mostly consisting of bales of hay, the ceremony was on the front porch. Ginny's sister and her current boyfriend held a hangman's noose. The maid of honor's dad escorted Cleo up onto the porch while holding a broken-down shotgun. A tape on a cassette player performed the bride's march. Afterward, there was a cookout. A lot of family and friends were there and everybody had a great time.

"In 1987, we moved to Tingley, Iowa, and we bought a little house there. It was a little retirement [and] farming town. It was a very small town. They had twenty kids in town one year and the town was going crazy trying to figure out what to do with them. You could tell that it was a retirement town.

"A lot of people in the town thought that I was strict with my boys. I guess I had rules that other moms in the area didn't have. I didn't let them run around without me knowing where they were."

Ginny remembered her boys as chivalrous, opening doors for her, holding out a chair at a restaurant. She said there had been a sibling rivalry, but nothing out of the norm. "They got along and they fought like normal brothers," she said. "They were very protective of one another. They could pick on each other, but they didn't like it when anyone else picked on the other. They had a lot of the same likes and interests. The only difference was that Chris was a lot more like his dad."

Cyril had physical and mental difficulties while growing up, his mom noted.

"Cyril, if you were ever to have seen a picture of his real father, he's identical to him. Cyril's never met him. We contacted him once and he didn't even want to know about him. That was pretty hard for Cyril to deal with, growing up. Cyril had a weight problem when he was growing up, so naturally he got picked on—a lot. He was also extremely intelligent. When they tested him once, he was five points above gifted. So, needless to say, he was pretty bored. And the school system down there isn't prepared to deal with kids like that.

"Cyril was one of those kids that, if he liked you, you knew. And if he didn't like you, you knew that, too. He didn't mince words. He showed respect to his elders, as long as they showed it back. He wouldn't take any crap.

"He had a hard time dealing when he was younger. He had a behavior disorder. He had a hard time with the fact that his real dad didn't want anything to do with him. He'd get frustrated and have mood swings. One of his teachers was wonderful. Sometimes he would just cry, and she knew what the reason was. She would take him out in the hall and talk to him and let him get himself back together before she took him back in the room.

"Cyril was never in trouble with the law—but Chris was. Chris had one of those personalities that you just had to like. He was like Tabatha. When he met someone, he was quiet at first, but it didn't take long for the quiet to go away."

Speaking of Cyril's younger brother, Ginny noted no physical or behavioral problems. She said, "Chris could chat a mile a minute. He had blond hair, blue eyes.

Cute, and he knew it. Tall. He was probably a good six feet. And he had the personality to go with it, and everybody liked him."

Sometimes Ginny would get letters or small packages from her girls. When Tabby was little, she sent her mother a cassette tape of herself singing. She gave a half-hour concert, singing along to some clumsy organ accompaniment, perhaps provided by herself.

At the beginning of the tape, Tabby said, "Here's the tape I promised you. It's me singing. I'll start with the song I was telling you about—the one I won second place for."

In a high, piping voice, which sometimes sounded as if it were straining the limits of her upper vocal register, Tabby then sang "I Believe," yet her pitch remained strong and on key. She sang: "I believe that for every drop of rain that falls, a flower grows." This was followed by other inspirational and church-approved songs.

CHAPTER 7

Vermont Law School: 1985–88

In the autumn of 1985, Kevin Bryant was twenty-seven years old. He was born on February 22, 1958. Kevin's life had centered around two things: bad health (a congenitally bad heart) and—like the Bassetts, who had raised Samantha and Tabatha—the Community of Christ Church.

Kevin's dad, Vivian, was an official with the church. Vivian Bryant and his wife Joyce lived in Penfield and belonged to the Pittsford branch of the church. In fact, Vivian Bryant knew Essie Bassett from church get-togethers dating back to the 1950s.

Kevin had always been smart as a whip, but he had been held back by his bad heart. He was nicknamed "AV boy" as a teen because, in school, he was frequently seen pushing audio-visual equipment. He graduated from Penfield High School in 1976, by far the smallest boy in his class.

At age twenty-seven, he had achieved his bachelor

degree and was ready to enter law school. There were only a few independent, private law schools in the country—that is, not affiliated with a university. In 1985, Kevin was accepted at and attended Vermont Law School, the only such school in Vermont.

Kevin was not the sort of guy to strike terror in anyone's heart as he walked down the street. He was five-two—five-four with his shoes on—and bespectacled. He did not radiate a picture of health, but he was neat, both in grooming and in dress. His black hair was always freshly combed.

Tabatha's father, Leroy Bassett, who had known Kevin ever since Kevin was a little boy, had always assumed that he was unhealthy just from the looks of him. "Kevin had always been kind of sickly," Leroy said years later. "His health was not the greatest. I lived on a farm. He lived in the city. I thought city folks were strange anyway."

Vermont Law School's "Mission Statement" proposes: "To educate students in a diverse community that fosters personal growth and that enables them to attain outstanding professional skills and high ethical values with which to serve as lawyers and environmental and other professionals in an increasingly technological and interdependent global society." Its motto, *"Lex pro urbe et orbe"*, means "Law for the community and the world." The nineteen-building, thirteen-acre campus was small and beautiful, located in the village of South Royalton, on the banks of the White River, in a National Register Historic District. There were only a little more than six hundred full-time students and less than forty full-time faculty members.

Although it's unknown if this factor entered into Kevin's thinking when he was looking for law schools, Vermont Law was considered one of the top law schools for women anywhere in the country. Even back in the 1980s, more than half of the students were women. The student body was a tad older than at most law schools as well, with the average age being twenty-eight. Age-wise, Kevin fit right in.

It was a new school. When Kevin first began attending classes there, the school was only thirteen years old. Kevin completed a three-year program and earned his J.D. degree, which qualified him, depending on his passing of the bar exam, to practice law anywhere in the United States.

CHAPTER 8

A Working Lawyer

During October 1989, when Tabatha Bassett was thirteen years old, Kevin Bryant passed the bar exam at the age of thirty-one and was licensed to practice law in New York State. A few months later, after a short search, Kevin Bryant landed a job.

It wasn't the best job. Low pay. High turnover. Okay for a guy fresh out of school. He accepted a position as a staff attorney at a local branch of Hyatt Legal Services, once a regionally well-known chain of law offices.

Hyatt, the chain, was called "the McDonald's of the legal profession" by *Barron's* magazine. The chain of law offices was cofounded in 1977 by Joel Z. Hyatt, who had earned his J.D. only the year before at Yale Law School. Hyatt, the man, was named by *The American Lawyer* as one of the ten most influential attorneys during the 1980s for his pioneering efforts in making the legal system work on behalf of middle-income families. Briefly involved in politics, in 1994, Hyatt was Ohio's Democratic nominee for the Senate. Today, Hyatt is the CEO of a start-up cable network that he established with former vice president Al Gore. According to the newsletter of Stanford Graduate

School, where Joel Hyatt was a teacher, Hyatt Legal Services "helped revolutionize the legal services delivery system by making legal care affordable and accessible to middle- and lower-income families." The founder flourished, the law offices not so much. They were less than glamorous, but that was where Kevin landed a job. Everybody was inexperienced, or otherwise troubled. In a sense it was like working at McDonald's. When anyone seemed too sharp and had been there for too long, coworkers wondered why they hadn't moved on.

In 1986, KRON-TV in San Francisco reported: "Since 1977, Hyatt Legal Services has grown into the largest law firm in the U.S., serving mainly middle-class clients out of storefront offices. While Hyatt's growth has been spectacular, former Hyatt lawyers have claimed that the incentive to take on new clients causes heavy workloads and high staff turnover, and charged that in the Bay Area, Hyatt hired two attorneys under suspension by the bar. Although the firm's system works well for some clients, it may be inappropriate for more complicated cases, such as contested divorces." So, the impression was that Hyatt generated a lot of business, and if it did make a lot of money, it did so through volume. They also were not too picky about the lawyers they hired, it seemed.

In June 1993, Kevin Bryant became a partner in the Hyatt's office in Greece, New York. His supervisor there was a man named William R. Shero (pseudonym). A swinging bachelor with a steady income, Kevin bought himself a Mazda Miata. After a couple years on the job there, Kevin bought the house on Pennicott Circle in Penfield. The house was in a perfect location. It was only about a mile from where he had grown up, and where his mom and dad still lived. It was a big house; so to help pay the mortgage, according to neighbors, Kevin frequently invited people to come live with him.

When his supervisor separated from his wife and was in the process of getting a divorce, Kevin invited Shero to take one of the bedrooms. As a result, they became housemates for a while.

CHAPTER 9

The Community of Christ

So how did the world of a small-town teenager and a middle-aged city lawyer intersect? The answer is, they shared a common faith. Asked if her entire family belonged to the Community of Christ Church, Samantha Bassett said, "Oh yes—and then some! It's an important part of our lives."

Both the Bryants and the Bassetts were active in the Community of Christ Church, which had congregations both in Greenwood, in Steuben County, and in the Rochester suburb of Pittsford. The church mission was to "proclaim Jesus Christ and promote communities of joy, hope, love, and peace." Although this was not the same church as the Church of Jesus Christ of Latter-day Saints (LDS), headquartered in Salt Lake City, Utah, there were similarities. Both churches, for example, traced their roots back to the early nineteenth century and proclaimed Joseph Smith—a resident of Palmyra, New York, only fifteen miles from Penfield—to be their first leader.

According to church literature, the Reorganized

Church of Jesus Christ of Latter-day Saints was founded on April 6, 1860, in Amboy, Illinois. Their headquarters has moved several times, but, ever since 1920, it had been in Independence, Missouri. A new temple/headquarters in Independence was opened in 1994. The church's "original temple" was in Kirtland, Ohio, and was maintained as a historical site.

Members of the Community of Christ Church did not call themselves Mormons, and will correct outsiders who erroneously refer to them as such. (There are two reasons why this is a touchy subject. For one thing, the term Mormon connotes for many people a belief in polygamy. Members of the Community of Christ are supposed to believe in monogamy. Also, they do not believe that the term "Mormon" was "part of the original church." They referred to themselves only as Christians.)

The Church of Jesus Christ of Latter-day Saints (referred to as LDS, Mormons) and the Community of Christ were the two largest denominations in the Christian "Restorationist" movement. At least, originally, these denominations believed that the true Christian Church died out in the early second century C.E., and was restored by Joseph Smith's ordination and his subsequent founding of the original LDS church. The Community of Christ had since abandoned this belief.

The church was originally known as the Reorganized Church of Jesus Christ of Latter-day Saints but it was agreed at a 2000 conference in Kansas City, Missouri, that this was quite a mouthful. So, by a vote of 1,979 to 561, it was agreed to change the name to Community of Christ. The new name took effect on January 1, 2001.

From an outsider's point of view, the Community of Christ seemed more greatly in touch with the modern world than the Mormon Church. For example, they did not baptize or marry by proxy their ancestors. They rejected the "Eternal Progression" theory, which was believed by some LDS membership in the nineteenth century: "As man now is, God once was; as God now is, so man may become."

They criticized Brigham Young's practice of "blood atonement": that if persons who commit murder are executed so that their blood is spilled upon the ground, then they might obtain forgiveness for their sins. Although, to be fair, that doctrine was no longer emphasized by the Mormons, either.

The Community of Christ Church rejected the sexism of the Church of Latter-day Saints. Women had been ordained since 1984. The leadership of the C of C Church has been gradually moving in a more liberal and ecumenical direction.

According to their Web site: "The C of C does not have a formal creed that its members must accept." However, a consensus existed on the following beliefs:

They viewed God as the "eternal Creator, the source of love, life, and truth." Most viewed God as the first element of the Trinity. They considered Jesus Christ as the "living expression of God in the flesh." They believed in Jesus' crucifixion and resurrection. Most considered Jesus to be the second element of the Trinity; some Jesus and God as two different persons. Most perceived the Holy Spirit as a person and as the third component of the Trinity. Some considered the Holy Spirit to be the "continuing presence of God in the world." Salvation and eternal life in heaven after death were available to all who accepted the Gospel. Salvation was by belief and works. The Book of Mormon referred to being "restored to Grace, according to your works." The Doctrine & Covenants also encouraged "works" for salvation. People who did not accept the Gospel would be given a second opportunity after their death. God's revelation continued to expand in the present day. They had eight sacraments: blessing of children, adult baptism by immersion and the laying on of hands, confirmation of membership, The Lord's Supper (Communion), marriage, administration to the sick, ordination to the priesthood, and the evangelist's blessing. Both women and men were eligible for ordination and assignment to all offices within the denomination. Members were expected to tithe by giving 10 percent of their after-tax earnings (in excess of that needed for basic living needs) to the church.

Kevin's family helped operate the church in Pittsford and members of Tabatha's family were officials in the Greenwood church. Church activities, for both adults and children, allowed members of various churches to get together.

"There are three churches in our area group," explained Samantha Bassett. "There's the Buffalo branch, the Rochester branch, and the Greenwood branch. We would get together every once in a while, as a church. We would have services together, and afterward we would have what we called pot luck. Everyone would bring a dish to pass and we'd all eat together."

Tabatha, known for her singing voice, did not sing in the church choir because there was no choir. The congregation was too small. If there had been a choir, there wouldn't have been anyone left to listen to it. Tabby did sing solos during services, however, and after she moved away, her singing voice was missed by the other members of the church. Ginny Winebrenner has taken credit for Tabby's love of music: "With all my kids, I sang them to sleep at night."

The Bassett girls were involved in their church in many ways—they would help set up before an event, help clean up after, and do just about any task that was asked of them.

According to Kevin's father, Vivian, and Tabatha's uncle the Reverend Terry Smith (husband of Leroy Bassett's sister Carolyn), the Bryants and the Bassetts had known each other for fifty years. Tabby's grandmother Essie Bassett first met Vivian Bryant, Kevin's father, back in the 1950s, and the two families had known each other through church get-togethers ever since.

And so it was that one summer during the 1990s, Kevin Bryant, son of the minister of the Rochester branch of the Community of Christ Church, first took special note of a pretty blond teenager named Tabby Bassett, who was the granddaughter of his father's longtime friend Essie Bassett.

CHAPTER 10

Tabby Gets Married
and Moves Away

In 1993, Samantha Bassett graduated from Greenwood Central School. "There were twenty-four kids in my senior class," she recalled. That fall she attended Graceland University, the Community of Christ–affiliated school in Lamoni, Iowa, where her dad had gone and where she had attended church get-togethers in the summer. As it turned out, though, Sam only lasted at Graceland for three weeks. She was terribly homesick, missed her boyfriend, and back to Greenwood she came.

Tabatha graduated from Greenwood Central School a year later, Class of '94, and her senior class was no larger than Sam's. Tabby had started life small, and she had stayed that way—even fully grown, she weighed barely one hundred pounds.

Tabby was one of the prettiest girls in town, with her honey-colored mullet. However, she did have flaws, most obvious of which were her crooked and discolored teeth. There hadn't been enough money for braces, but she didn't seem self-conscious about the imperfection. She still smiled with her lips apart, but photographs remember her as a young woman prettier with her mouth closed.

By the time Tabby finished school, she was already dating the man who was to become her first husband: Arnold Martin (pseudonym). He was a Canisteo kid, "about her age." According to Samantha, "I think they met down at our neighbors. He used to go down there and hang out and that's where they met." Arnold was Tabby's date for her senior prom.

Following graduation, during 1995 and 1996, Tabby worked for two years as a waitress at J.C.'s Café, which was just a little diner on the main street. "She didn't have to wear a uniform or anything like that. She could wait tables in whatever she was wearing," her sister remembered. While waitressing she studied to be a nursing assistant but flunked the test.

In August 1996, Tabby married Arnold at the Howard Community Center, in Howard, New York. Ginny was there for the wedding of her daughter. One guest brought a camcorder to the rehearsal, wedding, and reception. That video became the permanent record of the event.

The Howard Community Center was used for dances and meetings. It was a rectangular cinder block building, all right angles and white paint. At one end was a window in the wall that opened to the concession stand. Above the window was a sign with a Coca-Cola ad at the top, and listed up there was the extremely limited menu and prices. At dances and the like, you could get hot dogs, pop, chips, junk food.

The rehearsal for Tabby and Arnold's wedding took place at 4:00 P.M., Saturday, August 24, 1996. There were lots of large windows and sun was streaming in. There were about twenty people there, dressed in sport shirts and jeans. Some were in shorts.

A majority of the people there were overweight—in sharp contrast to the slender young bride-to-be, in her loose-fitting dark shirt and tight white pants. For the rehearsal the community center was set up for that night's dance. The dance floor had been cleared. All of the furniture, folding tables and chairs, had been pushed up against a wall.

Next to the concession stand was a white board, where management wrote, in black marker, an advertisement for whatever the next event to be held at the community center was going to be. For Tabby's wedding rehearsal, the sign read, ROUND AND SQUARE DANCE BY THE STARLITE RAMBLERS ON AUG 24, 8-12.

Arnold looked tall and gangly standing next to Tabby. He was skinny, too. He was on the shaggy side, needed a haircut, but at first glance a decent sort of young man—the Greenwood equivalent of a catch. Befitting the bride-to-be, Tabby was the center of attention at all times. She gestured broadly. Like a stage actress, her facial expressions were slightly exaggerated. She was playing to the crowd, relishing her moment in the spotlight. In contrast, Arnold seemed slightly embarrassed, like he would have preferred to be in the parking lot with his best man and ushers—fairly typical for a bridegroom at his own tense-but-dull wedding rehearsal. Someone had given Tabby a small bouquet, a compact bunching of short-stemmed flowers. It was really unnecessary but something for her nervous hands to hold during the rehearsal ceremony.

The camcorder's microphone couldn't pick up intelligible voices, unless they were very close by, and the camera person chose to give the rehearsal ceremony some space, standing far to the side and at the back of the room. But the song after the ceremony—played and sung by a young man at a piano—came through, loud and clear. It was "Let It Be Me," the beautiful Everly Brothers song, a sentimental favorite of the young couple.

When the ersatz check-your-watch ceremony was over, Arnold and Tabby did an about-face and headed toward the exit—he walking fast, she skipping. No one else moved from his or her place. Tabby flung her bouquet over her shoulder without looking back. The flowers soared up in a high arc and then came down with an echoing thud, in the center of the empty dance floor.

The tape goes all blue for a moment and then it is the next day, the real thing. The letters and numbers in the bottom right of the screen tell us that it is now Sunday, August 25, 1996, at one o'clock in the afternoon.

A four-tiered wedding cake rested on its stand in front of the concession stand window. Replacing the casually clad handful of people who had been at the rehearsal was a full house of sharply dressed folks for the actual wedding. There were maybe eighty people there, sitting in ten rows of eight chairs apiece.

And it must have been warm. Although no one was fanning himself or herself, it might have been a little late in the season for that, none of the men were wearing jackets. Arnold's usher crew was wearing white shirts and clip-on ties. Those ushers were videotaped in action, helping little old ladies to their seats. They were taking their jobs seriously, obvious by their tightly erect posture. They were doing their best to demonstrate adequate gentlemanliness.

Actually, there were two men in the room with jackets on—the minister and the lanky groom, Arnold. The groom was wearing a white tuxedo jacket with tails over black pants. It might have been the same outfit he wore when he took Tabby to her prom.

The white board sign that had advertised the "Round

and Square dance" now said, in a feminine hand, CON-
GRATULATIONS KITTEN AND CUDDLES. The bride had not yet
entered, and the organ player was warming up the
crowd with the theme from *Gone with the Wind*.

The ceremony began, Tabby entered from her
hiding place behind the concession stand. On her
left arm was her grandfather Carol, who was several
inches shorter than she was. On her right arm was her
father Leroy Bassett, who towered above her.

Tabby was dressed in a full wedding gown with veil.
The dress was formfitting to her curvaceous figure.
From the entrance on, the veil gave Tabby trouble. If
the video was any indication, she was forced to spend
much of the day doing everything with one hand because she was adjusting the veil with the other.

The camera person got in closer for the actual wedding ceremony than for the rehearsal. Because of the
zoom, viewers of the tape could see Arnold and Tabby's
faces as they exchanged vows and gave each other
rings. Again "Let It Be Me" was played. This time it
turned into a sing-along. The bride sang along, too.
Her eyes were closed as she tilted back her head to sing,
appearing blissful through her parting veil.

The ceremony over, there was applause as Arnold
kissed his bride and they headed to the back of the
room for the reception line. This time Tabby did not
skip. There would be no skipping in those sparkly
white shoes with the extremely high heels.

The camera focused on Tabby's face during the
entire reception line. Everybody got a hug and a kiss.
A woman came up from behind Tabby at one point and
gave her some distressing news—perhaps Arnold was
in the parking lot with his friends instead of wherever he was supposed to be. For a flashing instant,
she was "Bride-zilla." She wagged a finger and told
that woman what to do in no uncertain terms. Then,
flick, like the switch had been turned from off to on,

Tabby met eyes with the next person in the reception line and her face lit up with a grin. She was hugging and kissing everyone again, seemingly mindless of whatever was upsetting her a moment before.

The tape then cut to the outside. The professional photographer was doing her job. The entire wedding party and close relatives had gathered in the sun. They lined up in various combinations, stood up straight, squinted into the sun, smiled, and the photographer took their picture.

Someone had apparently informed the best man and the ushers that they had to get through the photo session before they could remove their clip-on ties, and the thought of freeing themselves from that simulated noose had them antsy.

A photo of Arnold with the maid of honor, Samantha, and the other bridesmaids was taken, and then the photographer asked for a picture of just Tabatha with the best man and ushers. The men whooped and hollered and moved in to get a good spot near the bride.

"Come on, boys, you can all be huggin' on me," Tabby said. "I love the attention!"

After that last shot of Tabby and the boys, the photographer said, "That's it," indicating that she had all of the photos she needed.

"All right!" exclaimed the groom's buddies, and off came the clip-on ties.

Then everyone, except for the camera person, left. The bride stood alone in the sunshine for a moment. She looked at the camera and slowly stuck out her unusually long tongue. She didn't stick it out in the conventional "fresh" manner, though. Bridal Tabby unfurled her tongue, stretching it at the roots. Speaking only of the action as a physical anomaly, and without religious symbolism, one could call the movement of Tabby's tongue serpentine. Her lips were parted as she wagged her tongue, as if she were doing a dead-on impression of Gene Simmons, the lead singer for the rock group Kiss. She retracted the tongue with a grin and the scene ended.

Then the videotape took us back inside, where the band, a quartet, had set up—drums, guitar, bass, and vocal. The singer was a woman, the others men. They were all in their forties. Perhaps they were the Starlite Ramblers. The guitar player stepped up to the mike and without introducing himself or the band, everyone already knew who they were, he said that Arnold had a request for the first number. For the first dance the bride and groom would dance to the Spencer Davis Group classic "Gimme Some Lovin'."

As soon as the song started, the newlyweds stepped lively onto the dance floor and began to dance rock style, without touching. And the many overweight spectators sat and applauded mildly. With that, the camera person put the camera away, thinking perhaps that the time for recording was through and the time for partying had begun.

When Tabby and Arnold were first married, Arnold was still studying engineering at Alfred. Soon after, he took a job at a processed-food manufacturer in Avon, New York, a town in Monroe County, just south of Rochester.

The Bassetts did not like the idea of Tabby moving away, but if she had to go someplace, they were glad it was to the Rochester area, because there was a Community of Christ branch there.

Vivian Bryant, the minister there, was a friend of Essie's, going back a long time. The Bryants would look after Tabby in the big city. Now a new congregation would get to hear Tabby's beautiful singing voice during Sunday services.

According to Tabatha's aunt Lorraine Warriner, Tabby was eager to leave little Greenwood and move to the big city. "She wasn't a small-town girl," Lorraine said. "She liked the excitement of having more things to do."

Tabby's grandmother and sister disagreed. They didn't believe that Tabby was overly restless living in the Southern Tier. She went to Rochester because her husband got a job there, it was as simple as that.

While Tabby was getting married to her high-school sweetheart at the Howard Community Center during August 1996, the Rochester branch of the Cleveland-based franchise Hyatt Legal Services discontinued operations.

Out of a job, Kevin Bryant went into private practice and opened up his own office in the Rochester suburb of Greece, which butts up against the northwest side of the city. Kevin C. Bryant Law Offices was located on Ridge Road West.

When Kevin learned that Tabatha Bryant, the pretty blonde he remembered from summer church get-togethers, was moving to Avis Street in Rochester with her young husband, he did one step better than look after her. He gave her a job. Not long after moving to Monroe County, Tabby was gainfully employed as a secretary at the Greece law offices of Kevin C. Bryant, Esq.

At Kevin's office, Tabatha worked on wills, real estate closings, bankruptcies, civil lawsuits, misdemeanor criminal cases. The law office was an exciting world. Some of Kevin's clients were well-known, some famous, and some notorious. There were prostitutes and pimps and gangsters, who all led wild lives. It wasn't long before Tabby realized she was happier in her work world in Greece with Kevin than she was in her domestic world with Arnold in Avon. She loved going to work. She dreaded going home.

* * *

Tabby and Arnold Martin had only been married for about a year when trouble brewed. They fought. When Tabby complained to her grandmother about Arnold, she always made it clear that her husband was not physically abusing her. It was verbal abuse. They were arguing. A lot. And she'd had enough.

Tabby asked Kevin to handle her divorce for her, and he agreed happily to get her a divorce-lawyer who could do the job quickly.

Arnold Martin, now without a wife, eventually left his job in Avon, New York, and moved back to the Southern Tier to do computer work at a hospital.

CHAPTER 11

The Bride in the Red Shoes

The transition went this way, and it happened in a matter of months: Kevin made Tabby his employee, then his client, then his live-in girlfriend, then his wife.

On December 26, 1997, Tabby and Kevin—who was only two months younger than Tabby's mother—were married in Fairport, New York. It had been only sixteen months since she had gotten married for the first time, to Arnold, in the Howard Community Center.

In Fairport, for her second wedding, she wanted to tweak the notion that she, being a divorcée, was no longer pure, so Tabby became one of the few brides to be married in red shoes. One of Kevin's sisters told Tabby that brides couldn't wear red shoes, but this only served to make Tabby more stubborn. She took her vows, from the ankles down, with a Jezebel-like defiance.

Tabby's sister remembered that the wedding was at "a real nice place. Maybe a country club. It was a country-club-kind-of-place. About one hundred people attended.

"I don't remember if there was a band or a deejay, but there was dancing. Most of the family was there.

Gram was there. Grampa was there. He had to get in a tuxedo, his first ever. I remember he needed help getting dressed," Samantha said with a laugh.

Unable to attend the ceremony were Tabby's mom and stepdad, Ginny and Cleo Winebrenner. They had been to Tabby's first wedding, but not this one.

"It was the day after Christmas, and, because my husband and I are disabled, we have an extremely limited income," Ginny said, "We just didn't have the money to go to New York. The times when we did go to New York was when we had managed to save a couple hundred bucks, or Tabby had sent us a couple hundred bucks."

To the best of her recollection, the groom had never impressed Ginny much. Years later, she wouldn't be able to think of anything nice to say about Kevin.

"Kevin has a lot of problems, both mental and physical," she said. "But I never liked Kevin, so you can't go by me. I never cared for him. I found him very cold and empty."

Despite the lack of warmth between Ginny and Kevin, the two were always civil with one another. They did not fight. Kevin was Tabby's choice and Ginny had to respect that.

"I didn't have to like him. I didn't have to live with him," she said.

Kevin and Tabby honeymooned in the Cayman Islands.

Tabby wasn't the only one of Ginny's kids to marry in the 1990s. In 1999, Cyril lived with Ginny's sister Sharon for a couple months and he was working at McDonald's in Monticello, Minnesota. It was there that Cyril met the woman he was to marry.

Ginny doesn't remember if the bride was working at McDonald's or if she just came in because she knew someone, but Cyril and Patty met in a McDonald's. Not too long after that, Cyril and Patty married. Next came a baby boy named Cleo.

Ginny recalled the time. "He's named exactly after my husband. My son didn't give his wife a choice on the name," she said with a laugh. "We call him 'Little One.' Little One is a miracle for me. He looks exactly like Chris. And he has Cyril's personality. He's the perfect combination of the two. I keep telling Patty that she's in for a world of fun when he grows."

CHAPTER 12

The Brotherhood of Misogyny

Tabby found that being married to Kevin was a tough adjustment. She was used to hanging around with friends her own age. She ended up being around Kevin's friends who were old and not all that friendly.

Ever since she had started coming around Kevin's Penfield house, she could tell that Kevin's housemates and friends didn't like her. One of those friends was William Shero (pseudonym), a divorced man in his late sixties who had worked with Kevin.

Years later, Shero recalled: "Well, we were both attorneys at Hyatt Legal Services, a nationwide franchise out of Cleveland. I was the senior attorney and he was my protégé. I was the manager and he was an employee. We handled all kinds of cases. I worked there for five or six years in the early 1990s. Kevin was already working there when I got hired. We became friends. Kevin bought a house out in Penfield, and I was living in an apartment. I had just gotten a divorce. He had room, so I lived in his house with him for a time.

"Kevin and I mostly went out to dinner—and that was about it. We went to a movie every once in a while, but not too often. We didn't really hang out together too much. I was there before she came into the picture.

"Kevin bought the house out in Penfield because his parents were out there and he wanted to be close to them. And his cousin lived with us. We were the three bachelors. Then when she came along, the cousin moved out. I forget his cousin's name. He was a nice guy, a real nice guy. The cousin moved out and then I moved out, and left the two of them alone. And after that, I lost track. You know, I didn't give a shit. If you are a bachelor, you can't mix with the lovebirds. It's a different world.

"So Kevin met Tabatha. She was a piece of shit. He met her and she was married. She was like a cheerleader. You know, a young airhead. She came into the house. He helped her get a divorce; then they got married.

"After she moved in, I moved out and moved back into an apartment, but for a time I was living there with the two of them. For about a month, and that's about it. I was living in the house with him, and he, they lived together there before they were married.

"Kevin was a great guy. He is a great guy. He's a piece of work, very intelligent. Unfortunately, he always had a problem—well, not always, but for as long as I knew him—we used to talk about relationships with women. I had had a divorce, and other friends had problems with women.

"He got married, and, unfortunately, it was to the wrong individual. During the month I was there, I couldn't understand how he got hooked up with a lowlife like that. She had problems. I could tell she wanted to have a family or something. She had the first baby. She wasn't much of a mother. She induced a premature birth by not drinking too much water. I remember Kevin told me she was fainting. She was, you know, she was weird. Then she had the second baby. Then she came to the office, bringing the two babies. Strange, strange. Then I guess she took up with this guy. I didn't know what the hell was going on."

CHAPTER 13

Root Canals and Crownings

One thing Kevin took care of right away was Tabby's teeth. Because they were snaggled, they had never been given high priority on Tabby's vanity meter. Neglect had caused her teeth to go from bad to worse. The nerve had died in one of the top front teeth, and that tooth had discolored. Many of her teeth now caused her constant pain.

Tabby needed a full dental overhaul, and so Tabby underwent a series of root canals and crownings. Her appearance improved tremendously. The new smile was just the first step in Tabby's playing of her latest and greatest role, that of lawyer's wife.

Her hair was cut and allowed to remain straight. And she completely changed the clothes she wore. According to Tabby's sister, her behavior did not change when she married Kevin, but her dressing style sure did.

"I didn't notice a change attitudewise," Samantha said. "But she did feel that she had to be, appearance-wise, the lawyer's wife. She wore a lot of suits. She really toned down, because before she dressed pretty

wild. I don't mean wild bad. I mean she liked to wear
funky clothes. She had this pink dress. It came to . . .
well, it was real short. And it had polka dots on it. She
would wear big, long earrings that dangled down to her
shoulders. She wore makeup and everything was real
bright. After she married Kevin, she kept her old
clothes in her closet, but I never saw her wear them a
whole lot."

Tabby's mom agreed that Tabby loved the change in
class her marriage brought. "For Tabby, the whole
idea of being the wife of a lawyer, the whole persona,
fascinated her," Ginny said.

Persona was one thing, and real life was another. It
didn't take Tabby too long to realize that life in the big
suburban house was not the heaven-on-earth that she
had dreamed about.

"She loved it, but only up to a point. She was having
trouble with the fact that she was never around people
her own age. Everybody was Kevin's friends," Ginny
said.

Infidelity entered the picture right away, according
to Ginny: "She told me in the first six months that she
was married that she thought Kevin was having an
affair, but she couldn't prove it. Something about a
hotel room and bubble baths and champagne."

Tabby attempted to gain information through cyber-
sleuthing. She read her husband's private electronic
communications, Ginny said. "Then Tabby said she
read his e-mail and she knew who it was—but she still
couldn't prove it, because she couldn't tell if he was
really having an affair or if he was just mouthing off on
the e-mail. He wasn't happy that she had gotten into
his e-mail account."

Despite these domestic disputes, Tabby became
pregnant twice and had two kids—Kevin C. Bryant
Jr., known as K.C., in 1998, and Steven in 2000.

And still Kevin wasn't making ends meet and she had

to work. After a time she had to work two jobs. Kevin's folks looked after the babies a lot. In addition to her duties at Kevin's office, Tabby took a second job as a teller at the Manufacturers and Traders Trust Company Bank (M & T Bank) in Perinton. As a teller she worked the "drive-thru" window, and gave lollipops to drivers who turned up their radios so she could better hear the music.

On weekends she sometimes chose not to be with Kevin and Kevin's friends. Instead, she would pack the kids in the car and head down to Greenwood. Actually, Tabby already returned regularly to Steuben County on weekends, both before and after she had her boys. She would visit her family and attend her old church in Greenwood. According to her old boss Andy Carbone, she often made a point of stopping back at J.C.'s Café to say hello to her old customers and coworkers.

Befitting her position as the wife of the boss, and mother of the boss's children, Tabby was promoted to head secretary at Kevin's office.

CHAPTER 14

Tackle Frisbee

Letchworth State Park, "the Grand Canyon of the East," is thirty-five miles south of Rochester. It is certainly one of the most scenic places in New York State. The park lies beside the Genesee River Gorge, which is more than six hundred feet deep in some places, overlooking the river as it courses past three major waterfalls between cliffs. Picnicking, camping, hiking, and horseback riding are some of the preferred activities.

When Essie Bassett heard that Ginny was coming for a visit and bringing Chris, she knew where they should go: Letchworth. And so, it was at this park that the Winebrenners and Bassetts, two families with Ginny in common, decided to hold their 2001 reunion.

During July 2001, the Winebrenners—Cleo, Ginny, and Chris (Cyril stayed in Iowa with his wife and son)—came to New York State to celebrate Chris's eighteenth birthday. Ginny took Chris to visit his sisters in New York. The Winebrenners stayed at Kevin and Tabby's house in Penfield and drove down to meet Samantha at the park.

Only on one occasion, that Ginny can remember, did all four of her children get together in one place. The girls were visiting Graceland University for a church event and Cyril and Chris visited them there.

Samantha admitted a few years later she had not really known her brothers very well. She, for one, was not disappointed that Cyril hadn't come. She described Cyril as "not my favorite person. He was arrogant, even when I first knew him when he was younger. He was kind of a know-it-all, and I usually don't like people like that."

For the visit to New York during summer 2001, the focus was on Chris, the birthday boy. Both of the girls brought Chris a birthday present, wrapped and festooned with bows.

"For his birthday we bought him a new outfit and took him to New York [State]. It was Chris's vacation and part birthday present," Ginny said. "Sammy bought him a little jeweled knife. Tabby bought him a shirt with a dragon on it. He had such a blast."

At Letchworth, alongside the Genesee River Gorge, they had a cookout and a picnic. But the thing that everyone remembered best and most fondly about the day was when the Bassett girls and Chris, along with Tabby and Kevin's son K.C., played a rollicking game of what they called "tackle Frisbee." It started out as normal frisbee, the girls and Chris just throwing the disc around, playing catch. Then Chris began to intercept throws that were supposed to go from Tabby to Sam or from Sam to Tabby. Tackle frisbee, as it turned out, had no rules. Most of the action involved both girls and K.C. ganging up on Chris to get him off his feet.

"He was so much taller than the girls that he could just reach up and grab the frisbee. After a while of that, the girls decided that they were going to get even, and they tackled him to get the Frisbee away from him," Ginny recalled. "Then little K.C. would jump in the middle and pretty soon everybody was tackling everybody—gently, of course. They were having one heck of a good time."

The next day they all went to Niagara Falls and crossed over into Canada, where they visited Marineland Park.

"We visited flea markets that day," Ginny recalled. "It was a little bit of here, there, and everywhere."

Sammy's boyfriend at the time was a stock car driver at Woodhull Raceway, a small Southern Tier dirt track. One evening they went to the track to see him race. That visit would turn out to be the last time that the Bassett girls would get to play and interact with their brother Chris.

CHAPTER 15

A Bad One

In 2001, Chris Winebrenner lived with his brother, Cyril, for a couple of months.

"While they were staying together, they had gotten into an argument. I don't know what it was about. I never asked. I figured that was between the boys," Ginny said.

Chris moved back to Minnesota, living not far from home, and was working at a McDonald's. Cyril was working at Lakeside Casino, in Osceola, Iowa. He was a dealer there.

Ginny's sister Denise and her husband, Jimmy, both worked at the Lakeside Casino. Denise was a dealer and Jimmy worked security.

"Cyril got hired on and he wanted to be a dealer. That's what he got hired on for, and they trained him. He could deal all the games," Ginny said.

It was autumn; Thanksgiving approached.

"My husband had gone deer hunting, and he came back on a Friday," Ginny said. "That Sunday, Chris was going to stop over and see him before he went to work at McDonald's. Well, they called him in early at McDonald's, so Chris called us and said he'd see us afterward.

"Well, we heard the helicopters go, and me and Cleo were saying, 'That must have been a bad one.' About an hour and a half later, we got a call from the hospital that Chris had been hurt in a head-on collision. They thought we should get there right away."

They got in the car and Cleo somehow managed to drive down to the hospital. Chris was in the intensive-care trauma unit. He had been driving a compact car and had crashed head-on with a truck. He was being treated for massive trauma to the head.

"For the first three days, they said we couldn't talk to him, and we couldn't touch him. The only thing we could do was go in once a day and say, 'Hi. We're here. We love you.' That was it. We couldn't actually touch him because he would react. And with the head injury, they didn't want the added stimulation.

"Cyril couldn't get there until Wednesday night. That was the same time my daughters got there. I had called them and told them he wasn't going to make it. So they were all there. Cleo and me hadn't had any sleep, so they sent us home, and we wanted someone there all the time.

"By Wednesday evening they said we could talk to him all we wanted. He could have visitors. And on Thursday morning, he died—and that was Thanksgiving Day," Ginny said.

Samantha recalled, "Mom called to tell us that Chris had been in an accident. He was in ICU. Tab and I flew out. They said for a time that he was getting better. Then he wasn't and they said there was nothing they could do and it was just a matter of time. So we took off his life support, and he died."

The whole family gathered for Chris's funeral. Ginny's dad was there, and the man, who had spent a lifetime in industrial hard-facing, was not acting himself. He recently had been diagnosed as suffering from dementia.

"My dad was there, even though he wasn't too sure who I was," Ginny said, adding that his senility was "only getting worse."

Chris's November 27, 2001, obituary in the *Elk River Star News & Shopper* read:

> Christopher L. "Chris" Winebrenner, 18, of Mount Ayr, Iowa, formerly of Big Lake, died Thursday, November 22, 2001, as a result of an automobile accident. His funeral service was held November 24 at Dare's Funeral Service in Elk River. He is survived by his parents, Cleo and Ginny of Big Lake; grandfather, Cyril Hentges of Blackduck; brothers and sisters, Samantha Bassett, Tabatha (Kevin) Bryant of Rochester, N.Y., Cyril (Patricia) of Jasper, N.Y., Rick of Osceola, Iowa and Charlie of Indiana; Nephews, Steven and Kevin Bryant and Brian Winebrenner; special aunt, Tammy (Russell) Hentges of Princeton; cousin, Emmy Lu (Brian) Howard of Big Lake; and many other aunts, uncles, cousins and friends. Memorials are preferred.

Chris's death started a family tradition to celebrate his birthday, which was July 15. Ginny said, "We have a special thing we do every year on his birthday. Chris always wanted to go to the casino, so we saved nickels. We were going to do that when he turned eighteen, but we took him to New York instead. Now we still save nickels and on Chris's birthday we take someone else and they get to be Chris for the day.

"I know it sounds morbid. Last year, 2004, we didn't do it because we couldn't afford it, so my niece Jamie went to the casino and spent twenty bucks. She said Chris had no luck at all."

After Chris's death Ginny located the knife that Samantha had given Chris for his eighteenth birthday, but the shirt with the dragon on it that Tabby had given him couldn't be found.

"I don't know what happened to that," Ginny said.

After Tabby returned home following Chris's funeral, she and her mom talked on the phone frequently—certainly a lot more frequently than the once-a-month they had spoken when Tabby was a child.

"Tabby and I talked a lot," Ginny remembered. "She would call me once or twice a week. Sometimes she would call me up and just say, 'Mom, you're awesome.' I'd say, 'I love you, too.'" And she'd say, 'Well, gotta go,' and hang up. That was kind of the norm for her."

When Tabby and Kevin were having marital problems, a situation that grew progressively worse, Tabby would call her mother in tears and they would have long conversations.

"We would talk for three, four hours sometimes," Ginny said.

Sometimes when Tabby was having trouble getting her boys to go to sleep, she would call her mom so Ginny could sing them to sleep, the way she had sung her to sleep when she was a baby.

CHAPTER 16

The Mini-Breakdown

For Cyril, however, things weren't that great at home. He and Patty were having problems. It had always been tough for Cyril to relax, but now he was having more trouble than ever.

The death of his baby brother did nothing to help Cyril's already fragile state of mind. During 2002, Cyril Winebrenner struggled with his emotional and mental stability. Eventually that mental health collapsed.

Samantha remembered: "He had a nervous breakdown. He was in Indiana at the time, I think. He was in the hospital and he couldn't remember anybody or anything. So Patty and Cleo and little Cleo went out there, because they were living in Iowa at the time, and he didn't know them. One of Cleo's brothers was up there, so they stayed with him. He called Tabby one time and asked if he could come stay with them until he got things sorted out."

Ginny remembered it this way: "Cyril and Patty were having problems. Patty left and moved back up here with her mom. Actually, we went down and we moved her up here, because she couldn't afford to move on her own. Cyril was . . . I'm not sure. He said that [he and Patty were breaking up because] he was working a lot and he asked us to come down. I said you'll have to put Patty on the phone. Patty'll have to tell me that this is what she wants or we're not doing it. I always try my best to stay out of my kids' problems. I wanted to be there if they needed me, but I didn't want to get in the middle of it. So I talked to Patty and Patty said yes. She had already had 'Little One.' So we went down and picked her up. We rented a trailer and dragged it back up here to her mom's.

"Cyril worked down there for another month and then he moved to Indiana. He had brothers there; well, they were Cleo's sons from a previous marriage. He moved out there with them, and then he stayed with Cleo's sister and her son Brian for a while.

"In October, I got a call, around midnight. It was a collect call, and when I asked from who, I heard Cyril's voice say, 'I don't know.' He had completely lost his memory. He didn't know where he was. He was terrified. After talking to him for a little while, I got him to hand the phone to someone else. He had wandered into a hospital. He had seen a big cross. It was a hospital in Crown Point, Indiana (which is just south of Gary, only about twenty miles from Chicago).

"Cyril put me on the phone with a hospital attendant and I asked her to go get a doctor, get somebody to come get him and take him to the emergency room. She went and got a security guard, who came on the phone and said he would take him to emergency; then he gave me the numbers I needed to make sure he got there okay.

"We were in Minnesota and we drove there with his wife. Because he was married, she was the only one who could do anything. They were still married at the time. The doctors said that Cyril had had what they called a 'mini-breakdown.' They said that his memory would eventually all come back, but that it would take time.

"Cyril was eventually put in a mental-health facility. They kept him for a couple of days. He wasn't violent. He wasn't suicidal. He just didn't know who he was, and he was scared. After two days my husband went there and picked him up. He brought him back. We were staying at my brother-in-law Danny's until we could get things back on track.

"Cyril didn't remember me. He didn't remember Patty. He didn't remember his son. He didn't recognize any of us. He got on his cell phone and he just started going through the numbers. He just started calling people and talking to people, trying to figure out who he was.

"He came across Tabby's number, because he and Tabby used to talk quite a bit. He talked to her and she asked to talk to me, so he put me on the phone and Tabby said, 'Okay, Mom. What's going on?'

"So I explained it all to her, and she said, 'Okay, now he makes sense.' I gave her back to Cyril and they must have talked for an hour. When they got done, I asked him if that helped any. 'No,' he said, 'but she seems to like me.'

"I said, 'Well, she should, she's your sister.'

"And he said, 'She said I could come up and stay with her. She told me to think about it. Next time I talk to her, what should I tell her?'

"I said, 'That's your choice. You can either come back to Minnesota with me, you can go back to Iowa, or you can go back to Minnesota with Patty. Or, you can go to Tabby's. You can do whatever you want. The choice is yours. You have to make that decision.'

"He said, 'But I don't know where I belong.'

"I said, 'I know that—but you have to have a place to start. You decide where you are most comfortable.'

"So he called Tabby back and Tabby called me. We

didn't have the extra money to get him there. Chicago to New York is quite a ways. So (in September 2002), Tabby sent us a hundred dollars so we could get to New York and get back. So we took him to New York and we spent a couple of days there, getting him settled in. Then we went back to Minnesota. We never did see him after that—until after Tabby was gone."

This wasn't the first time Tabby had invited a troubled sibling to come and live with her family in the house on Pennicott Circle. A few years before, Samantha had been having problems and had stayed for a spell with the Bryants.

So, Cyril, once again remembering who he was, was the latest in a series of houseguests of Kevin Bryant. From living in mobile homes all of his life, he found himself in the large, two-story suburban home on Pennicott Circle.

He was the houseguest of his sister, a "lawyer's wife," and her much older husband. The guy was as old as Cyril's dad. At least.

CHAPTER 17

Baby Doll

In November 2002, twenty-two-year-old Cassidy "Cassy" Green was tired of having a boss. She had worked at the escort services, sharing her hard-earned money with a guy who took none of the pounding, who only answered the phone.

She decided that she was going to set up her own escort service, and she knew what she was going to call it: Sunset Sensations.

Settled on the name, she had to come up with a location. She didn't have the money to run it out of a motel. She didn't know anyone with a house who'd be willing to go into business with her. That left mobile homes.

She would operate Sunset Sensations out of a trailer home in the Bloomdale Mobile Home Park, on Routes 5 and 20, in Bloomfield, Ontario County, New York, near her home. She was a lifelong resident of Bloomfield, with a mom who was local. One might think that Cassidy A. Green would go to another town, where she was a stranger, to start up her escort business. But travel wasn't in Cassidy's makeup.

Bloomfield, population 2,349, spread out over six-teen square miles. Like many of the small towns south of Rochester, it was on land originally inhabited by the Seneca Indians. About three-quarters of the land there is used for farming and the average house costs more than $100,000. That was in the village. Outside of town, where the mobile home lots were, the average cost was not nearly that high.

Cassidy had great entrepreneurial plans. She was going to advertise on the Internet, show off how great her girls looked in fishnet stockings and corsets. When she wasn't feeling so optimistic, she would think about what to do if the escort business didn't work out right away. She figured she would supplement her income by selling coke to those who frequented adult enter-tainment establishments.

She tried to do it all on her own, but she soon fig-ured out that she was going to need to call in an expert or two. There was paperwork to do, something about "doing business as" (DBA) papers. It was beyond her. Cassidy realized she needed help filling out the business papers to set up the business. She asked a guy, who said she needed a lawyer for that sort of thing. Did she know one? No.

Then, so her story goes, she said, no big deal, she could look one up in the phone book. She planted a finger of fate randomly on the page for attorneys and her fingertip fell on the name of Kevin Bryant, who had an office on Ridge Road in Greece.

Greece was a suburban town adjacent to northwest Rochester—not really in Cassidy's neck of the woods. She was a girl from the southeast of Rochester. Greece was in the far opposite quadrant of the county.

There is no reason not to trust Cassidy's "finger of fate" story, but it should be noted that when Cassidy showed up in his office, Kevin already had a keen interest in escort services, strip clubs, and other aspects of the sex biz.

Like many longtime bachelors, Kevin did not seek out sex in the most romantic of manners—he usually went out and paid for it. Or sex came to him. Sometimes it was a blow job in the office, other times he spiced things up with drugs and by gaining access to a crudely exotic locale. The info Tabby had picked up about her husband regarding the champagne and the bubble baths was no doubt correct. Back in those days, Kevin's lifestyle may have been described as "swinging," or the result of a "one-track mind." In politically correct terms, he exhibited symptoms of sex addiction.

Kevin didn't enjoy getting off in a cool and professional manner; rather, he dug the whole scene. He liked to call for more than one girl at a time. He tried to keep his trysts with escorts entertaining, both for himself and for the women he employed. The average woman who kept Kevin company was not known for her attention span, so Kevin tried to keep things as interesting as possible, even if it cost a few extra dollars. Motels, group scenes, and drugs kept the girls from getting bored.

Cassidy Green had come to the right place. Five-foot-two-inch Kevin Bryant happily helped the suitably diminutive escort fill out the papers for starting up Sunset Sensations. In December, Bryant notarized a business record filed with the Ontario County clerk when the company was started.

Cassidy liked going to the lawyer's office, and it wasn't just because Kevin looked to be a potential source of income down the line. She had another reason to look forward to her visits to the Greece law office. Working there (and living in the lawyer's home) was Cyril Winebrenner, brother of the lawyer's wife. Cyril had been down on his luck, but the bad luck had done nothing to harm his looks, which remained healthy enough to suit Cassidy.

As fate would have it, Cyril was in Kevin's office working his part-time job when Cassidy came in, with wide eyes. She had papers to fill out for an escort service.

Winebrenner and Green hit it off. Patty and his son were a long ways away. He was starting a new life. Ginny had done it. And so, Cyril and Cassidy began a romantic relationship. Soon after, Cassidy also moved in with the Bryants, sharing a room with Cyril.

Cassidy sometimes did waft in the breeze of an ephemeral ambition, but she lacked social upward mobility. She was a whore and a drug dealer. She was in constant need of money for dope, which would either go up her nose or into a crack pipe. She taught the joys of a cocaine/oral sex combo. It wasn't long before Cyril was also a cocaine addict.

This wasn't the only seduction going on in the house. Kevin was drawing his wife into his world of sex addiction. It was no longer enough to have a wholesome world at home and a smarmy world on the outside. He wanted the worlds to join.

When he had his group sex scenes with drugs and professional girls, he wanted Tabby there to join in the fun. When he got head from the stripper who worked out in Scottsville, he wanted Tabby's breasts in his face.

Whether the idea of sexual experimentation was appealing to Tabby, or she saw it as a last desperate attempt to save her marriage, Tabby went along.

* * *

Back home, things were not going great for Cyril's mom and dad.

"Cleo and I were both disabled," Ginny revealed. "The bottom of my husband's heart is deteriorating. He has severe blood vessel and vein disease. He had a quadruple bypass in 2002. The bypass helped, but all of the little arteries in his heart are blocking up. And he's losing circulation to his spine. . . .

"I got hurt at work in August 1994. I was working at the factory that makes the Gummi Bears. I was a machine operator. A roll of film fell off a machine and it weighed about seventy pounds. I tried to catch it with my left arm and it pulled everything out. They did surgery and removed my first left rib. The workman's comp wouldn't pay and held it off for so long that the surgery didn't work. Now if I do one sink of dishes, I can't feel a glass in my hand anymore."

Speaking of fate, she added, "Since I'm left-handed, it affected my left side. It was amazing. I saw fourteen specialists and every single one of them was left-handed. Even the lady that did my final exam for Social Security was left-handed. I've found that a lot of your specialists are left-handed, and a lot of your crafters, too. Most people who do design are left-handed. The only reason I know that is I'm left-handed and I design," Ginny said with a laugh.

CHAPTER 18

Tabby's Boyfriend

According to a family member, Tabby met the man who was to become her boyfriend, in "an establishment." Kevin said Tabby met Richard Oliver (pseudonym) in Nookie's Tavern (pseudonym), a strip joint in Henrietta.

It makes sense, because Richard worked right around the corner. The circumstances of that meeting are sketchy, but it is difficult to imagine them in a wholesome light. No matter what Tabby and Richard's relationship became, it probably started in a somewhat sordid fashion. Eyewitnesses described Tabby as an "amateur lap dancer" at Nookie's Tavern, a description that is open to interpretation.

Suffice it to say that, in early 2003, Tabatha Bryant began seeing Richard Oliver. A beefy blue-collar worker with a "Mr. Clean" shaved head, he was in his late forties, even older than her husband. He was even older than her mother. She had been forced to visit Kevin's world of vice. She had been stripped of her role as suburban lawyer's wife and mother and had been forced to fulfill a threesome with her husband and a hooker. Now she would make something of her latest visit to Kevin's world. She met a guy that she liked. The irony must have pleased her. While being systematically degraded by Kevin Bryant, she had discovered the man who might very well replace Kevin in her life.

Richard worked the night shift as a machine operator at a local factory. His job was at Schlegel, where they made industrial brushes, conveyor rollers, gasket seals of rubber or silicone, and various kinds of locks. Richard worked the night shift, midafternoon through eleven.

Tabby's teller job at the M & T Bank was only part-time. She had Tuesdays and Thursdays off. It was during those days—before Richard Oliver went to work in the middle of the afternoon—that he and Tabby would get together. Most often she would go to his place.

The affair heated up even further on Valentine's Day when Richard told Tabatha that he thought he was falling in love with her. After that, the frequency of their romantic trysts increased.

While Tabatha was seeking romance outside the home, things inside the home were kinkier than ever. February 22, 2003, was Kevin's forty-fifth birthday, and there was a party on Pennicott Circle. According to a "Notice of Intent" later filed by Monroe County prosecutors, Kevin "partied with a dominatrix stripper, two escorts and approximately twenty guests. . . . His two young sons were in the house at the time."

According to a co-worker at Tabby's bank, Tabby herself hired the women for Kevin's party. But Tabby wasn't home for the dominatrix party. She and Richard Oliver were out having dinner.

CHAPTER 19

Army of One

In March 2003, Cyril Winebrenner decided he needed some discipline in his life. He left the Bryant home and joined the army. Cyril had hoped that the disciplined world of the military might help him get his head back on straight.

But that did not turn out to be the case. Cyril, in fact, was just as much a misfit in the army as he had been elsewhere. Before five weeks was up, the army decided that they wanted no more of Cyril Winebrenner and he was discharged.

His military service had lasted only one month. Although Cyril later would claim that he was discharged because his asthma would not allow him to complete boot camp, there are indications that Cyril's lungs weren't the only part of his body that was having trouble with army discipline.

His attempt to get his head back on straight hadn't worked; then his stint in the army was over. He felt as if shame and anger had dominated his life—always had, always would. When he returned, he reunited with

Cassidy Green, but their relationship became volatile. According to Cassidy, Cyril was a changed man after this latest failure. He was hostile toward her, and the world and he began to beat her.

CHAPTER 20

A Legal Problem

In early June 2003, things were volatile on several fronts in the house on Pennicott Circle. Kevin saw Tabby as a threat that needed to be dealt with soon; Cyril began to hit Cassidy; Tabby had had enough of Cyril and Cassidy in her house.

She had agreed to take Cyril in because he was family, and he needed a break. But she hadn't banked on Cassidy being in the house, and the two of them were strung out most of the time.

The situation finally exploded when Tabatha kicked Cyril and Cassidy out of the Bryant home. One version of the story was that Tabby accused Cyril, now out of his head with coke addiction, of stealing $2,000.

Right around that time, Kevin began to think of Tabatha more coolly than ever. The situation was simple. He was a cuckold. She had to go. She was a legal problem, a problem to be taken care of. She was a problem that needed to be "disposed of."

She couldn't be allowed to take the kids. Perhaps she had already told him that she and the boys were going to split. Maybe she thought there was room for her and the boys in that house near Hilton that she had been visiting regularly.

She felt no guilt over her infidelity. She knew enough about Kevin's lifestyle, before and during the time that she became a part of it, to know there was no way she was doing anything to her husband that he hadn't already done to her—repeatedly.

On weekends Tabby still put the boys in the car and drove down to Greenwood. On Saturday nights Tabby, Samantha, Essie, and the boys would go to the local quarter-mile track for the stock car races. The driver Sam had been dating had become her fiancé, and one of Woodhull's winningest drivers.

CHAPTER 21

Tabby's Tail

Maybe it was the time Kevin visited his sons at their day-care center and one kid asked if he was the boys' "other dad." Whatever his inspiration of the moment, in June 2003, Kevin Bryant decided that he would be seeing his wife one day in court, and he wanted to have evidence on his side when that meeting took place. Perhaps he was already contemplating filing for divorce. He feared that she was about to leave him and he wanted to arm himself for what would be the inevitable custody battle.

In his practice, Kevin knew about private investigators. He worked with plenty of them, but he was hesitant to hire one who had been in his office. Tabby might recognize him and figure out what was up. He needed a stranger, so he called Louis Falvo, of the Falvo Agency, Statewide Investigations.

Although they had never met, Falvo's reputation preceded him. Kevin knew that Falvo did good work. He was a member of Associated Licensed Detectives of

New York State and a former regional director of Upstate New York. Falvo's background was in military intelligence (ONI, Office of Naval Intelligence, to be exact), although he wasn't exactly chatty about that part of his life. He had been a licensed private eye for more than twenty-five years, and was considered tops in his field.

As it says in Falvo's online advertisement: "Our commitment to client service and the utilization of the best technology available has made us a premier investigative agency." And Falvo lent some of that high technology to the services he provided for Kevin. Kevin said that he suspected that Tabatha was having an affair and he wanted proof. Falvo knew what to do.

Between June 13 to July 1, 2003, on seven occasions, the private investigator tailed Tabatha as she sneaked out to visit Richard Oliver. During those seven surveillances, Falvo accumulated the evidence Kevin needed.

Falvo did what he was hired to do. He had proven conclusively that Tabatha was having an affair. Clearly, Kevin thought, she was unfit to be a mother. After each day and evening of surveillance, Falvo gave Kevin a call and reported on the day's activities.

Then, on July 2, 2003, following his final day of surveillance, Falvo gave Kevin an in-person report. Falvo could have told Kevin until he was blue in the face that Tabby was trysting regularly with a boyfriend, and it wouldn't have had the effect of the visual aids Falvo brought with him.

Falvo's was a multimedia presentation. First there were photos. Then out came the videotape.

"VCR?" Falvo asked.

"Sure, right in here," Kevin replied.

Falvo played a tape for his client that showed Tabatha meeting a man in a shopping plaza, walking and holding hands, getting into her car with him, disappearing into his house, going to a party. All Tabby with Richard Oliver.

Nine days after Kevin watched the video, he filed for divorce at the Monroe County Clerk of Court's Office. The divorce papers would never be served.

CHAPTER 22

Something in Mind

Sometime during the first half of July, a cocaine dealer named Donny "Rocky" Sands (pseudonym) visited the Bryant home and spoke with Kevin. According to Rocky, who apparently knew Cyril, Kevin tried to hire him to kill Tabatha.

Rocky refused; he wasn't a killer. But, Rocky said, he was willing to help.

"I could plant cocaine in her car and arrange for her to be arrested," Rocky suggested.

Kevin liked the idea. With a cocaine arrest on her record, Tabatha would be discredited in future divorce proceedings.

But Rocky's plan never came to fruition.

Sometime during that same time period, either just before or just after the visit from Rocky, Kevin received a visit from Tim Hunter (pseudonym) and Jennifer Larch (pseudonym). He was probably a pimp and she a prostitute. According to Jennifer, she was an "escort" and her boyfriend a "bouncer."

According to Jennifer, Kevin was a client. They'd

met at group coke-and-sex scenes in local motels. She knew Kevin had a bad heart and had had a couple of open-heart surgeries. She'd seen the scars on his chest to prove it. Jennifer was impressed by how little Kevin was—just five foot two tops. One time early that summer, Jennifer was doing an outcall at Kevin's office. He discussed with her, as he had done with Rocky, his plans to end violently his marital woes. She didn't get it at first. Kevin, Jennifer said, told her he'd pay $500 up front for the purchase of a good piece, plus $4,500 later "when the job was done." She asked him if he was planning to kill his wife. He said he was.

The discussion had taken place in Kevin's office. While Kevin was making his pitch, he had gestured to the picture of his wife on the wall, the one he said needed taking care of. Jennifer took note of the woman in the photo, a pretty blonde. Jennifer didn't spend a lot of time thinking about unloved wives—it was bad for business—but she focused on this unloved wife for a moment. This face registered: the wife whose sickly husband wanted to bump her off. Jennifer liked the cute blond woman's face. She thought that Kevin's wife looked like a nice girl.

Kevin, of course, had wanted sex, but Jennifer was no longer in the mood to become intimate with Kevin. She was creeped out by his deadly business proposition. Later, while Jennifer took a walk, Kevin had repeated his offer to the bouncer Tim. Jennifer's boyfriend said sure, he'd buy a nice piece. Tim grabbed the $500; then he grabbed Jennifer. They split, never looking back. Kevin was $500 lighter and he hadn't even gotten his rocks off. Did he think he was all set, that the deal was done?

CHAPTER 23

When the Party's Over

As the first two weeks of July passed, Cyril Wine-brenner and Cassidy Green were very strung out. Their coke habit was worse than ever. They were doing a lot of "partying all night." The acceleration of their collective habit was causing a monetary crunch for the young couple, as evidenced by Tabby kicking them out for stealing money.

On the one hand, you have a pair of junkies panicky over drugs, selling coke—day and night—and snorting up the profits. They are desperate for blow, desperate for money, money to buy blow.

On the other hand, you have a middle-aged man, with a midlife crisis, who preferred to be in control, and he was losing control. Witnesses have suggested that, for Kevin, the question was no longer what to do, but how to do it. And how to get away with it.

By the middle of July, life was one never-ending party for Cyril and Cassy. It had been going on for days, drugs all night, make a run, sell some, blow some, have a beer, almost out of cigarettes, no toilet paper. The $5,000 offered to do the deed must have seemed like a million, almost enough to just stay high forever and ever. . . .

Tabby somehow managed to get semen on her during the evening of July 13, but the DNA was never matched. (Although it may have been checked against that of Richard Oliver only.)

Assuming that the semen did not get on Tabby's body postmortem, what was Tabby doing during the last hours of her life? Tabby and Kevin were sleeping apart. Her boyfriend hadn't seen her in a couple of days.

CHAPTER 24

Car Trouble

In the early-morning hours of July 14, 2003, Cassidy Green, her heart pounding, drove the getaway car south toward West Bloomfield. But the going was not easy. She'd gathered up her nerves and had her earlier navigation troubles under control, but now the Monte Carlo was misbehaving.

As Cassidy would put it later, the car had been cranky in general, but now it was behaving downright sick. There were electrical problems. The battery was going dead and power was dwindling. Cassidy lost the ability to turn the headlights up to bright. They got the car home, but barely.

Cyril put his bloody T-shirt, jeans, and the down-filled leather jacket he had been wearing in a bag. He then asked his friends Emily Gibbs (pseudonym) and Vinny Bennett (pseudonym) if he could borrow their car. They said okay, and Cassidy and Cyril got into the friends' car. Cyril brought the rifle and the bag of bloody clothes with him.

They drove south, away from West Bloomfield, and into

the rural area known to the residents as the Township of Bloomfield—"township" to distinguish it from the village, where the population was dense, comparatively.

The first item to be chucked was the shirt with the dragon on it—the disposal of the bloody T-shirt defies explanation. Cassidy could have disposed of the shirt anywhere. Police were not chasing her. No one was following her.

The shirt could have been stuffed in a Dumpster, buried in a shallow grave in any secluded area, thrown into any of the many wooded areas in the township. Cassidy could have simply tied the dragon shirt inside a plastic bag and thrown it into a garbage can anyplace away from the crime scene.

If Cassidy had chosen to do any of those, Cyril Winebrenner's bloody shirt probably would never have been seen again. Instead, she dumped the shirt on property belonging to a man named James Green. It was no coincidence that Cassidy and James had the same last name. James Green was Cassidy's uncle.

Cassidy and Cyril drove down Stetson Road and pulled the car over to the shoulder of the road. One of them got out and walked into the woods a bit, leaving the shirt hanging from a tree limb alongside a path in the underbrush, which was mowed regularly. All in all, it was a lousy hiding place. But if ever there was a couple prone to bad decision-making, it was Cyril and Cassidy in the hours and days following Tabatha's murder.

After getting rid of the shirt, they cruised to Wesley Road, where the leather jacket was hurled into a drainage tunnel. The final piece of clothing, the jeans, was chucked into the bushes along a stretch of Silvernail Road, which ran parallel to Stetson Road.

They then drove to a gas station to put gas in Emily and Vinny's car. They pulled into a roadside bar and grill for a drink. It was the sort of place where most of the men in there would be wearing red-plaid hunting garb in a couple of months, whether they'd been hunting that day or not. And many of them had a cigarette lit all the time. The bar was typical of those in that neck of the woods. It was an area where the smoking-ban laws hadn't really taken effect. In big cities across New York State, it was illegal to smoke in a public place, even a bar, and the sidewalks outside establishments were often filled with folks having a smoke before quaffing their next pint of lager. In the rural areas, like Bloomfield, the law was in effect but often wasn't enforced. As Cassy and Cyril had their drinks, several people at the bar smoked cigarettes, and ashtrays were welcomingly in place for them.

The couple's nerves were shot. They must have been jumpy as they smoked and drank, struggling to get a handle on it so they wouldn't attract attention. After the drink, Cassy drove Cyril to his car, which was parked on Clay Street. He took the rifle and put it in his car. According to Cassidy, she never saw the rifle again, at least not as a free woman.

CHAPTER 25

Kevin's Initial Interrogation

Whenever a wife is murdered and the husband reports the crime, it is good police work to eliminate the husband as a suspect first, and that was the intention here. When the first sheriff's deputies and investigators arrived at the scene, the questioning of Kevin began immediately.

Interrogation began in the driveway in front of the Bryant home. Among those interviewing the grieving husband was Deputy Bridget Davis.

Kevin told his interrogators that he had been in bed upstairs at the time of the murder, but he had not been asleep. He had been reading a Tom Clancy thriller. He'd gotten a phone call from a female ten minutes before the attack, but didn't know who it was or what that was about. According to Vivian, Kevin also said that one of his sons had heard the loud pop downstairs and had alerted him that something was wrong. If both stories were true, then Kevin was both awake reading and had to be told something was wrong by one of his sons. This would indicate that he was extremely slow to react to the emergency. He told police that he heard gunshots and then heard his wife scream, "Oh, my God!"

Kevin said he went downstairs immediately and found his wife dead, just as police found her a few minutes later. Kevin talked about his wife's affair, and he also kept looking up at the night sky.

"There's a full moon tonight," he noted. "The full moon brings out the craziness in people. If you're on the edge, it can make you go insane."

He said that he and his wife were having financial difficulties as well. And he added that he had no idea who would want to hurt her. He told investigators that he was an ordained pastor at the Community of Christ Church in Pittsford.

The interrogators kept returning to his marriage problems. Kevin admitted that sexual boredom had become a problem and he and Tabatha had tried experimenting sexually, an attempt to spice up their relationship. Kevin said that he convinced Tabatha to have a threesome with him and another woman. They had gone together to strip clubs such as Nookie's Tavern. He said that Tabatha had found a boyfriend at the strip club and that this had angered him. He admitted that his fury only grew when she suggested that they have another threesome, a different kind. The scene Tabby wanted to make involved Tabby getting between Kevin and Richard, her husband and her lover, in some hot two-on-one action. Kevin kept coming back to Tabby's boyfriend.

Kevin repeatedly spoke of Richard Oliver, probably because he wanted to cast suspicion in that direction, but that was not the effect it was having on his interrogators, who remained glued to him. The attempt to eliminate Kevin as a suspect was unsuccessful.

Kevin's interrogation continued several hours later at sheriff's headquarters in Downtown Rochester. The questioning was pretty much continuous, with breaks being taken only for meals. Kevin was served first breakfast and then lunch as the repetitive questioning stretched on for seventeen hours.

For lunch (and maybe for breakfast also) the suspect and his interrogators left sheriff's headquarters in Downtown Rochester and went to a nearby restaurant. Kevin said later that it was during the lunch break that he felt a migraine coming on. That headache, he would claim later, had become intolerable by the time his interrogation concluded.

Kevin got the drift. He was a suspect. His comments about Tabby's boyfriend became more pointed. A couple of times, Kevin gave up on the comparatively subtle tactics he had used earlier. He stopped merely mentioning Richard's name and began to hint strongly that Tabatha's boyfriend could be the killer. The sheriff's investigators were barking up the wrong tree.

As the number of hours that he had been under interrogation got into the teens, Kevin began to express concern about the welfare of his sons. They had been picked up and taken home by Kevin's parents, but . . . He felt like his place was with them, not with law enforcement answering the same questions over and over again.

"Look, if you have any new questions, you can ask me. Otherwise, I want to go home to see them," Kevin said.

"Just a few more questions," replied fifty-two-year-old investigator Paul T. Siena, who would become lead investigator.

As dinnertime approached, Kevin decided that he had had enough.

"Look, you're either going to arrest me right now or I'm going to leave. What are you going to do?" Bryant said.

"You're not under arrest," Siena replied.

Kevin left.

CHAPTER 26

Hearing the News

As Kevin was being questioned, the authorities were informing Tabatha's kin. Until her closest relatives were informed of her death, the news media would not be told the identity of the victim. It is done this way so that no close relative of a recently deceased person learns of their loved one's demise through the media.

No mother or father, the professional edict goes, should learn, by hearing it on the TV news, that their son or daughter is dead. And that meant that Leroy Bassett, Tabby's dad, had to be informed before the press could be told who the victim was.

When Leroy Bassett's name came up, his daughter Samantha said lovingly, "He's such a good guy." Leroy remarried after breaking up with Ginny. Like Ginny, he'd had a second family.

He spent many years in the army, but he didn't make it to retirement. He remarried a woman named Becky, who had five daughters of her own. If that wasn't enough, they also raised five foster children.

At the time of Tabby's death, Leroy and Becky were

living in Florida, the house not quite as noisy as it once had been. But July 14, 2003, happened to be Leroy Bassett's fifty-first birthday. That was part of the reason law enforcement took so long to reach him with the bad news. It was a broiler of a day and Leroy and Becky spent the morning at the beach with Becky's sister. After the beach the trio played miniature golf and had dinner. Leroy didn't get home until 10:30 that evening. It wasn't long before the phone rang. Leroy expected it to be Tabatha, calling with birthday greetings. Instead, it was a parent's worst nightmare.

"It's Sam. Are you sitting down?"

"Why?" Bassett said.

"I have some bad news"— Samantha paused— "Tabby has been killed."

Leroy couldn't say a word. He put the phone down and went into the bedroom, where he told his wife the bad news.

"You hear about it happening to others, but you never expect it to happen to you," Leroy later said.

Becky thought she must have misheard and made Leroy repeat what he had said.

"He had to repeat it a few times, because I didn't believe it," Becky Bassett said later.

Then Leroy and Becky lay together on the bed and cried.

Upon hearing the news of Tabatha's death, employees at the Manufacturers and Traders Trust Company Bank where she worked—in the town of Perinton— were emotionally overcome.

The bank's manager sensed immediately that to operate that day under these conditions was unfair to the employees and possibly even constituted a security lapse. He closed the bank and the weeping employees were given the day off to grieve.

* * *

Samantha Bassett recalled later how she learned the bad news about her kid sister: "On Monday night, about eight or eight-thirty, Kevin called Gram. I was working. He said that there was something he had to tell Gram and I about Tabby. And that was all he said.

"So he drove down. I was still at work when he arrived and he told Gram that Tabby had been attacked while she was asleep, and killed. I guess it was okay, because at the time we didn't think he had anything to do with it. But the fact that so long of a time went by. I mean, his parents knew what happened and they never called. A whole day had passed, practically."

Sam didn't know or didn't care that Kevin had endured seventeen hours of interrogation and a real or feigned migraine before making the drive from Penfield to Greenwood to tell Gram and Sam the tragic news personally.

"All of Gram's kids were at the church reunion, so, yeah, I had to make phone calls. I called my mom. I told my mom about two kids being dead. I had to tell her when Chris died, too."

Ginny remembered: "We were dealing with the fact that Chris's birthday was coming up the next day. I had gone to bed. It was almost midnight and my daughter Samantha called me.

"She said, 'Mom, are you sitting down?'

"I said, 'Well, no.'

"She said, 'I think you better sit down.' I said okay and she said, 'There was a break-in at Tabby's house and Tabby was attacked and it was fatal.'

"I said, 'What?' She told me again. I said, 'Is Tabby okay?'

"She said, 'Mom, she didn't make it.'

"And I said, 'Is she okay?'

"After that, I don't remember if my husband took the

phone or if I finished talking to her. I found out on Chris's birthday, so it was a double whammy. I've had a hard enough time just dealing with Chris's birthday."

Reverend Mike Allen, a Pittsford, New York, colleague of Vivian and Kevin Bryant at the Community of Christ Church, told reporters that Tabby loved to lead spirituals.

"She had a beautiful voice," he said.

Reverend Allen said that he knew there were strains in Tabby's marriage, but he had been under the impression that she and Kevin were attempting to work out their difficulties. As far as he knew, Tabatha and Kevin had planned to attend a church-sponsored family camp on the weekend after Tabatha was murdered.

Ginny and Cleo decided not to tell her father about Tabby's death. He had gone to Chris's funeral and had not been sure what was going on. His senility had progressed even further and a decision was made not to tell him. He wouldn't have remembered who Tabatha was anyway.

CHAPTER 27

Monday Morning
Press Conference

Rochester reporter Amy Cavalier remembered going to the office on the morning of July 14. She hadn't made it all the way in the door when she learned that there had been a murder in Penfield.

Amy never had to deal with anything like this before. Her previous experience was as a reporter at a public radio station in Oswego. Amy knew nothing about covering a murder. For her, it would be full-speed ahead, figure it out as you go. She remembered the most important rule of journalism: "First find out: who, what, where, when, and why!"

She was twenty-seven years old at the time. She was born and raised in Oswego, a town of about twenty-five thousand, located in upstate New York on the shores of Lake Ontario and the Oswego River. After graduating from Oswego High School, she attended the State University of New York (SUNY) at Oswego. An outdoor enthusiast—she lived to ski—Amy graduated with a degree in journalism in 1999. During her senior year of college, Amy interned at WRVO-FM, a public radio station that served an eighteen-county region in upstate New York. Shortly after graduation, she was hired as a full-time news reporter/producer for the station. Cavalier earned numerous Associated Press and Syracuse Press Club awards for her on-air work. In January 2003, Cavalier was hired as a reporter with Messenger Post Newspapers. The small family-operated company distributed weekly newspapers in the suburbs of Monroe County and a daily newspaper, the *Daily Messenger,* headquartered in Canandaigua, New York. By April 2003, she was the full-time *Penfield Post* reporter. Three months later, Tabatha Bryant was murdered. It would be Cavalier's job to cover the story as it unfolded for both the weekly and daily newspaper. Cavalier's work for the *Penfield Post* had been featured recently in a book, *Memories of the Home Front,* published by Atria Senior Living Group. Her article on two local women's memories of life during World War II was included in a compilation of over seven hundred testimonials from women residents living at Atria communities nationwide.

In the next three years, Amy would get a better education in law, the justice system, and life than her education at SUNY Oswego could have ever prepared her for. On that first Monday morning, she was informed that the Monroe County Sheriff's Office would be holding a press conference, and so she immediately left for the Pennicott Circle gathering. Amy arrived at the residence at about 9:30 A.M.

Reporters and sheriff's cars lined the front of the house. The white house was hidden partially from the street by tall evergreens. The front yard was cordoned off with police tape and the garage door around the corner was open, revealing a minivan parked inside.

There were still a few minutes before the press conference was scheduled to begin, so Amy filled the time

by canvassing the neighborhood, trying to get neighbors to talk to her. For Amy, the residents of Pennicott
Circle painted a more complete picture of the folks in
number 2. One neighbor told Amy that the Bryants had
had other people living with them from time to time.

"One of the boarders might have been the wife's
brother, but I couldn't swear to it," a neighbor said. The
mailbox at the house was for Bryant, and the neighbors
referred to the apparent victim as Tabatha.

The same neighbor who had heard the major arguing two-and-a-half-hours before the murder said that
she did not want her name printed in the newspaper,
and then revealed to Amy a little bit about the apparent victim. She said she and her young blond neighbor had spoken on several occasions.

"She told me she wished she did not have to work as
much and could stay home with her children more,"
the neighbor said.

Amy and the other reporters learned that sheriff's
deputies responded to a 911 call from the home at
12:01 A.M. July 14. When they arrived, they discovered
a homicide victim—a female in her twenties.

Undersheriff Daniel Greene held the press conference. He made it clear that the sheriff's office did
not believe this to be a case of random violence. On
the contrary, Greene said, they believed that Tabatha
appeared to be the intended target.

"We are pursuing all leads at this point," Undersheriff Greene said at the press conference. "We're
doing everything we can, including knocking on neighbors' doors."

One of the neighbors who talked with investigators
during that process reported hearing "major arguing" between 9:00 and 9:30 on Sunday night, two-and-
a-half to three hours before Kevin Bryant reported his
wife's murder. The neighbor, however, could not swear
that the arguing was coming from the Bryant house.

According to Monroe County Sheriff's Office captain Theodore "Ted" Wright, Tabatha's murder was the first in the town of Penfield that he could recall in more than forty years. He said the last one he could clearly remember was the murder of Pamela Moss back in the early 1960s.

In 1962, James Moore, a landscape gardener, raped and strangled fourteen-year-old Moss. Her body was found two days later in a water-filled gravel pit. Moore confessed and was given a life sentence without the possibility of parole.

"Her body was found in the Dolomite Quarry, off Panorama Trail," Captain Wright said. That would have been only a few miles from the Bryant murder scene.

By noon, through neighbors and a check of property tax records, Amy had verified that Kevin Bryant, an attorney, lived in the big white house with his wife, Tabatha, and their two children. At the press conference, reporters had been told that the couple's two young sons were unharmed.

CHAPTER 28

An Emerging Picture

The next day, Tuesday, July 15, 2003, TV news and the Rochester newspapers for the first time identified the victim. The positive ID had been made public by the Monroe County Medical Examiner's Office.

The deceased was Tabatha Marie Bryant, born October 8, 1976. The medical examiner's report indicated the victim had been shot and stabbed.

Following Kevin's seventeen-hour interrogation, the sheriff's office had not lost interest in him. They went to work, hard, trying to find out all there was to learn about Kevin C. Bryant, attorney-at-law. One of the first routine checks was into records at the Monroe County Executive Office. It was here that investigators learned that Kevin Bryant had filed for divorce papers only days before his wife's murder. Later, reporters learned Kevin had not yet served her the papers and the couple's pastor indicated the couple was planning on going on a weekend retreat through their church, the Community of Christ Church, to try and reconcile.

With that piece of information, Amy Cavalier worked

to get a fuller picture of Tabatha. She began by attempting to contact the Community of Christ Church in Pittsford, where it had been reported that Tabatha attended church and sang in the choir. Amy couldn't find the church in Pittsford. The church turned out to be located on Pittsford-Palmyra Road, just across the town line in Palmyra—but she did get a number off the Internet for a church by that name in Greenwood, New York.

"I called the phone number, but I didn't get a minister," Amy recalled. "Instead, I found myself talking to Lorraine Warriner, Tabatha's aunt."

Lorraine, sister of Leroy Bassett, Tabatha's father, told Amy how her mother, Essie, raised Tabatha. Amy learned that Essie Bassett had raised Tabatha and her older sister, Samantha, in the small town of Greenwood. Lorraine said, "Tabby was a happy child, much like she was as an adult. She was bubbly and always in the middle of everything. She loved everyone, and loving love. We just can't understand who was so angry with her that they would do this. I've never known her to have any enemies.

"She loved her boys. I don't know what they'll do without her." About Tabby's initial move from Greenwood to Monroe County, Lorraine said, "I think she was excited. She wasn't a small-town girl. She liked the excitement of having things to do."

Knowing very little, Lorraine said she and the family were shocked by the news.

"Kevin is just beside himself," she added.

PART III

CHAPTER 29

Jennifer Gets Deposed

A couple of days after the murder, Jennifer Larch looked at a newspaper and there she saw a photo of a woman she recognized. It was Tabby, the nice-looking woman whose small husband wanted her killed. Jennifer knew she had a story that law enforcement was going to be very interested in hearing.

A man who used to be a Livingston County sheriff's deputy had once hired Jennifer as a baby-sitter. She got in touch with him and said she needed to tell someone about a murder. Was there someone there who would listen to her? Investigator Tyler Barrus invited her into the sheriff's station to tell her story. Barrus had Jennifer take an oath to tell the truth, and with the help of a stenographer, he got her story on paper in the form of a "supporting deposition."

If she had been caught lying, she wouldn't have been charged with perjury. Instead, she would have been guilty of a less frightening "class A misdemeanor under the laws of New York State," which stated that it was illegal "for a person, in and by written instrument, to knowingly make a false statement, or to make a statement which such person does not believe to be true."

Here is Jennifer Larch's deposition, which she signed and dated July 18, 2003, four days after the murder:

My name is [Jennifer Larch]. I am twenty-eight years old. I live at [address deleted]. I just moved in there with my boyfriend [Timothy Hunter], about two days ago. Before that, we had been living at his cousin's house on Ross Street, in the City of Rochester.

Over the last eight years I have been working as a dancer at Foxy's in Scottsville. I have not really danced since last summer, though. I still go in on occasion when I need money and do paperwork and waitress or other odd jobs.

If any of my old customers are there I can do some table dances and make a little extra money. The last time I actually went to work at Foxy's was last week on Thursday or Friday.

Last summer I actually got let go from Foxy's. I was having a problem with crack cocaine. I ran into a girl I knew from Foxy's named [Lynnette]. Her name is [Lynnette Harrison]. I don't think that is her real name, though. No one uses their real name.

Lynnette used to dance at Foxy's about five years ago and that is how I knew her. The meeting happened around February, the first week. We got to talking. She was saying that she has a crack problem, too, and asked me if I needed any money.

I told her that I did. I gave her my number and told her to contact me if she had any ways for me to make money. I had been living at my sister Jacqueline's house at the time. Lynnette called me later on that night. She asked me if I really wanted to make some money.

I said I did. Somebody came and picked me up and brought me to the Microtel (a motel) in Henrietta. Lynnette was there. I ended up staying there with her for the next three weeks. That was how I started in the escort business.

Lynnette did not run this service. In fact, I don't even know the name of it. I know it is run by a girl named Sue. I had Sue's number at my house. During that three-week period of time, Lynnette and I were working together. We were dancing and doing whatever else it took to make money.

We had been moving around between the Red Carpet, the Dorkat and the Microtel during that whole period. I was basically hanging out the whole time with Lynnette. Basically we would get a hotel room, then call Sue and tell her that we were available. She would call us and give us a name and a number to call to set it all up and then the guy would come over. Lynnette would do outcalls but I never did that.

One time during this three-week period of time I had been out shopping. This was, I think, about a week or so after Valentine's Day. When I got back to the room there was already a guy in the room. Lynnette introduced me to him as Kevin.

Kevin had brought Burger King for us. It was early morning, like breakfast time, 9:30 or 10:00 AM. We all sat down, ate, and then had sex.

Kevin is a really small man. He is about 5'2". He has scars all over his chest from all these open-heart surgeries. Lynnette had warned me that he had had open-heart surgery a few times, so to take it easy. I know that she had seen Kevin on prior occasions.

When he left the hotel room, he left a business card. The card is either white or beige and it says Kevin C. Bryant. The card has an address and a phone number on it. I'm sure that it says Attorney-at-Law.

A couple of weeks after that, about a week after St. Patrick's Day, I had been at Lynnette's house on [deleted] Street in the City. We were there with her friend Chrissy. I don't know her last name, or if that is her real name.

A guy named Howard came over. I don't know his last name either, but he was just coming over to get high, anyway. Nobody had any money. We decided to call Kevin because he has money. I think Chrissy called him. She called him on his cell phone, the same number off the business card, I think.

We set something up with him. Chrissy and I met him at the Day's Hotel across from the Gates Pub. On this occasion I think he may have already had a room. I'm pretty sure about that. I remember Chrissy going in first and me putting make-up on in the car.

They must have already had the money worked out by the time I got up there. I remember going in the room and there was cocaine everywhere in the room. There were full bags and piles and empty bags and stuff all over the place.

There was actually two different rooms connected. When we got there Chrissy ended up going into the connected room. I remember that there were two guys, a girl, and a golden retriever type dog in the room.

All of the people that were there were white. The girl was real young and had blonde hair. She looked like she was only like sixteen or seventeen years old. The guys looked to be thirty-five to forty. Kevin gave us money and we went in and got a room. This was early morning again because we had been up smoking [crack] all night long.

When Kevin had first given me his business card he had said that I could call him any time. I decided to contact him and see if he would be willing to have just me come see him instead of me and Chrissy or me and Lynnette. I wanted to make the money for myself.

I had only done these things through the escort agency for three or four weeks. I had picked up four clients from the agency that I started seeing on a weekly basis strictly through me and not through the agency. Kevin was one of these four clients.

The only time that I actually met with Kevin through Sue's escort service was the first time at the Red Carpet. Every time after that was on my own—including the time at Day Motel. After the time at Day Motel I misplaced [his card] somewhere and I had no contact with him for about two months.

Over that period of time I had been staying kind of from house to house, between my sisters on [name of street deleted], my mothers house in Lakeville and in my car at Foxy's parking lot. My sister told me that about three different times a guy named Kevin had called.

My sister knows that I am doing escort work and that Kevin was a client but I don't think that she knows anything about him more than that. My mother had told me the same thing, that a guy named Kevin had called for me at the house in Lakeville.

I have no idea when these calls were made to my sister or my mother. I never called him back. I was kind of straightening up a bit and I did not need the money that bad anymore. Kevin was just a client.

My boyfriend Tim Hunter had just got out of jail a while ago but we had finally got back together around the beginning of June. On June 23rd I got stopped out in Penfield by the Sheriff's Department. I got a bunch of tickets and my car ended up getting impounded. Tim and I had got back together. I needed money. I started calling a couple clients back to get some money. We were really desperate.

On Tuesday, July 1st sometime in the afternoon I think that it was probably later in the day, like 4:00 PM. I called Kevin Bryant at his cell number. I called from Tim's cousin's phone at [address deleted], Rochester.

I said, "Hey, how you doing. Do you want some company later on tonight. I need some money."

He said that he had just taken his kids to the doctor and was either on his way home or on his way to the office. At any rate, he told me to meet him at his office at 8:00 PM. I wrote his office address in my address book. He had given Tim directions while on the telephone.

Tim drove me to the office at about 8:00 PM and came back and picked me up after about an hour. Kevin's office was located by the Red Lobster on West Ridge Road. They had just put up a Krispy Kreme across the street.

When I got there the door was locked but there was a magazine stuck in the door jam [*sic*] so that the door would not close. The main entrance is on the east side of the building. When you go into his office building, Kevin's office is on the main floor on the left side as you go in.

I went and knocked on his door. Kevin answered the door. He gave me a bottle of Jack

Daniels as I came in. As soon as I got the bottle I began to slosh down as much of it as I could. He said he had to go to his car to get some stuff.

I just hung out in his foyer and waited for him. He came back in with his red duffel bag. We went back to his office. He sat at his desk and started opening mail. He got a large wad of cash out of a bank envelope, the kind you get when you cash a check.

He was showing the money off in his hands. He was flipping through the wad of cash and he said sarcastically that he "only had $7,500." He paid me my $150. Then he started talking about his wife and how she was cheating on him. He said she had come home once at four in the morning. He said that he had found out she was seeing some guy each Tuesday and Thursday. And he told me that he wanted to start seeing me each Tuesday and Thursday. I was getting kind of drunk but I can remember that he was getting really upset about it. His face was turning all red.

He finally laid down a blanket on the floor. He had got it from somewhere in his office. We had sex. He really only fingered me and ejaculated on my chest.

He said, "Call me this time next week." And I left.

On Tuesday, July 8th, I called Kevin Bryant from my friend Robin's house again. I called the same cell phone number from Tim's cousin's phone. This was about 7:30 or 8:00 PM. I talked to Kevin. I asked him if he wanted some company.

He said, "You won't believe it. I'm on my way to the office right now. Come on over as soon as you can."

Tim took me over to Kevin's office once again.

Tim stayed in the car outside this time. I went in and met Kevin in his office foyer. He said he had to run outside and get his stuff. He went outside for a minute. As soon as he came back in he dropped off his red bag in his office and we both sat down. I had brought the traffic tickets with me. He was looking for a rubber and had made copies of the tickets.

He said, "Who's the guy in the car?"

I told him he was my bouncer.

Kevin said, "Does he do any side work?"

I told him that Tim worked for Buckley Movers.

Kevin said, "That's not what I mean, Jennifer."

I said, "So what do you mean?"

He said, "Never mind."

I pressed him a little bit and I said, "What are you talking about?" I was thinking that he was looking for a bouncer or something.

Kevin said, "I need to get rid of someone."

I said, "Who?"

He did not say anything. He just kind of smiled a bit.

I said, "You're not talking about killing your wife?"

"Yes, I am," Kevin said.

I was awestruck because he was dead serious. He asked me if I thought the guy out in the car would do it.

He said, "I will give you $500 right now to go out and buy a piece and $4,500 when it's done." He said, "If you can find someone to do it I'll take care of your tickets. I'll get your car out of impound, pay any fine you have, and represent you in court. That will be your commission."

I said, "Are you out of your fucking mind?"

He said, "No. If you can't find someone to do it can you at least find a clean gun?"

I said, "No, I can't do that." I told him that I could not do any sex stuff right then, but asked him if he could pay me anyway and I would come another time and take care of him. He agreed. He paid me $150 and I left.

I went outside to the car. Kevin told me he was going to come out and talk to Tim. He followed me outside, Kevin got into our truck and I just took a walk. I did not want to know anything. When I got back Kevin was not in the car. I saw him go back in the office.

When I got back to the truck. Tim told me that Kevin had asked him if he would kill his wife. Tim told me that Kevin had given him $500. We pretty much took the money and left. We were able to get our apartment the very next day.

I found out on Monday (July 14) or Tuesday (July 15) that this woman got killed. I recognized her picture in the paper as being the same woman I had seen pictures of on Kevin's office wall. I could not believe it. I got sick to my stomach. I've been throwing up for three days.

I met with Investigator Tyler Barrus from the Sheriff's Office and told him everything I know about Kevin Bryant. I turned over the tickets that Kevin had copied as well as a couple of beat up pages from my address book to him.

Jennifer's statement ran four typed pages. Each had been signed and dated by Jennifer. Investigator Barrus has signed and dated the final page, adding "20:35," or 8:35 P.M., the time at which the document was signed.

CHAPTER 30

Saying Good-bye

On the same day that Jennifer gave her deposition—Friday, July 18, 2003—H. P. Smith and Son Funeral Home in Canisteo held visiting hours.

"I'd say there were one hundred seventy-five to two hundred people in attendance," said Tom Smith, owner of the funeral parlor. "That's above average for any funeral we've had. The death was quite far-reaching, in that both sides of the family are very large and both had many friends. The young age of the deceased also makes a big difference here. Those that live till they're ninety years old have usually outlived their friends."

The next day, Saturday, July 19, 2003, Tabatha's funeral was held in Greenwood. So many people attended the service that the small country church couldn't hold them all. At Kevin's request, Tabatha's uncle Terry Smith, a minister, delivered the eulogy.

Smith had practiced as a marriage and family therapist for twenty years in Hornell, New York, before moving to Columbus, Ohio, to work as a minister to young

adults and families in the Grove City Community of
Christ. Terry received his master of family therapy degree
from Southern Connecticut State University and was a
certified family-life educator. He'd been an advocate
for healthy families in the Grove City and greater Columbus communities, and, at the time of the murder, he
served as president of the Columbus Marriage Coalition,
which he helped to found. Terry and his wife, Carolyn,
were elders in the Community of Christ. They had four
grown children and one granddaughter.

According to funeral attendee Michael Hartwig,
who married into Tabatha's extended family, much of
the town of Greenwood came to the funeral. Hartwig
described Tabatha as "friendly, very vivacious, outgoing, and always willing to do a lot for other people." In
attendance was Tabby's grief-stricken grandmother
Essie Bassett, who had raised her from the time she was
a baby in her always-full house on Route 248. And so
was Ginny Winebrenner, Tabby's mom, who had only
become close with her daughter in the era of cell
phones and unlimited long distance. She had to grieve
over the loss of another child to a violent death, and
she had to worry about a third child, Cyril, who had
been having serious mental problems the last time
she saw him.

Ginny worried that Cyril's disappearing act in the
wake of Tabby's death wasn't a symptom of another flip-
out, another breakdown, mini or otherwise. Ginny
tried to have optimistic thoughts, none came.

She knew that because of the way Cyril felt about
Tabby—"They had been so close that it was scary"—
something had to be wrong with Cyril or he would have
been at his sister's funeral. There were no happy reasons for Cyril's absence.

At Tabatha's funeral tension between Ginny Winebrenner and Kevin's parents was running high. Ginny
recalled, "Kevin's mom came up to me to tell me she

was so sorry, yadda-yadda, and Kevin's dad watches her like a hawk. Every time she would get near me, he would get between us and get in the way. He did not want her talking to me. That didn't surprise me. He was the type that would say 'Jump.' And she would say, 'How high?' She was cowed by him. He ruled the roost. He was a jerk.

"Tabby called me once, she was so angry. She said that Kevin's dad told Kevin that he needed to make a will up saying that everything would go to Kevin's dad and he would dole it out as he thought Tabatha needed it. You can imagine how that went over. Kevin's dad once said that if Kevin died, he would allow Tabby to raise the boys. Him and Kevin are two of a kind. He may be a minister, but I would be terrified of him."

On the other hand, the tension that had existed between Ginny and the Bassetts—the family she had once been a part of—was lessened by the tragic occasion.

"Up until Tabby's funeral, the Bassetts and I didn't talk at all. Now we do, and they are wonderful people. I can now call and cry on their shoulder. The same is true with my ex-husband. We didn't talk at all until the funeral and now we do. We get along better now than we did when we were married, I think," Ginny said.

Following the funeral, Tabatha was buried in a Greenwood cemetery—home again.

The next day, WHEC-TV 10 in Rochester reported, "Tabatha Bryant used to bring her two young boys to church retreats. Extended family members say that, at three and five years old, the boys don't understand what's happened. Husband Kevin is having a hard time, too."

Kevin's father, Vivian, spoke to the reporter after the funeral and described the aftermath of Tabby's murder: "One of the boys woke Kevin up after hearing a shot.

Kevin went downstairs and found his wife dead. She had been shot and stabbed."

The reporter made it clear that Kevin was not a suspect in the murder. At least that was the public story. Behind the scenes Kevin remained the investigation's prime suspect—not that they weren't chasing down other leads. The victim's brother was missing, for example. Investigators needed to get in touch with everyone who had been in touch with Kevin—and that included Cyril Winebrenner, who was strung out on coke and hadn't shown up for his sister's funeral.

The Rochester *Democrat and Chronicle* (D & C) had reporters searching for someone, anyone, who might know something about the woman who had been killed. They talked to Sharon Brown (pseudonym), who had been Tabatha's coworker at Kevin's office. Sharon began working as a secretary in Kevin Bryant's law office in 2000, at which time Tabatha, the boss's wife, was already the head secretary in the office. Sharon said to the D & C reporter, "Tabby had two kids and she had to juggle between her kids and going back and forth to work. Those kids were her heart. She would do anything for them." Brown called Tabatha outgoing and cheerful—and had assumed that Tabatha was older than she was. "She was really mature," Brown said. "She had herself together."

Debbie Proud (pseudonym), a friend of Tabatha's from Greenwood, had been a regular customer at J.C.'s Café, where Tabby had waitressed. Days after the murder, Debbie recalled for a reporter Tabatha's outgoing demeanor: "When Earl came in, she'd give him a big hug. When Mike came in, she'd yell out, 'Hey, Mikey.'" Describing Tabby's demeanor, Debbie said, "She had a zest for life. She was high on life."

CHAPTER 31

Frightened Neighbors

The little corner of Penfield where the Bryant family lived was now the home of some very frightened neighbors. There was a killer on the loose. Cars cruised by slowly. Were they sightseers, or maybe the killer returning to the scene of the crime? Nerves were raw. Phones were ringing constantly. Strangers came to the door.

The Bryants' neighbors received phone calls and visits from reporters that first week as well. Christine Kenny (pseudonym) was a neighbor of the Bryants, who lived just a few doors down on Pennicott Circle. Days after the murder, when interviewed by local reporters, she recalled Tabatha as a devoted mother.

"She loved her boys and wanted to stay home and take care of them," she said. "She used to walk her kids around the neighborhood all the time."

Kenny told local reporter Patrick Flanigan that in 2002 Tabatha had held a party for the neighborhood in order to meet her neighbors. Because of her two kids and two jobs, Tabby had not had an opportunity to meet her neighbors, so she created an opportunity.

"She never got a chance to meet anybody," Kenny said. "Her social life wasn't the best. It was her way of getting to know people in her neighborhood."

Kenny said that Tabatha had expressed her desire to quit her jobs and become a stay-at-home mom.

Speaking four days after the murder, Christine Kenny admitted to being nervous about her own safety: "Until they find out who did this, it's hard to justify anything. If you can't feel safe in your own home, what's the world coming to?"

Kenny was also interviewed by Amy Cavalier, working for the *Daily Messenger.* During that interview she said about the neighborhood, "It's real quiet with mainly families living here. I'm here full-time, and it's almost too quiet."

Cleo and Ginny Winebrenner got back to Minnesota on a Monday. Still, no word from Cyril.

Ginny remembered: "When we got back from the funeral that Monday, we stopped at my brother Jerry's first because Tabby had had Chris's ashes, and Jerry had picked them up and taken them back from Tabby's funeral, and he was hanging on to them for me.

"And they said that we should call home because Cyril had been trying to reach us. I had even called the police because no one had heard from him. I wanted them to help me find him so he could go to Tabby's funeral, but nobody could find him.

"We went back home and Patty told us that Cyril was coming in on a bus. I said okay, and we went up on a Wednesday to pick him up at the bus station, and that was the first time I had seen him since his breakdown.

"During the time since I'd last seen him, Cyril had gone into the service and he was out. I mean, he was in the service for a month, two months, something like that. He got a medical discharge. I assumed it was because of his asthma, but Cyril absolutely refused to talk about it, so I have no idea. He wouldn't talk about anything at all that happened when he was in the service. He wouldn't even mention it, so I don't know what went on. It wasn't very often that he was that closed mouthed about something, so something happened, but I don't know what it is."

Ginny let Cyril stay in her trailer in Osceola, the same town—population 4,659 spread out over six square miles—where Cyril had worked as a dealer at the Lakeside Casino.

CHAPTER 32

Cassy Sells Blow to Rocky

Donny "Rocky" Sands was the drug dealer who had been to the Bryant house earlier in the month. While there, Rocky said, Kevin had asked him to accept money in exchange for killing Tabatha. Rocky had refused.

Kevin had then asked Rocky to plant cocaine in Tabatha Bryant's car and arrange for her to be arrested, which would discredit her in potential divorce proceedings.

When Rocky heard that Tabatha had been murdered, he knew immediately that Kevin, Cyril, and Cassy had been behind it. Although he was a drug dealer, he had his scruples—just as Jennifer Larch had hers—and on Sunday, July 20, 2003, he went to the sheriff's office with what he knew.

The sheriff's investigators asked Rocky if he was willing to help them break the case. Rocky said yes. He gave them information that would help them find Cyril and agreed to wear a wire while making a drug deal with Cassidy. Rocky hoped that while he was making the drug deal with Cassidy, he would be able to get her to talk about the murder.

Rocky twice bought cocaine from Cassidy. After the second buy, Cassidy was arrested and charged with drug violations. Investigator Paul Siena talked to her. He told her he wasn't that interested in the drug charges, what he was really interested in was Tabatha Bryant's murder. Maybe she knew something that would help. At first, Cassidy denied having anything to do with Tabatha's murder.

She better start talking and keep talking, she was told. As it was, she was every bit as guilty of Tabby's death as if she had wielded the knife herself. She could get the lethal injection. That is, unless she started talking.

Cassidy subsequently made two statements, which were transcribed and she signed. In each statement she swore that she had told the investigators everything she knew about the murder of Tabatha Bryant. It had been Cyril Winebrenner who killed his half sister. She did not mention that—according to what she had been led to believe—Kevin had paid Cyril to kill Tabatha.

On Friday, July 25, Ginny's brother Russ called and asked if Ginny and Cleo wanted to come up and help him and his wife.

"They were remodeling their house," Ginny said. "So we went there for a while, which was good, because I felt like I needed to get away. The doctor had said we should try to relieve as much stress on Cleo as possible, so we needed to move. And Russ and Tammy were worried about him and offered to let us stay with them till we could find a place of our own.

"Then, the next Friday, Patty called us and said that Cyril had been called in to talk to the police. Shortly thereafter, we learned that he had been arrested."

* * *

The general public was unaware of just how narrow the investigation into Tabby's murder had become. Tabatha's coworkers at the M & T Bank complained to the press that no one from law enforcement had been in to interview those who knew her at work. One of them might have seen something suspicious, but no one even bothered to ask, they fretted.

CHAPTER 33

Osceola

On August 2, 2003, two weeks after the murder, sheriff's investigators Paul Siena and David Vaughn traveled to Osceola, Iowa, to have a chat with Cyril Winebrenner. As it turned out, Cyril was right where they thought he would be.

Siena was the same investigator who had questioned Kevin Bryant at length the morning after the murder.

Winebrenner seemed calm at first, but he lost his pleasant demeanor when Siena informed him that Cassidy Green had confessed.

Meanwhile, Ginny Winebrenner was out of her head with worry: "I had called down there to the jail while they were talking to Cyril and I had even talked to Cyril once. I asked him what was going on. He said, 'They're just asking me questions, Mom. They just want to know what I know.' I said, 'Okay. Are you all right?' He said, 'I'm fine. We're having pizza.'"

As Cyril's interrogation continued, Ginny Winebrenner, left unappeased by her one brief conversation with

Cyril and the fact that they were having pizza, repeatedly called the police station looking for information.

"I had no idea what was going on," she said. "I knew that they were questioning him, but I didn't know about what. I knew that Cyril knew a lot about Kevin because he had worked for him. And I knew that Kevin didn't have a very good clientele. I called the investigating officer four times and I asked him to call me back and let me know what was going on. He never even bothered to call me back. What a jerk.

"I didn't find out until Patty told me that they had arrested him, and what they had arrested him for. It couldn't have been a bigger shock. I had no clue. My first thought was, no way. Couldn't have been. By the time I found out, Cyril was already on his way to New York, and I've only talked to him once since then."

By later in the day, many newspapers in the Northeast and Midwest were printing Cyril Winebrenner's name, saying he was the depraved killer who had mercilessly stabbed his own half sister to death.

Cyril didn't maintain his innocence for very long. Instead, he seemed determined to give the sheriff's investigators as detailed of an account of his sister's murder as he could. He would shirk none of the responsibility, he said. He had done it for money, money paid to him by Kevin Bryant. Kevin had fired the rifle and he had wielded the knife. He had been doing a lot of drugs at the time. He never said he was sorry.

Within a few hours the sheriff's investigators had begun preparing a thirteen-page statement detailing Winebrenner's participation in the crime.

CHAPTER 34

The Night They Raided
Sunset Sensations

Sometime during late July 2003, police from Monroe, Ontario, and Livingston Counties raided a trailer home on Routes 5 & 20 in West Bloomfield, New York. The home—the principal inhabitant of which was a man named Jeff Null (pseudonym)—was, according to paperwork filled out by Kevin Bryant, the headquarters for an escort service operated by Cyril Winebrenner and Cassidy Green. Both of these parties had stayed, off and on, at the Bryants' Penfield home during the six months before Tabatha's murder.

A neighbor of Null's, Paul Brass (pseudonym), later told a WHEC-TV reporter: "Oh yeah, there were a lot of cops in there last week. They raided that trailer over there. I don't know what they took out or how long they were there. I just know there were a lot of cops there. They had the driveway on the other side of the house shut right off.

"A lot of people used to come and go from that

trailer over there. At night. Nobody liked to be seen during the day around there," Brass added.

Null told the law enforcement officials that Winebrenner and Green also stayed at the trailer on occasion, in addition to it being the listed address for their escort service.

CHAPTER 35

Uncle James Finds a Shirt

Around the same time as the raid on Sunset Sensations, James Green—Cassidy's uncle—was riding his tractor through his land. He maintained a series of paths through his grounds and periodically took the large riding mower along those trails to keep the weeds from taking over.

From his perch atop the tractor, he saw something black clinging to a tree. He switched off the engine and climbed down to see what it was. It turned out to be a black T-shirt.

He brought it inside and showed it to his wife, Roberta. It must belong to a kid they know, they assumed. What else was there to think? Who else is shedding clothes out there? Probably a friend of their girls during a party or something.

Uncle James's wife, Roberta, washed the shirt and kept it. So when sheriff's investigators rang the doorbell some weeks later and asked if they had found anything unusual on their property, they said, yeah, a shirt, we washed it. Here it is.

CHAPTER 36

Cyril's Voluntary Statement

On Saturday, August 2, 2003, Kevin Bryant and Cyril Winebrenner were charged with second-degree murder. Winebrenner was still in Iowa; Kevin Bryant was placed in the Monroe County Jail.

The news of the arrests came as a surprise to all but those involved in the investigation. The sheriff's office said there was a good reason for not publicly naming any of the suspects before the arrests were made.

For most of that Saturday, Cyril was at the Osceola Sheriff's Department being interrogated by Siena and Vaughn, of the Monroe County Sheriff's Office.

By Saturday evening the thirteen-page statement made by Cyril confessing to his part in Tabatha's death had been typed. Cyril and two witnesses, Siena and Vaughn, signed it.

The heading on each page of Winebrenner's statement read:

VOLUNTARY STATEMENT, Town of Penfield, State of New York, County of Monroe. Date: 08/02/03. Time: 8:22 PM. Place: Osceola Sheriff's

Department, 220 Townline Road, Osceola, Iowa. I have been duly warned by Investigator Siena and Investigator Vaughn, who have identified themselves as a Monroe County Deputy Sheriff Investigator, that I have the right to remain silent and don't have to say anything if I don't want to; that anything I do say can be used against me in a court of law; that I have the right to talk to a lawyer before making any statement and to have him here with me; that if I can't pay for a lawyer, one will be given to me before I make any statement, if I wish. I understand what my rights are and am willing to make a statement. I do not want a lawyer at this time. No promises or threats have been made to me to induce this statement.

At the bottom of each page it read: "I have read this statement consisting of 13 page(s) and the facts contained therein are true and correct. I have also been told that swearing to a false statement can make me guilty of an additional crime."

There were then three spots for signing. Cyril signed each page on the line labeled, "Signed by person making statement." The other two lines were for the signatures of witnesses. Each witness had signed each page and written next to their signature the year of their birth. Siena had been born in 1951. Vaughn in 1977.

Cyril's signed statement then read:

My name is Cyril Winebrenner and I am 22 years old and I live at 1791 Truman Road, lot 15, Osceola, Iowa. The trailer there actually belongs to my mother, Virginia Winebrenner but I've been staying there for about a week now.

In September of 2002, I had bounced around from Iowa to Indiana (the typed word "Kentucky" had been crossed out and replaced by the handwritten word "Iowa"). I had some problems in Indiana and I had to decide where I wanted to stay. One option was New York where my sister lives with her family.

My sister, Tabitha [*sic*] and her husband Kevin Bryant, offered to let me stay with them until I got back on my feet.

(Author's note: Tabatha's name was misspelled with an *i* by the Osceola Sheriff's Department stenographer during much of the written statement. Although other corrections were made in the typed text, which will be noted as we go along, the spelling of the victim's name was not corrected, leading one to surmise that Cyril did not know the correct spelling of his sister's name or did not care if it was spelled correctly. For the purposes of this book, the spelling of the victim's name has been corrected following the first reference.)

Winebrenner's confession continued:

They live at 2 Pennicott Circle in Penfield, New York, 14526. Kevin and Tabatha have two kids, KC and Steven. I moved there in October 2002. After about a week and after I was adjusted, Kevin gave me a job working for him.

Kevin is an attorney and has his own practice. Kevin's practice is located at 1597 West Ridge Road, suite 202, Rochester, New York 14615. He gave me a job as a paralegal. It was an apprenticeship. I never got any formal schooling or degrees to be a paralegal, but I worked there full time.

Tabatha did paralegal work and accounting in Kevin's office, too. She also worked at the M & T bank as a teller. Tabatha worked less and less at Kevin's office since I started there. Everything was going fine at this point at home and work.

In November of 2002 I met Cassidy Green. Cassidy

came into Kevin's office, while I was working, with a guy named [Jeff Null]. Cassidy and Jeff came into the office to file a DBA for an escort service called Sunset Sensations.

Cassidy, who I call Cassy or "Baby Doll," started calling me, because she was interested in me. After a short time, we started dating. Cassidy is twenty-one years old and she's four-feet, ten-inches tall. She's thin, about 76 pounds, and she had brownish blonde hair.

Everything was going good with my relationship with Cassy. She moved in with me at Kevin and Tabatha's house at 2 Pennicott Circle in the beginning of February 2002. In the middle of February, I started to learn some things. I learned that Tabatha was having an affair with a male named Richard.

I have learned Richard's last name once or twice, but I can't remember it. I didn't say anything to anybody about Richard and stayed out of the middle of things. On March 4th, I left to go to the army.

I was at boot camp for one month and came home. I came home because of my asthma condition. I brought some clothing back from the army. I have a set of camouflage BDU's and two pairs of black military-issue combat boots. One pair is new and has never been worn. (Author's Note: BDU is Battle Dress Uniform.)

In the beginning of April 2002, I moved back into the house with Kevin and Tabatha. I went back to work at the law firm. Cassy was still living at Kevin's house and we continued to date. I wasn't home for long when Kevin became aware of Tabatha's affair. Kevin asked me and Cassy about it. I told Kevin that I knew.

Kevin showed me proof that he had. He had pictures of Tabatha and Richard kissing and [others] of them together. Kevin said that he had hired a private investigator and that the investigator had followed Tabatha and Richard and gotten the photos.

Kevin was livid and started getting obsessed with getting rid of Richard. Kevin kept saying he wanted to kill Richard. Kevin talked about this for a couple of weeks. Kevin never talked about details on how he was going to kill Richard.

Every time Kevin brought up the subject, Cassy and I told him that he would get caught and that there were better ways to handle it. Kevin would never really respond to that.

After Kevin got off the kick about Richard, he started talking about Tabatha. Kevin would make comments on a daily basis like Tabatha was out of control and that Kevin had to have her taken care of.

Kevin would say things like he wanted her taken care of and that he wanted her out of the picture or he wanted her to go away.

Kevin also asked for our help in getting information for a divorce. Cassy and I took pictures of Richard's car at Kevin's house. I gave Kevin the photos but wound up discarding the negatives.

Around this time, Kevin had been seeing a few prostitutes. There were a couple girls that would come to the office and go into Kevin's office with him. [Connie Kraft] (pseudonym) and [Lynnette Harrison] were two of the girls that would come to the office that Kevin paid to have sex with. Cassy also told me about two girls from [Nookie's Tavern] that Kevin had seen.

Kevin bought cocaine for me on a regular basis. I'd say it averaged out to about once a week. As far as I know, Kevin was giving the cocaine to the prostitutes.

At this time period, Cassy and I started doing cocaine together. We would snort it. We started doing one eight ball a day between the two of us. (Author's Note: An "eight ball" is one-eighth of an ounce of cocaine, approximately three-and-a-half grams.)

Cassy was also working for Kevin at his practice doing secretarial work. We also started dealing cocaine to support our habit. We had quite a few sources of cocaine and Rocky was one of our sources.

I had met Rocky through Cassy between April 4th and April 6th. I also bought a brown van and a 1990 maroon Grand Am within two weeks of coming back from the army. In the beginning to the middle of May, I introduced Rocky to Kevin Bryant. Rocky needed help with a family court issue.

Things were OK around the house and didn't start to get bad until the middle of May. Kevin and Tabatha were arguing more and more.

Both of them were going out more. They would hang out at Nookie's in Henrietta. Tabatha had met Richard at Nookie's.

It was about this time that Kevin became obsessed with killing Tabatha. I was around Kevin all the time and he would talk about Tabatha a lot. Kevin would say that Tabatha needs to be taken care of and needs to learn her place.

Kevin started complaining that Rocky ripped him off of three grand and never did his part. I always thought that Rocky was just his client. I didn't know the extent of Rocky and Kevin's relationship until Kevin started complaining about Rocky ripping him off.

I asked Rocky about ripping Kevin off just a short time after I learned about it. Rocky said the money was over a dump truck ordeal. I just let it go after that, even though it didn't make sense.

Once Vinny Bennett and I were at Kevin's office, and Kevin gave me a manila envelope with the private eye photos of Tabatha and Richard. I guess it was for reference material. I think that Cassy has the envelope still, but I haven't seen it in weeks.

Kevin started talking about taking care of Tabatha more and more. I ignored this talk. Kevin would talk about this every day. Kevin said a few times that he would pay $5,000 to have Tabatha killed and pay $15,000 to have Tabatha and Richard killed.

Then Kevin even said that he would pay half of Tabatha's life insurance to make her go away. Once Kevin said that the sooner the problems went away, the higher the bonus. Kevin said that he would take care of all the other issues.

Kevin would make these comments to me when I was alone. Cassy told me that Kevin would make comments to her as well. Kevin would also talk about it to me and Cassy when we were together.

Kevin didn't say any details at that time. He would just repeat the above things over and over. I would never respond to him. I would change the subject or ignore it. Kevin would say these things daily.

Kevin would talk about this at the office, the bar or the car. He wouldn't talk about it at home because Tabatha was still there. Kevin talked about it so much that Cassy and I moved out at the end of June.

The atmosphere of the house was bad. In my opinion, Tabatha was mistreating the children. Kevin and Tabatha were arguing more. I was starting to have a lot of resentment for the situation in the house.

Kevin was starting to put a lot of pressure on us to do something about Tabatha. Kevin said he didn't care how, but wanted the problem taken care of.

I came up with an alternative to killing Tabatha around that time. I thought that if Tabatha could get arrested for having cocaine with intent to sell in her van that she would go to jail for a long time.

I talked to Cassy and [Vinny] (Bennett) about the plan. Kevin gave Cassy $1500.00 for us to buy cocaine to set Tabatha up. We got two ounces of cocaine with the money and Cassy bagged it up into about two hundred $20 bags.

The plan was to put cocaine in Tabatha's mini-van and then call the cops to have her pulled over. Vinny had a key to the van and was going to help. Once, Vinny and I found Tabatha's van at Nookie's and planned on planting the drugs. We never did go through with the plan, and wound up blowing some and selling some of the cocaine.

Kevin was also having a problem with a male client named Kim Saunders. Kim was upset with Kevin and [Kevin] told me that he might need a cleaning crew for him. I told him that I would help because it entailed just hurting Saunders. I asked Vinny if he would help if need be, but he declined. Nothing ever came of the Saunders issue though.

Somewhere around the beginning of June 2002, Cassy and I moved out to [Jeff Null's] trailer at 8066 Route 5 & 20 in West Bloomfield. Cassy and I had one bedroom. Jeff was a friend of Cassy's and she had lived with him before I met her. Jeff stayed in his bedroom.

Vinny Bennett and his girlfriend [Emily] stayed

in the other bedroom. I don't know Emily's last name. Vinny and Emily moved in at around the same time that we did.

Cassy and I were still snorting cocaine. We were still doing about an eight ball a day or maybe a little more between the two of us. We were still dealing cocaine to support our habit.

I stopped working for Kevin when I moved out. Cassy quit working for Kevin, too. I told him I needed a vacation and wanted to get away from the ruckus for a while. I did do some contracting work for Kevin after I left his office. I only did three or four separate jobs for him.

There was another plan to get Tabatha sick and make her go to the hospital. Cassy and I had met this girl named [Robin Batarr] (pseudonym). Robin bought a lot of cocaine from us and would hang out at the trailer and party.

Robin had some pills that were intended to help someone stop smoking. Robin gave us one pill and it got crushed up. I was going to put the pill in Tabatha's drink so that she would test positive for drugs at the hospital. It didn't work because when the pills got mixed with the Peachtree and orange juice, blue chips formed around the glass.

There were a number of phone numbers that we used to get a hold of Kevin and Tab. I always called Kevin on his cell phone. He said at one point that he had another cell phone for just in case. I never had the number for that though.

Sometime around the middle of June, I bought a 1985 Monte Carlo. The car is a two-door and it is a dull pink. It has scrolling pin-striping down the sides and an Alpine window decal. The car also has a really loud muffler, because the muffler is disconnected.

One of Cassy's friends sold the car to us. The deal was for $500, but this girl was getting twenty bags [of cocaine] from us and getting it off the price of the car. I don't know the girl's name. Cassy made the deal. The car was in my name. The plates from the van were put on the Monte Carlo.

The van was sold to Toby's dad for $100. I don't know what Toby's last name is, but he is a friend of mine. They live over by Hemlock, but I don't know the street.

I bought a 1990 Pontiac Grand Am. The Grand Am is a maroon or a dark red and it's a two-door. I got the Grand Am from a friend of Kevin and Tab's named Rich Sutera. I paid $750.00 and drove it for a couple months.

The Grand Am blew a head gasket. The car was towed over to Tim's house, who is Toby's brother. Tim is a mechanic and he did some work on the Monte Carlo for us.

Actually the Monte Carlo blew an engine within the first week we had it. Tim's brother provided the new engine for the Monte Carlo. Tim fixed the car and charged Cassy.

Tim was supposed to fix the Grand Am, too, but he wouldn't because we still owed him money for the repair work on the Monte Carlo. The Grand Am has been at Tim's house ever since, and should still be there now.

Around July fifth or sixth, Kevin brought Cassy home from a family picnic. I don't know what time it was. I was sick and didn't talk to anybody for about a week. Kevin said he wanted to talk to me. We went for a walk to the back of the grain bins.

Kevin said that the situation had gotten out of hand and that something had to be done immediately. If I didn't take care of it then myself, Cassy would be a liability that he couldn't deal with.

Kevin said that my parents, wife and son could be just as much a liability. I asked him what that was supposed to mean.

Kevin said for me to just take care of the situation or I will find out what it means. By this time, we were back at the car. Kevin got in and drove away. I know that Kevin was talking about killing Tabatha.

Initially a part of the running narrative, Cyril later added parentheses to the following comments and initialed the change, establishing the next two sentences as an aside: "I want to tell everyone that I am not trying to get out of this or the guilt associated with. I fully understand the severity of my actions and I'm prepared to take the punishment what ever is deemed fit by my peers."

The narrative then continues:

I did not tell Cassidy about this. I didn't think she needed to know, I started trying to solicit people that might be able to get me a gun. On one occasion, I asked Vinnie to get me a gun, and he said that it would be expensive. He was going to try.

I also asked Toby what he would charge to make a silencer.

The next sentence originally read: "He has a machine shop and military background." It was changed and then initialed to read: "His Dad has a machine shop and military background."

Toby said that he didn't have the materials and would need the cash up front. He thought $300 would cover the materials. I didn't give him any money because of the timeframe to make the thing and I was concerned about our situation. (Cyril later wrote in an addition to this sentence: "And possible reprocussions [*sic*]."

A few days later, I'm not exactly sure which day it was, I was at the trailer with Cassy, and it was at night. Cassy and I were in the bedroom and she asked me what I was going to do about the situation. I knew that Cassy was talking about killing Tabatha.

I looked at Cassy and told her that I didn't know what I was going to do. At this point I was basically trying to figure out how I could get the whole situation to go away, and have nobody get hurt. For the next couple of days, I kind of just put the whole thing out of my mind.

Cassy and I were having problems in our relationship. I was trying to concentrate on me and her, and how to make things better between us. We were doing a lot of cocaine in those few days and Cassy and I were selling a lot also.

On Sunday July 13, 2003 I got up at about 1:00 or 2:00 in the afternoon. It got to be later in the evening, and I was playing on the internet and watching TV, when Cassy came into the bedroom and told me that she had talked to Kevin on the phone and that it had to be taken care of today. I knew that Cassy was talking about killing Tabatha.

I asked what the hell was going on and she told me that she didn't know, but that he wanted it taken care of today. Cassy said something that spooked me. I can't remember exactly what she said but it was something to the equivalent of Kevin saying, "or else."

A short time later, around 10:30 or 11:00 PM, Kevin called the trailer. Kevin talked to Cassy, and

afterwards, Cassy came in and told me that we had
to go.

I knew that Cassy had a .22 rifle that she had
gotten from her father. Her rifle was in the trunk
of the Monte Carlo, and was actually supposed to
be for protection. We had some problems with a
drug dealer named [Rocky], and the rifle was for
protection against him.

It was between 10:30 PM and 11:00 PM and we
left the trailer in the Monte Carlo. I was wearing
blue jeans and a dark tee-shirt and black combat
boots. Cassy was driving and we drove directly to
Kevin and Tabatha's house.

We sat pretty much in silence. Cassy had asked
me why I was so upset. Basically I was trying to prepare for what was about to happen. I knew that we
were going to Tabatha's to kill her, and I told
Cassy that I was trying to prepare.

I was intending to kill Tabatha and trying to get
my head right. We got to Kevin's house at about
11:30 PM. Cassy pulled the Monte Carlo into the
driveway. The Monte Carlo had a specific sound
and a loud muffler. The exhaust is broken and the
muffler doesn't work right.

Cassy turned the car off, and we got out of the
car. Just before I got out of the car, I put a pair of
latex gloves on. Cassy had gotten the gloves and
gave a pair to me.

I went into the trunk and got the .22 caliber rifle
out. This was Cassy's rifle. I carried the rifle and
Cassy and I walked through the gate together,
and I went to the sliding glass door.

I checked the doors and they were locked. Cassy
went to the side garage door and it was unlocked.
Cassy walked inside the garage and I walked in
after.

Cassy said, "It's not here, we have to go." I asked

her what she was talking about, and she said, "it's not right. We got to go." I don't know what she was talking about, but the door into the kitchen was locked. Maybe she was talking about a key, but I don't know.

Then we walked back into the driveway, and got into the Monte Carlo. I put the rifle in the back seat of the Monte Carlo. I took the gloves off and put them in the pocket of my blue jeans. The gloves were the style that you would pull out of a box.

Cassy was still driving at this point and she drove to the Noco gas station on Browncroft Boulevard. Cassy pulled up to the store and the store was closed. The pay phone was on the side of the building. Cassy used the phone, but she didn't say who she was calling.

I had a vial of cocaine and I was getting ready to do some blow. I figure there was a tenner in the vial. That's about a gram-and-a-half of cocaine.

Cassy drove back to Kevin's house. Along the way, Cassy said that she had called Kevin's cell phone collect from the pay phone and now everything would be open. I assumed that she was talking about the doors to Kevin's house. (Author's Note: The transcript originally said "I know" but was changed and initialed to "I assumed" by Cyril.)

We drove back into the driveway and stopped. Cassy turned the car off, but stayed in the car this time. I put a new set of latex gloves on and got out of the car.

I went directly to the sliding glass doors. I checked the doors and saw that they were open. I was carrying Cassy's .22 caliber rifle. I walked into Kevin and Tabatha's house and into the kitchen.

As I walked into the house I closed the sliding door behind me. I knew that Tabatha had been sleeping on the pull out bed in the living room, because Kevin had told Cassy. Cassy had relayed the information to me.

I also knew that Kevin and Tabatha had been having marital problems and that Tabatha slept on the couch from time to time. I walked through the kitchen and toward the living room entrance.

There are two doorways that enter into the living room. One doorway enters the living room from the kitchen, and the other enters the living room from the hallway that leads from the kitchen to the front door.

I looked through the living room doorway from the kitchen and saw that Tabatha was sleeping on her side, facing to the left. I could see Tabatha's face and I looked at her sleeping and realized that she was my sister.

I was having a hard time with the fact that I was there to kill my own sister, and I started thinking that I couldn't do it. I realized that I couldn't pull the trigger.

I was standing there looking at Tabatha, when Kevin came down the stairs. He looked at me and told me to do it. I told Kevin that I couldn't go through with it.

Then Kevin started arguing with me saying stuff like I had to, and to go ahead. I put the butt of the rifle down on the floor and leaned it up against the door jam [*sic*] of the left entrance to the living room.

Kevin was getting upset, telling me that this was the time, and things like that. I started to walk toward the sliding door, when Kevin grabbed the rifle and shot.

There were five rounds in the magazine of the rifle. Kevin shot at least two and maybe three rounds. I think that three were fired because later,

I pulled the magazine out and there was one round in the chamber and one still in the magazine.

Tabatha started screaming and I freaked out. I grabbed a large butcher knife from the rack in the kitchen, and ran into the living room. Tabatha was still on the pull out bed, and I just started stabbing her.

I'm not exactly sure how many times I stabbed her, but I remember stabbing her in the throat and how she started rolling around on the bed. I was stabbing her as she rolled and kept going until she stopped moving and stopped screaming.

There was blood splatter on my clothes, and I don't know if Kevin had gloves on also. I walked out of the living room and into the kitchen. I was still holding the butcher knife as I walked.

Kevin stuffed an M and T bank envelope of money in my back pants pocket. Then Kevin handed me the rifle and told me to get rid of everything and go.

I ran out of the sliding doors, and back to the Monte Carlo. I got into the passenger side, and Cassy started the car, turned on the lights and drove off. We drove to West Ridge Road.

I put the knife in the backseat passenger side on the floor of the Monte Carlo. I changed my clothes and put the bloody clothes in the back seat floorboard area.

I can't remember if I changed while Cassy drove or at the first stop we made. The first stop that we made was at the Hess station on West Ridge Road. We got gas and cigarettes.

I counted the money in the envelope and counted fifty one-hundred dollar bills. There was $5,000.00. Cassy had asked how much was there. I told her how much money was in the envelope.

There were only hundreds in the envelope of money that Kevin had given me.

We had to spend the money because the guy didn't have change for the hundred. We bought a carton of Marlboro Reds and multiple packs of Newport 100's.

Cassy tried calling Kevin from the Hess. Cassy used the pay phone. I don't know which phone Cassy tried calling. I don't think she got a hold of him.

Then we left and Cassy was driving still. We made two other stops at gas stations. I don't know which gas stations they were. Cassy tried to call Kevin from a pay phone at one of the gas stations. She didn't get a hold of him.

I used the pay phone at the other gas station. I tried calling Kevin, but I couldn't get ahold of him either. I can't remember if I tried Kevin's home or cell phone.

We then drove home. Cassy was driving south on Route 65 and I threw the butcher knife out the window around Mendon Ponds Park. I was on the passenger side of the car, and threw the knife as far as I could. The overall length of the knife was about twelve to fourteen inches and the handle is wooden and brown.

We went back to Jeff Null's trailer. We were in the house for about ten or fifteen minutes. I went right into the bathroom. I saw some blood on me on my left hand and arm.

I started freaking out. Cassy gave me some baby wipes to clean it up. I cleaned the blood off. Cassy said that we had to get rid of everything. I went to the living room and grabbed a garbage bag from atop the refrigerator.

Cassy and me went back out to the Monte Carlo.

I put the bloody clothes into the garbage bag. We then drove away and Cassy drove again.

We got a mile down the road. The alternator belt broke on the car. We went back to the trailer and asked Vinny and Emily if we could borrow their car. They agreed to let us use the car if we put gas in it. We agreed.

We transferred the jacket, the garbage bag, and the gun into Vinny and Emily's car. I held the stuff between my legs in the front passenger seat. Cassy drove and picked out the spots to get rid of the clothes.

As we were driving, I was cleaning the gun with baby wipes that Cassy gave me. Cassy would pull over into spots and told me what to get rid of where. I did what she told me.

We got rid of one item at a time. The jacket went into a storm drain right by a stream. All the other items were placed wherever Cassidy pulled over. I don't know the spots.

We then went to the Hemlock Sugarcreek and filled the car with gas. I paid for the gas with a one-hundred dollar bill. We drove to Toby and Tim's house. I put the .22 caliber rifle that was used to shoot my sister Tabatha Bryant in the trunk of the Pontiac Grand Am. I'm not sure why I put the rifle in the trunk, and didn't throw it away. Then Cassy and I went back to the trailer.

I went to our bedroom and Cassidy came in with me. Cassidy said I had to leave. I told her I didn't want to leave. Cassidy said that she would take care of New York and when it was OK to come back she would let me know. I stayed in my room.

That Monday morning at about 8:00 am, July 14th, Cassidy picked up two alternator belts for the

Monte Carlo. I gave Cassidy about $2,800 of the money I got from Kevin.

I took about $2,000 of Kevin's money and packed my black army bag and left. I also took my katana [author's note: a katana is a Samurai-type sword] with me. I drove to Ansonia, Pennsylvania. I stayed one night at a hotel that I don't remember the name of. The hotel was about a mile down the road from a bar called The Roadhouse on Route 6.

That Tuesday I went to the Great Valley Motel in Wellsboro, Pennsylvania. Bill and Julie Welch owned the motel. I paid them $260 to stay there for a month. I bought a microwave, refrigerator, TV and a Playstation for the room I rented.

I would hang out at the bar right next door called the Roadhouse. I tried calling Cassidy from the pay phone out front of the motel a couple of times. I spoke with her once and discussed how she was doing, etc. I did talk to her mother, Michelle, several times.

I stayed at the Great valley motel until the Tuesday of last week. I sold my Monte Carlo to Bill and Julie for $100. I sold the appliances to them, too.

I took the money and bought a bus ticket to Des Moines, Iowa. I arrived late on Wednesday. My parents picked me up and drove me home in Osceola. I have stayed at my mother's ever since.

I have never seen or talked to Kevin since that night at his house. I have talked to Michelle on several occasions. I have talked to Cassidy once since I returned to Iowa.

Cassy called me from a pay phone at my mother's in Osceola. I told her that I loved her and that I was waiting for her. Cassidy and I have e-mailed each other several times. We just talk about miscellaneous bullshit.

Then on August 1st, 2003 between 9:00 and 9:30 am, I was met at my house by Investigator Vaughn and Investigator Siena of the Monroe County Sheriff's Department.

They told that they were investigating my sister's death. They asked me if I would voluntarily come to the Osceola Police Department and talk to them. I voluntarily agreed to go.

We talked about my sister Tabatha. I eventually told them the truth about what happened and admitted all of my involvement in the death of my sister Tabatha Bryant.

I admitted that I was there when Kevin Bryant shot Tabatha with the .22 caliber rifle that I brought into the house, and I also admitted that I stabbed Tabatha Bryant numerous times with a butcher knife that I got from the kitchen of her home.

I then gave this statement to Investigators Siena and Vaughn with no threats or promises made to me.

I also gave Investigator Vaughn and Investigator Siena written consent to search my Monte Carlo that is located in Pennsylvania. I also gave Siena and Vaughn written consent to come to my trailer home in Osceola and remove the military combat boots that I was wearing when my sister, Tabatha, was killed.

That concluded Cyril's statement. Winebrenner signed it, every page of it, and the investigators had him brought back to Monroe County. They put him in a cell in the Monroe County Jail, which would be his home for a long time.

Cyril's thirteen-page statement eventually saw the light of day. Eighteen months passed and the contents of that statement were made public. However, it was in the form of severely whittled-down sound bites and pullout quotes.

It was around this time that reporters learned about the police raid on the "escort service" mobile home in West Bloomfield, which had occurred just before the arrests. Best at digging out facts for a time was local TV station WHEC. Another link between Cyril and Cassidy was established when unnamed sources close to Kevin's private practice told WHEC that Winebrenner and Green "frequently worked" at the Ridge Road law office.

Prosecutors were fresh to the case and refused to comment on what the motive for the crime might have been, when first asked by WHEC. But representatives from the DA's office did announce that the rifle used in the attack on Tabatha had been recovered. At this point the public first learned that the .22 rifle believed to be the weapon that was used to shoot Tabby had been a gift to Cassidy Green from her father.

CHAPTER 37

Three Busts

Sheriff Patrick O'Flynn told the gathered reporters that they were there because of Tabatha Bryant's murder, and that—despite the violence—he still considered Penfield to be a safe community. He reminded them that from day one he had pledged to get to the bottom of the case, and apologized for not being more forthcoming with information during his investigation, but he did not want to release anything that might have jeopardized the "successful outcome he was about to announce." He thanked the people of Penfield and the press for their patience and called the case "one of the most complex murder investigations I've seen in my twenty-seven-year career."

He then read the names of the three individuals who had been arrested: "One: Kevin C. Bryant, forty-five years of age, of Penfield—the husband of Tabatha Bryant. Two: Cyril Winebrenner, twenty-two years of age, of Osceola, Iowa—half brother to Tabatha—who is in custody in Iowa. Three: Cassidy A. Green, twenty-one years of age, of Bloomfield, New York, girlfriend to Cyril." The sheriff said that Kevin Bryant and Cyril Winebrenner were both being charged with murder second degree and Cassidy Green was being charged with manslaughter first and criminal sale of controlled substance in the third degree—two counts.

"At this time we are confident that we have all parties in custody relative to the homicide of Tabatha Bryant," the sheriff said. He then thanked his Criminal Investigative team, Undersheriff Daniel Greene, Captain Theodore Wright, Lieutenant Steve Scott, Investigator Sergeant Gary Caiola, Investigator Paul Siena, Investigator Dave Vaughn, Investigator Jeff Gerber, Investigator Kevin Garvey, Investigator Tyler Barrus, the Pennsylvania State Police Department, Iowa Division of Criminal Investigation, Osceola Sheriff's Department, Livingston County Sheriff's Office, Ontario County Sheriff's Office, the Rochester Police Department, the Monroe County District Attorney's Office, and the medical examiner's office.

Sheriff O'Flynn characterized the case this way: "This was a domestic dispute that escalated to the point of homicide."

CHAPTER 38

Tabby's Dad's Story

When Kevin, Cyril, and Cassidy were arrested for Tabby's murder, there was a flurry of activity at the *Penfield Post*. Reporter Amy Cavalier heard her boss saying something about the human angle, and the next thing she knew she had an assignment she wasn't relishing: get a close member of Tabby's family and get his or her story. The interview Amy got was with Leroy Bassett, Tabby's father, who was living in Florida.

When she called, Amy was pleased to find that Leroy was not annoyed at being disturbed and was willing to be interviewed on the record for her paper, which she knew he'd never heard of. Leroy told Amy that his name was Carroll Leroy, but he went by Leroy. He verified that he was Tabby's dad—and Samantha's, too, he pointed out—and mentioned up front that he had had a chance to spend some time with them after he got out of the military.

He ran quickly through Tabby's life, that she had graduated from Greenwood Central School and had gotten married, for a short time, to a man who lived in Canisteo. It didn't work out and they got divorced, after which time she "got to know Kevin quite well.

"Our families have known each other for forty years," Leroy continued. "My dad was pastor of our church in Greenwood. Kevin's dad was a member of the church in Rochester. There has been a lot of intermixing of families ever since I can remember. Somewhere in that link between both families being church members, Tabby met Kevin.

"They got married. I'm not sure how long they knew one another before they got married. I'd say it was probably a year, a year and a half, that they were in close contact before they got married," Leroy said. He forgot that Tabby had moved to the Rochester area with her first husband, when he added, "Tabby married Kevin in 1997 and moved up to Penfield with him."

What did Leroy think of Kevin, the older lawyer who was to marry his youngest daughter?

"I had known Kevin since he was a little boy and I had always thought of him as a sickly man. His health was not the greatest," Leroy said. He then admitted to a touch of prejudice against Kevin and his ilk. "I lived on a farm. He lived in a city. I thought city folks were strange anyway," Leroy said. "Kevin was different. Not in a bad way. There were just differences in family cultures. He and I got along fine."

Leroy had to admit that his impressions of Kevin Bryant weren't exactly those of an expert. He had known Kevin as a kid, and had seen him a couple of times because he married his daughter, but there was nothing in between. In 2003, Leroy was fifty-one, and for about thirty-five of those years he had lived far from both the Greenwood and the Rochester Community of Christ churches.

"I moved away in the 1970s, and hadn't been home in thirty years," Leroy said.

He said he never knew Cyril. He knew that Ginny had

remarried and had kids. He knew that she'd had a pair of boys and that the youngest one had died.

He and Tabby had talked on the phone at least once a week, if not a couple of times. "She always liked to call and keep me informed about her life," he said. "She always asked me about my mother"—referring to "Gram"—because they were so close. During those phone calls she never said anything to her father about being unhappy with her husband.

"Other than normal family spats and arguments, she seemed quite happy," Leroy recalled.

The Bryant boys, Leroy's grandkids, had come down to Florida twice to visit.

"She called me one night and said she had been to visit her mom in Iowa. Cyril came back with her. He and his girlfriend were staying with them. She didn't say much more than that. She did mention that she had gotten into an argument with Cyril and she had asked Cyril and his girlfriend to leave for one reason or another."

Leroy then gave his daughter a quick personality profile: "Tabby was all business, either working or playing, she was all business when she did something. Yet, she always had a smile, a good word for anybody. She was up front. She wasn't afraid to tell you what she was thinking. If she didn't like something about you, she would tell you about it.

"She could never turn someone away. She bought us plane tickets one time to come up for Christmastime. We went up to see them. Every three months pictures of the kids were sent.

"I don't think she had a harsh word for anybody—except for maybe me when she was mad at me. I was always the one that could make her mad. We were so alike. But she would try to get over it very fast. She had one of the best personalities of anyone I know."

Leroy knew that Tabby had two jobs, working in Kevin's office and as a teller at a bank. According to

Tabby, Kevin's business kept him very busy. He wouldn't get home many nights until nine or ten o'clock, sometimes even midnight, and he always blamed business.

Amy asked Leroy if maybe the age difference between Kevin and Tabby had contributed to their difficulties, but Leroy said he'd never heard anything like that. As far as he knew, age was not a factor.

Leroy told the story about hugging his wife, Becky, and crying after hearing the news about Tabby. After they had had their good cry, they called another couple in Florida.

"Then we tried to figure out how to make it to New York as soon as we could," Leroy recalled.

It wasn't long after they heard the horrible news that Leroy had an idea. He looked at Becky and they simultaneously said, "'Kevin's got to be involved with this.'

"Maybe it was because there was no other reasonable explanation," Leroy recalled. "It's not like he had ever done or said anything that would make us think he was capable of murder. It was just a gut feeling."

In the days following his daughter's death, Leroy felt like an outsider looking in. For one thing, he was in Florida, a long ways from the scene of the crime.

"I finally managed to get a liaison with the sheriff's department up in Penfield," Leroy said. "She was supposed to keep us filled in, but after I thought I had things fixed up, I never heard from her again."

Despite Leroy and Becky's hunch that Kevin had something to do with Tabby's murder, it was still a shock when he heard the news. Essie Barrett called her son, two days after the arrests, and said Kevin Bryant had been arrested.

"The thing that made it so shocking about Kevin was that I had known his family for so long and I still couldn't believe that something like that could happen," Leroy said.

After hearing that Kevin was the so-called mastermind,

Essie told her son that Tabby's half brother Cyril and Cyril's girlfriend had also been involved. She laid out the whole scenario as she understood it.

"That made me angry," Leroy said. "But I always ended up turning my anger back to Kevin. If it turns out to be true that Kevin paid Cyril to do it, I put my blame on Kevin more than anyone. He furnished the money for it, and most of our anger is toward him.

"I know his family insists that Kevin is innocent, and I can't say as I blame them. I would feel the same way if he were my son or child. I know I can't see any child of mine doing something like that."

Did Tabby ever give any indication that she and Kevin were headed for divorce?

"No. I don't think she knew that Kevin had filed for divorce. She never mentioned it to me. I think it was a surprise that Kevin was going to spring on her," Leroy said.

How did he feel when he learned that Ginny's son and his girlfriend were involved? Amy Cavalier asked.

"My reaction to Cyril and Cassidy was, whoa, some folks'll do anything for money. If the money is good enough, they'll do anything—right or wrong," Leroy explained.

Leroy said that he thought it was good that the Bryant boys had been sent to live with Kevin's parents. The advantage, he said, was that they lived so close that the boys would not have to live in an area they did not know.

"I know the boys have options," Leroy continued. "My mother would have taken them. My daughter, Samantha, would have. Even my wife said that she'd take them. It is important for kids to be around family they know. That way it's not so much of a trauma for them."

Leroy said he hadn't been in touch with Kevin's family at all, but he had talked to his ex-wife, Ginny, a few times. He said Ginny and Becky liked to chat because they were very talented with their hands and at crafts, and both excelled at crocheting. They liked to exchange patterns.

"You know all the time before the arrests we knew that Ginny's son and his girlfriend did it. Our family sort of knew they were suspects, but I don't think Ginny did. It just came as a terrible shock to her. She's in a sort of disbelief that her kid would do that to a half sister," Leroy said.

What punishment did he think Kevin deserved? Amy asked.

"If I had my say, I wouldn't want the death penalty," Leroy answered. "Two wrongs don't make a right. It's the easy way out for him. If he is found guilty, I'd like to see him sit and think about it forever. I think that's the way the family up in New York thinks, too."

Leroy said that he had come to accept the fact that Tabby was no longer with them, but he still wanted to know exactly who did it and why it was done.

"We've never heard any kind of motive as to why he'd do it or have it done," he said.

What was his best guess regarding the motive?

"The only thing I could visualize, and this is totally speculation, is if he told her he was going to get a divorce, and she said something like, 'You'll never see your kids again.' He was very proud of those two boys. That's the only thing I can think of that might have given him the motivation to do what they say he did."

Did he feel the matter had been laid to rest?

"I think in any murder there has to be a conviction in order for it to really be laid to rest," Leroy answered.

How were his efforts going to get up north and to attend Kevin's trial?

"It doesn't look like we are going to make it up," Leroy concluded. "The best we can hope for is daily contact with the family so we can keep track of what's going on in the trial."

* * *

Having interviewed the victim's dad, Amy continued in her pursuit of the human angle. She called Tabatha's aunt Lorraine in Greenwood to get a statement regarding the arrests, but Lorraine said that, presumably because Tabatha's half brother and husband were under arrest, she could no longer comment on the situation.

For many Rochesterians, including Amy Cavalier, Tabby's murder hit home. This had been true even before the arrests, but even more so after. Amy couldn't stop thinking about it, and she knew she wasn't alone. The reason: it just didn't make sense.

As was true for many others with whom she had discussed the case, Amy simply could not imagine how a middle-aged attorney, who once interned at the Monroe County District Attorney's Office, would consider murder an answer to any problem. There was much speculation in the initial days following the murder. However, the details that would emerge in the following two years would be more sordid than anyone could have imagined.

As Amy recalled later, "Looking back on it all makes me realize that there is no way I could ever imagine what was going on in Tabatha, Kevin, Cyril, or Cassidy's minds or lives. When I review the details of extensive cocaine use, hookers, adultery, and strip clubs that filled Tabatha and Kevin's lives, I realize I could never speculate what they were like or what led them to the events of July 13, 2003.

"I've wondered many times how this murder came to fruition. It baffles me that three people knew about this and not one of them stopped and said, 'Hey, maybe this is not such a good idea.' Even after all I've learned, the events of that night remain a mystery to me. I still have no idea what motivated these people to take the action they did."

CHAPTER 39

Whispers of a Double Life

Popular blogger Bob Lonsberry, an opinionated Internet Conservative, wrote that Kevin and Tabby's church had gone public quickly with their spin on things: how the Bryants were great people and lived on the straight and narrow.

"But that's not what some people were saying," Lonsberry wrote, citing that there were claimed eyewitness reports indicating that Kevin and Tabby were not on the straight and narrow at all, but were regulars at Nookie's, a strip bar. They were "pretty enthusiastic enjoyers of the topless bar and its goings on." Witnesses had come forward to say that the four people involved in the murder—Kevin, Cyril, Cassidy, and Tabatha—had all been in Nookie's together, having what appeared to be a marvelous time.

One might think that the statements about the Bryants were the work of overactive imaginations, but they had been corroborated by Kevin himself, who spoke to sheriff's deputies of his swinging marriage during the minutes and hours after Tabby's death.

Lonsberry wrote that the case called out for the death penalty. Those that read the blog had to wonder what was going on in the Bryants' marriage. It was unclear who was leading whom into the depths of debauchery, but strip joints—historically—were simply not a place where a man took the mother of his children to get freaky with the clientele. The behavior was more in keeping with the way a man treated his mistress, or the way a pimp treated his whore.

CHAPTER 40

A Blend of Burlesque
and Brothel

The modern "strip joint" is a blend of a burlesque house and a brothel, how much of each depends on the joint. In the old burlesque theaters, which dated back to before the Great Depression, women came onto a stage in showgirl costumes. As music played, usually a tune with a lot of bass and percussion, suitable for thrusting the hips, the women, piece by piece, removed their clothing. As this was going on, men cheered from an audience, the seating for which resembled that of a traditional theater. The act was known as a striptease because, to prevent police intervention, the dancers almost always disappeared behind the curtain before the audience got to see anything other than a curve here and a provocative shadow there.

In later years, the women removed their tops and exposed their breasts. If the law insisted, they kept their nipples covered with pasties. By the 1960s, there were communities that allowed the striptease artists, now referred to as strippers, to become completely nude. By this time most strippers did not work in theaters but either in nightclubs or bars. By the 1970s and the proliferation of pornographic film houses across America, the striptease theater was all but extinct, existing only in New York's Times Square and in certain sections of L.A. To better compete with the porn houses, where hard-core sex acts could be seen in gynecological glory up on the silver screen, the strip bars and clubs often had to offer "extras" in a back room. When a girl was not performing on the usually small stage, she would sit at the bar, get men to buy watered-down drinks at inflated prices, and try to coax them into a back room (sometimes the ladies' room) where sexual activity (usually oral sex) would take place.

In the 1960s strip clubs, there was the possibility of an actual band that played as the women performed their acts; since the 1970s, the "dancing" has almost always been done to prerecorded music. The nicer places had a disc jockey who catered the music to each performer's needs. In the cheapest roadside joints, a jukebox would provide the music and the customers got to choose the tune that backed their favorite woman disrobing. In the early days, management would pay the performers their income. By the 1960s, management got to underpay the talent legitimately—just as employers routinely underpay waiters and delivery people—by expecting the customers to tip the girls. The stage was set up so that the dancers and customers could get very close to one another. The women would dance close to the edge of the low stage so that the men could place dollar bills (or sometimes larger denominations) in their garters.

Beginning in the 1980s, there appeared a particularly upscale form of a strip joint called the gentlemen's club. The women were prettier and the drinks more expensive. The sound systems rivaled those of legitimate dance clubs, or discotheques. The stages were small and usually up against a mirrored wall so that the customers could see the dancer from all angles. There was almost always a silver pole that went from the stage floor to the ceiling. Around the pole the dancer swirled, writhed, and contorted herself, boggling the audience with brand-new ways to make humping motions. Customers at the edge of the stage held up money, and the dancer, while taking the cash, would squat, like a baseball catcher, offering a seemingly exclusive view of her feminine parts. If the bill was large enough, or the customer was otherwise preferred, a second view, this one from the rear, would be offered.

At the gentlemen's clubs, which attracted successful businessmen and professional athletes as customers, there was an activity known as the "table dance." For a price a man could commission one of the dancers to do her striptease not on the stage but at his table, a personal one-on-one performance. Although there might have been some minimal contact between the customer and the dancer (she might rest her hand briefly on his cheek), the man was not allowed to touch the woman. One quick feel and a bouncer would be on top of the situation with stunning swiftness. The table dance lasted the length of one song, at which time the customer had the option of purchasing another, and then another, until his wallet was empty. At the end of the night, management kept most of the money.

The table dance evolved into the "lap dance." Again a customer would purchase a private dance, but this time, after a rapid striptease, the woman would be in direct contact with the customer. With him sitting back in a comfortable but armless chair—and as before expected to keep his hands more or less to himself—she would shake her breasts very close to his face. She would turn her back to him and bend forward to give him a rear view. While in this position, hair hanging straight down, the dancer would reach back to caress herself. If law forced the dancer to wear a G-string during her lap dance, she would find an excuse to adjust it, pull it to one side for a moment, and give her customer a flash of pink. She would straddle him and whisper in his ear. If it was dark enough, and the man was being generous enough, she would sneak a quick feel of his crotch and allow her nipples to lightly brush his lips. Just enough to make an additional "dance" a necessity.

But those were about the limits in the high-end gentlemen's clubs that sprung up in many major U.S. cities—not that they always were followed. Some clubs allowed customers to rent out dancers at an hourly rate, and to move into the "champagne room" or the "VIP room," where another level of privacy could be achieved. It is not hard to imagine that, under these conditions, with a professional woman sitting for an hour upon the lap of a customer, that the line that separates striptease from prostitution could on occasion be broken. And, even in situations in which management strictly forbade sex acts in the club, there was always the parking lot or, in more urban situations, the roof.

Not to be outdone, lap dances quickly became a standard practice at the smaller joints, including roadside strip joints, such as the one in Henrietta where Kevin took Tabatha. They were cheaper but every bit as intimate—perhaps even more so. At establishments such as this, the limits were set by management and depended on how likely it was that an undercover cop was observing, and the moral attitudes of the women (usually not a factor).

Because the strippers were often under the control of a man who had a business interest in the establishment, or were otherwise dependent on a steady cash income (often for drugs), they tend to be an open-minded lot, not afraid to cross the line into whoredom as long as the price is right. The clientele was mostly made up of truckers, bikers, and regular guys on their way home from their factory jobs who were either hooked on the product or were using the strip joint to soothe a broken heart.

At many small-time strip joints, like Nookie's Tavern, whether they are in rural or suburban sites, the establishment served as a one-stop vice center. Have a nasty habit? They could take care of it for you. The decor was fairly predictable: small stage, mirrored wall, silver pole, bar, maybe an eight-ball table. Blow jobs were in the girls' room. You could buy pot or coke from the guy in the first stool, but you had to go outside to make the transaction.

In recent years it is true that the patrons of strip joints have become increasingly coeducational. It is not uncommon to see couples, mixed groups, and groups of lesbians enjoying the show, but married couples with kids at home are still a rare form of clientele. Why was Kevin taking the mother of his children to a strip joint and allowing her to give lap dances to strangers?

A husband wanting to spice up his marital sex life is one thing, even if it involves sanctioned infidelity. Kevin, however, must have realized that strip joints are magnets for misogynists. To these men, the strip joint was one of the few places left in America where you could publicly disrespect a woman (up to a point) and get away with it. Then again, Kevin was a fellow who'd had trouble with his relationships with women. Was it his own loathing, or the loathing of strangers, that Kevin wanted Tabatha to experience?

CHAPTER 41

Nookie's

Nookie's was near the intersection of two major roads in the southeastern suburbs of Rochester, in an area known for its chain restaurants and car dealerships. It was a small building, twelve hundred square feet tops.

Even if it was nighttime, it still took new eyes a moment or two to adjust to the dimness of Nookie's. It was dark, like a haunted house. There was yellowed white light and a dreamy helping of black light, which made the lingerie glow. Add in the bare, impossibly high breasts and the thumping techno music, and it was a heady mix. It was the work of the devil, a sound-and-sight seduction system.

As you entered, the door was guarded by a man in a black suit, black tie. The bartender wore identical garb. The doorman was also the bouncer and the cashier. With the exception of the bills that went into the girl's garters, or drinks bought at the bar, all transactions went through the cashier. The computerized cash register had icons on a screen that would be touched and the price for that item would come up. That's how you paid for lap dances. As a customer stood inside the front door, the stage was on the left, in the front left corner. It was lit from below and had the customary pole from stage to the nine-foot ceiling. There was enough room for the dancers to achieve altitude.

The bar ran across the entire back wall and had nine stools. The rest of the floor had been crammed with small, round tables for drinks and padded easy chairs—so many chairs that it was occasionally difficult for the waitresses to get to a back table to deliver drinks without a few slick upper and lower body moves.

Along the right wall, as a customer entered, were four booths, small cubicles with curtains that could be drawn. The booths would have looked familiar to Catholics, resembling as they did confessionals. A sign on the wall said that the price of a lap dance during the day was $25 for two songs. At night the cost was $25 for one dance. If that seemed like too much for too little— like it was supposed to—customers had the option of going into the booth with the girl at a rate of $65 for a half hour or $120 for an hour. The cashier pressed the appropriate icon on his computer screen and took all the money. What a customer tipped the girl in the privacy of the booth was up to him—or her.

All four walls were mirrored, and at any given time, there were nine women working: three dancers, who would take turns on the stage stripping to three-song sets, three waitresses, and three girls who hustled men in the bar for lap dances. The lap and stage dancers were often one and the same, and when it was not a girl's turn to do one, she did the other.

The girl on the stage perfected her moves on the pole, with the emphasis on acrobatics. She would begin each set wearing a tube top, short shorts, and a G-string. Platform shoes were popular. The girl danced her first song in all of her clothes. She removed her shorts after the first song, and her top after her third. Only for the third song was she clad only in her G-string. Of course, this was when most of the dollar-bill-in-the-garter action took place.

Girls twirled and twisted themselves around the pole. They twirled right side up, and sometimes upside down. When a customer approached the stage, arms to the sides, with a bill between the fingers, the dancer moved to the edge of the stage. She gave the side of the customer's neck a little breath. If the customer was wearing a T-shirt that was not tucked in, she might lift the shirt and give the customer a nibble on the belly. A dollar bought about fifteen seconds of attention. Everyone loved the attention. Then the bill went in the garter and the girl returned to the pole.

When one girl finished her three-song set, the interim would be filled by the fast-talking disc jockey, who reminded everyone how sexy everyone was. The next girl often sprayed the pole with Lysol and wiped it down with a paper towel before beginning her own set. The cleaning products were kept at the edge of the stage. Because it was common for the girls to press their breasts and buttocks against the mirror at the back of the stage, cleaning the mirrors in that corner became part of the show. After all of the three stage dancers completed their sets, there was a break and the waitresses—wearing microminis over black-light sensitive G-strings—cleaned the mirrors with plenty of Windex, and much shaking and shimmying. This gave a girl who might have been doing a half hour in the booth a chance to get her act together if she was due up next to dance on the stage.

The thing that made Nookie's special was the percentage of its clientele that was female. They ran a small ad in the sports section of the Rochester daily newspaper and not only did the ad mention the club's proximity to a nice motel, but also "couples welcome."

The female customers weren't just those who had come as part of a heterosexual couple—some of the women were in mixed groups, and there was often a group or two of lesbians in the house. Nookie's was not a bad place for a young lesbian to have fun, and the men in the club didn't mind at all watching girl-on-girl activity.

For a sex addict or a woman who felt she still had wild oats to sow, Nookie's provided a perfect venue.

CHAPTER 42

Cassy Speaks Again

On Wednesday, August 6, 2003, Cassidy Green made yet another sworn statement, this time an oral statement under an agreement with the district attorney's office. Immediately thereafter she testified before the Monroe County grand jury regarding her knowledge of Tabatha's murder. That brought to at least five the number of sworn statements Cassidy had made regarding the murder since she was arrested on drug charges. Cassidy's story had evolved over that time, a fact that would come back to trouble her.

She initially had put the predominant blame on Cyril. It was her boyfriend's anger toward his half sister that led to the crime.

During one of her earlier statements to prosecutors, Cassidy said, "Cyril often talked about hurting Tabatha and Cyril said he was going to 'fucking snap' and that he was gonna kill her."

The amount of guilt she assigned Kevin grew with each statement, and a new element, involving the envelope of money that was supposed to be on top of the file cabinet in the garage, appeared.

The following day, Thursday, August 7, a grand jury indicted both Kevin Bryant and Cyril Winebrenner for first-degree murder. The men originally had been charged with second-degree murder, but those charges were upgraded by the grand jury, which decided not to act in the case of Cassidy Green. She would remain in the Monroe County Jail until the outcome of Kevin and Cyril's cases.

The Monroe County District Attorney's Office then announced their theory regarding why Tabatha was killed. That office alleged that Kevin Bryant paid Winebrenner and Green $5,000, along with promises of future benefits, to kill his wife.

According to Assistant District Attorney (ADA) Michael C. Green, the motive had to do with the breakup of the marriage. Kevin had filed for a divorce from his wife just a few weeks preceding the murder. Cyril did both the stabbing and the shooting.

The .22 rifle used in the shooting was identified as belonging to Cassidy. The knife used in the murder had not been found. It was likely still where Cyril tossed it out of the car, somewhere in the Mendon Ponds vicinity.

"These are some of the most horrific allegations the office has seen in some time," Michael Green said. He added that Kevin and Cyril most likely were to be tried separately. Green reiterated that the DA's office had not yet decided whether to pursue the death penalty or life in prison without the possibility of parole in the men's cases.

According to DA Howard Relin, Cassidy's lawyer most likely would waive a hearing, scheduled for Penfield Town Court, at noon, on August 8, 2003, and ask that the matter be referred to county or state court in exchange for agreeing to remain in custody without bail until the other cases were disposed of.

Cassidy, it was alleged, not only owned the rifle used to shoot Tabatha, but she also drove the getaway car. She had been charged with first-degree manslaughter in connection with the killing and she still faced felony drug counts for selling cocaine to a police informant.

CHAPTER 43

Judge Marks: First Female County Court Judge

Patricia D. Marks first sought the nomination of her party for election to the position of Monroe County Court judge in 1984. She had spent years prosecuting felonies as an assistant DA and was confident that she could handle a judge's duties, but the move still constituted a risk on her part. No woman had run for the job before, and Marks was young, married, and had a child. It would be tough, she realized, to maintain a balance between the campaign and her family. Professional and personal relationships were bound to be strained. As it turned out, most of her worries were for naught. She won the election. Her family became her biggest supporters. Her friends remained loyal, and the scrutiny placed on her—because of her gender—helped her do her best.

"I now celebrate twenty years on the bench and thirty years of marriage," Judge Marks wrote in 2004. "I cannot imagine my life any other way."

* * *

Ten days after Cyril's plea—on Monday, August 18, 2003—it was Kevin Bryant's turn to be arraigned before Judge Marks. Kevin pleaded not guilty to charges of first-degree murder. As a show of support, many of Kevin's friends and former coworkers were in the courtroom, but none made statements after the hearing.

Kevin was ordered held without bail. Kevin's lawyers, John F. Speranza and deputy capital defender Thomas Kidera, reserved the right to request bail in the future.

Speranza, leader of Kevin's defense team, had gray hair. As is often true of defense attorneys, he wore it on the longish side. Always in a suit, he wore glasses, which he often held on the tip of his nose and peered down through.

Speranza had hoped to get Kevin freed on bail before and during his trial. But, on August 18, 2003, Judge Marks ordered no bail after Bryant pleaded not guilty to first-degree murder.

Before becoming the publicly hired capital-case defender in Monroe County, Thomas Kidera had performed the same role in Seneca County, in New York State's Finger Lakes region, nestled between Lakes Seneca and Cayuga. Kidera's most famous case while working in Seneca County was *People* v. *Eric Parsons* in 2002. After a long history of domestic turmoil, the twenty-five-year-old Parsons faced five counts of murder as he was accused of using an accelerant to set a fire that killed his wife and four children. The fire occurred at his wife's apartment in the town of Romulus. Although the prosecution considered for a time seeking the death penalty in that case, which would have been a first in Seneca County, Parsons was found guilty on March 19, 2003, of five counts of arson in the first degree and five counts of murder in the second degree. He was sentenced on May 6, 2003, in Seneca County Court, to two 25-years-to-life terms in prison.

Kidera, as would befit his role as a capital-case defender, had long advocated the abolition of the death penalty. In states in which the death penalty is legal, there is a racial bias, he had noted, and nonwhites tend to be sentenced to death far more often than whites. He had also noted that the number of death sentences varies greatly from county to county, where the death penalty is legal. In New York State, for example, 83 percent of the state's murder arrests were made in the downstate area—New York City and its three largest suburban counties (Westchester, Nassau, and Suffolk). Prosecutors there, some of whom have philosophical objections to capital punishment, have seldom sought the death penalty since New York brought back capital punishment in 1995. But in the upstate area, which would include Monroe County, which had only 17 percent of New York's murders, prosecutors sought the death penalty far more frequently. Indeed, 36 percent of the cases in which the death penalty was sought were tried downstate, and 64 percent were tried upstate.

Following Kevin's plea of not guilty, as had been the case with Cyril's plea, prosecutors had 120 days to decide whether or not to pursue the death penalty. That time limit could be extended, however, if the DA asked for an extension. Kevin was scheduled to return to court on December 1.

Court was adjourned. Kevin's mom and dad bolted for the courtroom door like they wanted to beat the traffic.

CHAPTER 44

Kevin's Other Legal Woes

In September 2003, Kevin's legal woes were not limited to criminal court. He had trouble in civil court as well—two lawsuits were pending against him.

Kevin was being sued for $2 million by Willie James Jr., of Rochester. Kevin's association with James began in 1995 when Kevin worked in the local office of Hyatt Legal Services. Bryant agreed to take on James's case, but it was eventually handled by Kevin's associate and onetime housemate, William R. Shero.

James had been arrested and was tried on burglary and other criminal charges. With Shero defending him, James had been convicted and sentenced to prison. Hyatt appealed, but James's conviction was upheld.

While serving his prison sentence, James had filed a complaint stating that he had received an inadequate defense. James was released in 1999 when a federal judge agreed.

In May 1999, U.S. magistrate judge Hugh B. Scott, of Buffalo, recommended that James's conviction be set aside, saying Shero's defense work had been "substantially deficient at every step of the proceedings." Shero surrendered his license to practice law in 2001.

James subsequently sued Bryant, stating that he was wrongly imprisoned because of the extremely poor job that Bryant had done in defending him. James was represented in the civil suit against Hyatt, Bryant, and Shero by Rochester lawyer Ron Berg. In August 2003, Berg said, "The case is now in the pretrial discovery phase. At this point Bryant's incarceration is not a factor, and it should be possible to depose Bryant in jail, if need be."

Berg noted that Bryant might be "judgment-proof," meaing that his client could not collect any money from Bryant because all of Bryant's funds were to be committed to his own legal problems. However, Berg noted, if Bryant had malpractice insurance, the insurance company would pay the judgment.

When a lawyer finds himself being sued for malpractice, it doesn't help if he is behind bars at the time.

"It's clearly not a good thing for the defense that one of the defendants is in custody. But it's not fatal to their case," Berg said.

Bryant and Hyatt were being represented in the lawsuit by a lawyer named James A. Hoare.

In the other lawsuit against Bryant, a couple, Albert G. and Dana R. Phillips (pseudonyms), from the town of LeRoy, in nearby Genesee County, had already won a $202,000 judgment from Bryant and his associate Shero, both of whom worked at the time for Hyatt Legal Services. The suit stemmed from the fact that Bryant and Shero had agreed to represent the couple in a legal case they were involved in. The pair of lawyers had then dropped out of the case without notice just before the Phillipses were to go to trial. Neither Bryant nor Shero had paid any money to the Phillipses, and lawyers for the couple were in the process of trying to collect the judgment money.

* * *

Besides the friends and the family of the Bryants, some of those most affected by Tabatha's murder and Kevin's arrest were Kevin's clients. Some were trying to find new lawyers who could take over where Kevin had left off. Others were trying to recover their legal files, many of which contained sensitive and confidential information, from Bryant's offices, fearing that those documents might fall into the wrong hands in the chaos and vacuum caused by Kevin's sudden incarceration.

CHAPTER 45

New DA

In the November 2003 elections, Assistant District Attorney Michael Green was elected the new Monroe County district attorney. Howard Relin, a Democrat, had appointed Green, a Republican, as an assistant DA years before. When Relin announced he would not seek reelection, Mike Green tried to get the Republican endorsement to run for the position.

They turned him down, instead choosing Anne Marie Taddeo, a former family-court judge, as their candidate. Green then switched parties, running and winning on the Democratic ticket. It was one of the only races the Democrats won that year in Monroe County.

Reporter Amy Cavalier covered the race for district attorney closely, so she already had a good working relationship with Mike Green when they again came into contact with one another before and during Kevin Bryant's trial. She always found him to be a fair, accessible, and responsive public official.

Green—no relation to the defendant Cassidy Green—was a youthful-looking man of average height, with sandy blond hair. Despite his youthful appearance, he carried himself with an air of maturity. Soft-spoken and well-measured, yet confident and approachable, he exuded an aura of calm.

In Green's first statement following his election, he said that, under his leadership, his office would be run in a nonpolitical fashion.

He said, "(The current DA, Democrat) Howard Relin has always run it that way. His appointing me as first assistant district attorney in 2001 is proof of that, knowing he may have been handing the job to a Republican. The decisions we make and the work we do here is just too important for it to be a political job. Those decisions need to be made on justice and merit. We've had a tremendous conviction rate in the past two years, and I think the reason for that is because of the cooperation between the police and prosecutors on those cases. I think we need to strive to accomplish that level of cooperation in all areas of the office."

He said his office would "aggressively prosecute violent felons and murder cases."

Describing his two-pronged attack on prosecuting drug offenders, Green said, "First, I will go after major drug dealers with long sentences and by seizing their assets. On the other hand, we need to use programs like Drug Court and Road to Recovery to get treatment and rehabilitation for nonviolent drug addicts. Rather than just warehousing them, we need to get them off the streets, learning, working, and being taxpaying members of society."

Green would be responsible for prosecuting all violations of New York State law, particularly penal law, which occurred in Monroe County. They also prosecute violations of motor vehicle and traffic law. Each year, the office prosecutes approximately thirty-five thousand cases—twenty-eight thousand involving misdemeanors and violations, and about five thousand to six thousand felonies.

CHAPTER 46

Sorting It Out in Court

On November 17, Cassidy Green was indicted on three charges of cocaine sales, stemming from the three undercover buys executed by Rocky. Chances that Cassidy would be able to beat these charges were remote, considering the crimes had been videotaped. These charges would eventually be used as leverage to get Cassidy to testify against Kevin and Cyril regarding Tabatha's murder.

Three days later, November 20, 2003, DA Michael Green discussed whether or not his office would seek the death penalty for Kevin Bryant.

He said, "We are in the process of looking at the facts and circumstances of the case, records of the parties involved, and the impact the case has had on the community. We've also met, and continue to meet, with the victim's family to get their input."

In the meantime, although it had been five months since the murder, Tabatha's father and stepmother, Leroy and Becky Bassett, still felt the pain of her loss acutely.

"Leroy still hurts about it, but he accepts that she's in a better place now," Becky said.

"I would like to know why it was done," Leroy said.

On Friday, November 21, 2003, Cassidy Green pleaded not guilty to her felony drug charges (possession and sale of cocaine) in Monroe County Court. Representing Cassidy was her well-known and flamboyant attorney, Felix V. Lapine.

The press learned from Lapine that she had stopped cooperating with prosecutors and could, as a result, face a more serious charge than the first-degree manslaughter charge she was then facing for her role in Tabatha's murder.

Lapine said his client had been cooperating with the DA's office in the homicide trial, but that prosecutors "jacked up" the proposed jail sentences so many times, she changed her mind.

"It does not appear to be to her advantage to cooperate with prosecutors at this point," he said. "She wants to extend her right to a trial on the manslaughter charges."

According to Lapine, he had told the DA's office that all deals were off, back in October. He said that the drug charges against Cassidy were "Mickey Mouse," and he accused the DA's office of trying to "hang a criminal record" on his client before the homicide trial.

Cassidy had done very well for herself by getting Lapine to represent her. One of the cases that made Lapine well-known in Rochester was his 2002 defense of forty-seven-year-old, down-on-his-luck businessman Bernard Sorrentino Jr., who was charged with the stabbing death on St. Patrick's Day, 2002, of his thirty-seven-year-old wife, Angela, in their Auburn, New York, home. In a classic case of overkill, Sorrentino stabbed his soon-to-be-estranged wife sixty-six times before slashing her throat. After Angela Sorrentino was killed, Bernard Sorrentino fled to Mexico and then Arizona. He led cops on a high-speed chase through the desert before he was apprehended two weeks after the murder. In his efforts to have Sorrentino acquitted, Lapine made an unsuccessful attempt to block the use of his client's statement, his criminal history, and other evidence at the trial. In the statement that Lapine tried to suppress, Sorrentino had said that after a brief sexual encounter with his wife, she had taunted him by calling him fat, ugly, and an assortment of colorful metaphors. When his wife told him to go ahead and commit suicide, Sorrentino said he blacked out, only to be reawakened by his dog tugging at his arm. At that point, he said, he realized that he had killed his wife and then he fled. Lapine's defense was based on the fact that Sorrentino was being treated for depression with the drug Prozac, and that this fact had diminished his responsibility for his crime. Sorrentino was eventually convicted of second-degree murder (murder without premeditation) by a jury that only had to deliberate for four-and-a-half hours.

For years, Lapine had been outspoken in his moral objection to the death penalty.

"It's clear that the death penalty is government-sponsored revenge," he once wrote in *Syracuse University Magazine*. "Government-sponsored killing desensitizes society to the idea of killing others. When we become that insensitive to killing, we debase ourselves just as any other murderer does."

Incidentally, in January 2005, the *Democrat and Chronicle,* the Rochester daily newspaper, would incur the wrath of some readers by publishing Lapine's poor ranking in law school at Syracuse back in the 1970s. Readers felt that Lapine's success since law school made his class ranking irrelevant, and one reader said that the reason he might have done poorly in school was the fact that English was not his first language.

Representing the DA's office at this hearing was

Thomas Brilbeck, who was sitting in for Timothy Prosperi. Brilbeck was a drug-crime specialist with the Monroe County District Attorney's Office in 2003 and represented that office in hearings concerning the fate of Cassidy Green. (In 2004, Brilbeck would be the Monroe County chief of special investigations.)

According to Brilbeck, "The grand jury feels confident that there is enough evidence to charge her with the class B drug charge."

The DA's office made it clear that Green was not facing the death penalty for her role in the murder, but her attorney, Lapine, said that that could change pending grand jury consideration. In other words, with Cassidy Green no longer cooperating with prosecutors, the DA's office was expected to present evidence against her to a grand jury, which could return a higher charge.

Meanwhile, Cyril Winebrenner was back in court with his attorneys, Donald M. Thompson and Peter J. Pullano. Among Pullano's previous clients were thirteen religious leaders arrested in a Rochester federal building on March 5, 2003, during an Ash Wednesday civil disobedience demonstration opposing the war in Iraq (Pullano's work on this case was pro bono), and an ex–police officer charged with sex abuse, for whom Pullano earned an acquittal.

Joanne M. Winslow also was in court. Winslow was an athletic-looking woman with a short haircut that featured bangs. She had recently recovered from a broken leg suffered when walking her dog. She was a member of the Rotary Club who would be honored one day at the Rochester Rotary Club Luncheon for her "commitment as Co-Chair of the LPGA Committee." The president of the Rochester chapter of the Rotarians commended Winslow for her "often behind-the-scenes work and dedication to this event." In addition to being a Rotarian in good standing, Winslow was the chief of the major felony bureau at the Monroe County District Attorney's Office, and she would lead the prosecution team in the case against Kevin Bryant.

Both sides wanted to extend the time for the DA's office to decide if Winebrenner's was a capital-murder case. Judge Marks said that she would make her decision whether or not to extend the 120-day period by December 1.

As this was going on, Kevin's license to practice law was suspended by a Grievance Committee of the Seventh Judicial District (Appellate Division of the New York State Supreme Court, Fourth Judicial Department)—judges J. P. Pine, Kehoe Hurlbutt, and J. J. Hayes presiding.

On November 25, 2003, Judge Marks ruled on the district attorney's application to extend the time period to file a notice of intent to seek the death penalty. According to the court report: "The parties signed a written stipulation in support of the State's application, wherein they stipulated that good cause existed to extend the time in which a written notice of intent to seek the death penalty must be filed. Defendant specifically waived any claim concerning the timeliness of the filing of a written notice of intent. During oral argument, the district attorney indicated to the court that the extra time was necessary for a determination on the merits of their case. Defense counsel also asserted that the investigation into defendant's background was ongoing and additional time was needed to continue that investigation. The instant [the] court held that although the statute did not anticipate a waiver or stipulation, it was required to make a finding that good cause existed for an extension. After review of the record, and in consideration of the evidence presented by both parties, it found the same."

The parties stipulated in writing that good cause existed to extend the time in which the state must file and serve a written notice of intent to seek the death penalty to January 20, 2004.

There was a court hearing on December 1, 2003. The press and a few spectators gathered, thinking the prosecution was going to announce whether or not it was seeking the death penalty in the case against Kevin. ADA Joanne Winslow asked Judge Marks for more time on the grounds that she needed to study further "the circumstances of the case and Kevin Bryant's background."

Judge Marks said, "I grant the prosecutors an eleven-day extension, and I'm scheduling the announcement of the prosecution's intent for December twelfth."

By law, the prosecution had to announce whether it was seeking the death penalty by December 16, as this was 120 days after Bryant's arraignment. If the DA's office failed to announce by that date, life in prison without parole would be the harshest penalty they could seek in the case.

The DA's office simultaneously asked for more time to decide whether they would seek the death penalty in the case against Cyril. They were scheduled to announce by November 21, 2003, but asked for more time to study the case. Judge Marks agreed to push back the announcement until January 20.

The pattern of delays continued. On December 12, 2003, outgoing Monroe County District Attorney Howard R. Relin was scheduled to announce his decision in court as to whether prosecutors would be seeking the death penalty as a punishment against Kevin Bryant, if he was found guilty of murder.

But that day's hearing was postponed until December 31, because one of Bryant's attorneys, John Speranza, was in the hospital due to an undisclosed illness.

Winslow said the prosecution joined with the defense in requesting the extension.

"It's the right thing to do to ensure that the defense

attorney has a meaningful role in this part of the process," she said.

Judge Marks granted the extension.

December 31, 2003, was DA Relin's last day in office. Addressing Monroe County Court judge Patricia Marks, he used the occasion to announce that he elected *not* to seek the death penalty if Kevin Bryant was convicted. As the district attorney made his statement, relatives of both Kevin and Tabatha were in the courtroom. Present were Tabatha's uncle by marriage, Richard P. Warriner, her older sister, Samantha, and several cousins. Although Relin called the crime one of "the most horrendous and despicable crimes ever committed in the county," his reasons for not seeking the death penalty were that Bryant had two young children, and that Tabatha's family wished that the death penalty not be sought. He said a death penalty case with appeals could linger for more than a decade, and the sordid details of the case could harm the two boys, ages three and five, once the facts were learned.

"Once the children are old enough to understand the situation, [it] will cause the children irreparable psychological damage if we seek the death penalty," Relin said. "All of us have great concerns for the children. Were it not for the strong feelings of the family, we would be seeking the death penalty."

Relin said that he had talked to Bryant, who had years before been an intern in the Monroe County District Attorney's Office. Relin had advised Bryant to plead guilty and to spare his children the pain that his trial would cause.

"I've told Kevin Bryant to consider avoiding a trial for the benefit of his children," he said. "The boys are going to suffer for the rest of their lives because of this."

The DA, however, said that even if Bryant did say he would plead guilty, there could be no plea bargain in a case of this magnitude. The DA added that his decision regarding Bryant—that is, not to seek the death penalty—would not affect the Winebrenner case.

Kevin had until January 12 to hire his own lawyer or to go to trial with the capital defenders—John Speranza and Thomas Kidera—who had been appointed by the court.

The local newspaper, the following day, reported teasingly that there were many facts about the Bryants' "lifestyle" that had not been made public. They did, however, report that when Winebrenner and Cassidy Green started an escort service, police said that Kevin Bryant had helped fill out the legal paperwork for it.

In the courtroom when the announcement was made was Tabatha's uncle Richard Warriner. Outside the courtroom he told the press how painful the situation was for the families, noting that Tabatha's and Kevin's families had known each other for four generations. The Bryants and the Bassetts, he explained, had, and planned to continue to have, a close relationship.

"We love each other," Warriner said. "That's what makes it so hard."

He added that the Bryants' young children visited his home in Steuben County for Christmas, that they were unaware of the allegations against their father, but that "they understand that [their mother] has gone to heaven."

Warriner said that he agreed with the decision not to seek the death penalty for Kevin, but that "the person or persons responsible for this act must be punished somehow. We don't feel [the death penalty] would add anything to it. It would only take away from the boys. Now we have to let the American justice system take its course.

"Tabatha's family has been traumatized by this terrible act of murder," Warriner concluded. "We miss her terribly. She was a beautiful young girl who loved her family, her kids, music, and church."

During the hearing on January 12, prosecutors had suggested that Kevin plead guilty to spare his family—particularly his two young children—the ordeal of a trial. Defense attorney John F. Speranza now said that he, too, had suggested this to his client, but Bryant had rebuffed the recommendation.

"This case will proceed to trial," Speranza said.

CHAPTER 47

The Toughest Decision
Any DA Has to Make

With a decision regarding whether to seek the death penalty in the case of Cyril Winebrenner scheduled for less than two days away, DA Michael Green, who had been in office for less than a month, spoke to the press about the matter on January 18.

Green said, "The decision whether or not to seek the death penalty in a case is difficult, if not the most difficult . . . that any DA is called upon to make."

Although his predecessor as district attorney, Howard Relin, had decided not to pursue the death penalty in the case against Kevin Bryant, citing Kevin's children as the reason, Green said that he would treat the Winebrenner case separately.

Green said, "This is a case where we have been in ongoing negotiations with the defendant and his attorney. Certainly, there are many factors we need to take into account." Although he did add that he would factor the feelings of Tabatha's family, which overlaps with Cyril's family, into his decision, Green concluded, "Capital-punishment cases could take many years, and family members could be dragged through the process."

On Wednesday, January 21, 2004, with Judge Marks out of town on judicial business—she was at a conference in New York City—the decision as to whether or not Cyril Winebrenner would face the death penalty if convicted was postponed.

Two days later, on Friday, January 23, 2004, DA Green said he would seek the death penalty if Winebrenner was convicted. The decision came after Judge Marks denied the district attorney's request for another 120-day extension.

Green said, "Before you put the resources into a capital trial, you've got to consider the likelihood that that sentence is ever going to be carried out. But at this point in time, I think, more than anything, this decision presents our desire to keep our options open.

"I do not rule out the possibility that the motion (to seek the death penalty) could be withdrawn at a later date. I anticipate that we will reevaluate this decision after the trials of the other two defendants are complete. Pending circumstances I cannot foresee, it will likely be the last time I will reconsider this motion. If we did not file the motion today, we would never have the option to reinstate it. It's important we keep all our options available. We have the option of withdrawing the motion anytime, right up until the jury comes back with its decision. We looked at the allegations, the defendant's involvement, the proof we have against him, his background, the feelings of the families and the procedural posture. This course of action reflects the seriousness of the allegations in this case, but it also leaves our options open procedurally. We would not file for it if it didn't seem like an appropriate option."

Tabatha's family, which had been in strong attendance in previous court hearings regarding Kevin Bryant's upcoming murder trial, were noticeably absent at this hearing.

But the victim's family had a message for the press, which they conveyed through Michael Green.

"They care just as deeply about Winebrenner's case as they do about Kevin Bryant's case," the district attorney said. The family, however, made no attempt to account for their absence at the day's hearing.

The district attorney added that Tabatha Bryant's family did not wish to seek the death penalty against Winebrenner, just as they did not wish to seek it against Kevin.

Green said that the feelings of the family were only one of the factors he had to consider, however. There was also the evidence that prosecutors would gather in the case against Winebrenner between that point and the trial, then scheduled to begin September 20, 2004.

The DA had said that he would have sought the death penalty in the Kevin Bryant case if it weren't for the fact that Bryant had two small children, whose lives could be affected adversely by their father's execution.

Was Green showing a double standard? After all, Cyril Winebrenner also had a child, the "Little One" back in the Midwest with Patty.

CHAPTER 48

Cassy and the Grand Jury

Cassidy Green was scheduled to appear in court on Friday, January 30, 2004, but the court hearing was postponed until sometime in late March at the request of her attorney, Felix Lapine. Lapine said that his request was due to "health issues" he was facing. It would not be the last delay caused by a defense attorney's illness.

Lapine was healthy enough, however, to discuss the significance of Cassidy's upcoming court appearance. "My client was under police custody at some point for about forty-eight hours, and she made a number of statements related to the drug charge that are the subject of contention," Lapine said. "The hearing will determine whether her statements were voluntary."

Cassidy's manslaughter charges were still pending consideration from the grand jury. She had been living in the Monroe County Jail for six months, after she had been arrested on drug charges. Since right after her arrest, she had been saying that she would cooperate with the DA's office when it came to the prosecution of Cyril and Kevin. However, with her drug trial approaching, Cassidy, under the advice of Lapine, who was trying to get a better deal, changed her mind about cooperating. Her last voluntary statement to the district attorney's office had been back in November 2003. Because of this, her case was put before the grand jury to reconsider the charges against her.

The grand jury wasted no time in responding to Cassidy's decision.

"The grand jury has ruled that there is enough evidence to charge Cassidy Green with murder in the first degree," DA Michael Green said. "Written statements made to police by Cassidy Green will be used against her in trial."

She had originally been charged with first-degree manslaughter for her role in Tabatha's death—driving the getaway car, supplying the gun used in the attack, and disposing of evidence after the crime was committed. That charge would carry a maximum penalty of twenty-five years in prison. Now, since she had announced through her attorney that she wasn't going to be cooperative, Cassidy was indicted for first-degree murder. The maximum penalty could be death—or, more likely, life in prison without the possibility of parole.

Cassidy was arraigned on Monday morning, March 1, 2004, before Judge Marks. Prosecutors told the press that they would decide sometime in the next two weeks if they would seek the death penalty if Cassidy was convicted.

On Tuesday, District Attorney Michael Green said his office might announce whether it would seek the death penalty against Cassidy at her next scheduled court appearance. That appearance took place on Monday, March 15. Before Judge Marks, DA Green announced that he *wouldn't* seek the death penalty if Cassy was convicted. The DA said Cassidy escaped a death penalty trial partly because she didn't pull the trigger in the slaying.

The DA added, "Justice is best served by pursuing a sentence of life in prison without parole. We considered the allegations, her background, all the facts and circumstances of the case, the resources that would be needed to pursue a capital case, the likelihood that this would result in a death sentence and also the family's wishes and feelings."

Lapine said he was not surprised by the DA's decision. "I didn't think they ever would [seek the death penalty]," he commented. The attorney then emphasized his belief that his client was innocent of the charges against her.

A date for Cassidy's trial was expected to be announced by the start of summer.

On the same day, in a separate court hearing before the same judge, Kevin Bryant's attorney John Speranza requested that trial dates for his client be delayed to allow him to review additional evidence. ADA Winslow said that results from some examinations from the Monroe County Public Safety Laboratory were still not available.

"This is a case that involves a lot of investigation," she said. "There were a lot of materials submitted and collected."

Judge Marks said that new trial dates would be set for Kevin Bryant once all the evidence had been turned over and reviewed. She then ordered all parties to appear in court every Monday until the trial began.

CHAPTER 49

DNA Mystery

On Friday, April 2, 2004, in what was called an attempt to establish a motive in Tabatha's murder, the Monroe County District Attorney's Office asked that Kevin be compelled to give a DNA sample.

Winslow wanted the DNA sample to compare against three separate pieces of evidence: 1) The semen found on the body; 2) skin cells in a rubber glove found in a bag of garbage on the curb outside the Bryants' home—since they did not have Tabby's blood on them, the state must assume that these were the gloves Cyril wore the first time, late on the night of July 13, 2003, that he tried, and failed, to get inside 2 Pennicott Circle; and 3) blood samples taken from the home. The sample, prosecutors believed, could be used to help establish a motive in the case.

It was also publicly revealed on this date for the first time that Tabatha was having an extramarital affair, and that her boyfriend's DNA already had been tested.

Kevin's defense attorney complained about the request for Kevin's DNA: "The fact of the matter is that's totally redundant because they knew of the existence of the boyfriend, he's already given a full statement, and they've already taken a DNA sample from him," said John Speranza.

Judge Marks took the weekend to give the matter some thought and on Monday, April 5, 2004, she ordered that Kevin Bryant supply a DNA sample. ADA Winslow told Judge Marks during the brief court hearing that she believed the sample produced by Kevin, when compared with semen found on Tabatha's body, would prove that Kevin had a motive to commit the murder. Clearly, the prosecutor's theory was that the semen sample on Tabatha's body did not belong to Kevin. But the semen did not match the DNA of Richard Oliver, and Oliver said that he hadn't seen Tabby for a couple of days at the time of her murder.

If the semen found on Tabby's body had matched the DNA of Richard Oliver, an additional test on Kevin's DNA would not have been necessary, since the producer of the semen would have been identified already.

Everyone in the courtroom assumed that the semen did not match the DNA of Kevin Bryant. If there was any chance that the semen would have matched Kevin's DNA, the prosecution wouldn't have wanted the test to be made. The prosecution had no interest in showing that the defendant had had sexual relations with the deceased soon before her murder, even if it had been true. It would have done nothing to help them show motive.

Joanne Winslow didn't want to tarnish the deceased's reputation, but Tabby's infidelity—perhaps her infidelities—were the problem that Kevin needed to solve. Winslow had to show that Kevin did not have to be deluded in order to be jealous of his wife's behavior.

Winslow said, "Tabatha Bryant was no longer in

love with her husband and had taken a boyfriend with whom she had sexual relations shortly before her death."

By law, the prosecution is not required to show motive when presenting their case. However, Winslow did point out, "Even though we don't have to prove it, juries always want to know it."

Defense attorney Speranza maintained that a DNA sample from Kevin wasn't necessary to prove what the prosecutors said they wanted to prove. The prosecution already had a DNA sample from Tabatha's boyfriend, Richard Oliver, and, using that, should have been able to determine if the semen on her body came from him.

Speranza argued, "This is an absolute red herring. Ms. Winslow said, 'We want to eliminate the boyfriend.' They have the boyfriend's DNA already."

Speranza insisted that there was more than one reason why the prosecution wanted a DNA sample from his client. They didn't just want to compare that DNA with the semen found on Tabby's body at all, but rather with the human matter that might have been retrievable from the surgical gloves found in the garbage. Without knowing whether or not that glove could be linked with any individual or individuals, Speranza argued that it could have been placed there before the murder was committed. Therefore, it was irrelevant to the case.

Despite Speranza's argument, Judge Marks ruled that Kevin must provide a DNA sample. She ruled that there was a "likelihood that it would yield credible evidence."

On the other hand, Judge Marks ruled that the DNA sample provided by Kevin could not be used for comparison purposes with skin cells found inside the rubber glove recovered from a plastic trash bag placed along the street in front of the Bryant home.

She said that any comparison between Kevin's DNA and cells found inside those gloves would be "meaningless" because "there was no other evidence on the gloves, such as Tabatha Bryant's blood, that would connect them to her death."

The judge ruled that Kevin's DNA sample could be compared to both the semen found on the body and the blood found in the home.

Winslow told Judge Marks that she would be presenting more information in the future about the glove that might lead the judge to change her mind regarding the meaninglessness of such a comparison.

About the attempts to ID the DNA sample on the body, Judge Marks recalled later, "The prosecution made an application to get a DNA sample from Kevin Bryant so that his DNA could be eliminated as a possible match with certain items of evidence. There were multiple problems in the types of evidence they were seeking to use for comparison. I ultimately ruled they couldn't use evidence unless they could link it to this crime. As far as I know, the semen was not identified."

At this hearing Judge Marks stated that she anticipated Kevin's trial to begin in August or September 2004.

On Monday morning, May 10, 2004, Cassidy Green's drug trial was scheduled to begin, but, just before jury selection began, a new deal was struck. Cassy's drug charges and first-degree murder charge would be combined and she would be charged with first-degree manslaughter (with a suggested penalty of twenty years in prison) in connection with Tabatha's death. The lesser charge, it was agreed, would be in exchange for her cooperation and truthful testimony against Cyril Winebrenner and Kevin Bryant. Whether or not Cassidy's eventual testimony was truthful would be up to the sole determination of the DA's office. And, according to the terms of the deal, the charges against Cassidy Green would not be reduced until after the DA determined that the testimony had been truthful.

"We would determine it based on the information we have and based on her testimony," Winslow said.

The deal had been offered previously to Cassidy Green's attorneys, but it had been turned down.

That summer, the city's Channel 10 News obtained documents that outlined witness accounts of Kevin's actions in the months leading up to the murder. The papers discussed Kevin's forty-fifth birthday bash at which he partied with a dominatrix stripper, two escorts, and approximately twenty guests while his sons were in the house. When Bryant learned Tabatha had a boyfriend, he threatened in April 2003 to have them both killed.

In the spring and summer of 2003, Bryant told his sons, "Mommy won't be coming home and Mommy is not going to be with us anymore."

The evidence also told of a conversation between Bryant and a fellow inmate at the Monroe County Jail about Tabatha's murder, in which, according to the court papers, Bryant said, "I did it."

CHAPTER 50

Preliminary Hearing

On Monday, July 12, 2004, Kevin Bryant's preliminary hearing began. The hearing was to determine whether sheriff's deputies had probable cause to arrest Bryant and whether statements Bryant made during the hours after the murder would be admissible at his trial.

First to testify were the sheriff's deputies who were the first to respond to Kevin's 911 call. They described finding Tabatha's body lying on the sofa bed on the Bryant's main floor, in the blood-splattered living room. According to the deputies, Kevin seemed calm when they arrived and was still on the phone with the 911 operator.

After the hearing, Speranza was asked by reporter Dave McKinley, of WROC-TV, the CBS affiliate in Rochester, if "cops had cause to detain Mr. Bryant for some seventeen hours, before charging him with a role in his wife's killing."

Speranza replied, "That's the sixty-four-dollar question, David, and the question is whether there was probable cause to detain him for those many hours and whether any statement was a derivative product of a principle or primary constitutional illegality."

In McKinley's televised report, he concluded, "Translation: did the cops do everything by the book? That's important as to what kind of evidence will be allowed at trial. Because while Bryant never signed a confession, he allegedly made statements to police. If the judge finds they didn't do their jobs by the book, though, those statements could be ruled inadmissible."

Previous to that day's hearing, the defense had moved to have the charges against Kevin dismissed. The grounds were that the charges against Kevin, as stated in his indictment, were duplicitous. Kevin's indictment stated that he'd "solicited, requested, commanded, importuned, and/or intentionally aided another person or persons to kill his wife Tabatha Bryant. The victim was shot with a rifle and stabbed multiple times with a knife. The defendant procured the commission of the killing pursuant to an agreement with a person or persons other than the intended victim to commit the same for the receipt, or in expectation of the receipt, of anything of pecuniary value from a party to the agreement or from a person other than the intended victim acting at the direction of a party to such agreement."

The defendant filed motions to dismiss the indictment on the grounds of insufficient evidence. He also asserted the indictment must be dismissed because it failed to list a cognizable crime and was duplicitous by charging conduct that was principal, accessory, and solicitor. In addition, the defendant asserted the language of the indictment might cause him to be convicted of the crime charged even if the jury did not reach a unanimous verdict.

Judge Patricia Marks reviewed the charge and the indictment before dismissing the defendant's motion. She wrote, "A count of an indictment is duplicitous when the count charges more than one offense. . . . The decision on whether an indictment is duplicitous rests on a careful analysis of whether the facts support the framing of the charge and whether the charge, as set forth in the indictment, expresses a single crime under the same theory. It is irrelevant whether the person charged in the count is the actual perpetrator or an accessory."

CHAPTER 51

Kevin Raises His Right Hand

In an attempt to show Judge Marks that the statements Kevin Bryant made during his initial interrogation on July 14 should not be used as evidence against him in his murder trial, Speranza called Kevin himself to the stand.

Kevin testified that sheriff's deputies had arrived at his home just after midnight and he'd been escorted to the driveway by a woman deputy. She'd asked questions and he'd answered them. Initially, Kevin testified, he didn't notice whether or not she was taking notes, but he knew that she used no artificial light to illuminate her notebook.

There was a male deputy also, but he came and he went. The woman deputy was with him at all times for three hours. Three times, Kevin testified, he'd had to explain what happened, why he'd called 911.

"They insisted that I stand so that I was looking away from the house. I kept asking about Tabatha's condition. I asked what they were doing to help her," Kevin testified. "I was wearing the T-shirt and shorts I'd worn to bed. I didn't have shoes on. I had no money, no keys in my pocket."

Kevin said he'd watched what was going on as he answered the questions, and he saw sheriff's deputies going from door-to-door, talking to the neighbors.

"They were also putting tape around the trees and the cars so [that] no one could get through," he said, adding that forty-five minutes or an hour after he went outside he was first informed that his wife was dead. "I was really just in complete shock, I didn't know what was happening; at times I was sitting, kneeling in the driveway, dry heaving in the grass next to the driveway, I was shaking.

"One of the officers asked me if I was okay. I said I had to call my parents to come get the kids. They wouldn't let me go back in the house, where the kids were. I tried to call my parents on my cordless phone, but couldn't because of my unsteadiness, or because it wouldn't connect. I said I couldn't get through and the police officer said they'd call. I gave him the number. I didn't speak with my parents at that time. The deputies told me that my kids were okay and that someone was watching them, but I couldn't see them."

About fifteen or twenty minutes after the deputy called Kevin's parents, they arrived. The two deputies he was with led him across the grass lawn to his parents. Kevin had hugged his parents, told them that Tabatha was deceased, and had asked them to take the kids.

"After a while my mother gave me a sweater to put on because it was a little chilly," Kevin said. His parents had stayed at the scene for ten or fifteen minutes and then they left with his two sons.

Kevin had told the deputies that he wanted to go home with his parents and his children, but they said no. He had to stay where he was and answer some more questions. "We need to talk to you," they had said.

Kevin testified: "After the children left, I stood in the

gutter on the north side of the house. There was an officer with me almost the entire time. They would come over, hang out with me, question me, then leave. The female officer would ask me, over and over again, what happened, even though she had already asked me twice at the bottom of the driveway. I repeated the series of events of what had made me call nine-one-one until I got to the end of the driveway. We were discussing things, matters of mine and Tabatha's life. They asked me about what had gone on that day, from Sunday morning until I called nine-one-one. I was asked to repeat the scenario five or six times between midnight and three A.M."

"How many times did you request to leave?" Speranza asked his client.

"Twice in the driveway," Kevin said. "Three to four times on the north side of the house. The answer was always no, we have to ask you questions; we'll have to see about that later. I was introduced by the female officer to Investigator Siena and one more. This occurred while we were standing in the street. The female officer introduced me to the investigators. She said, 'They will be handling the case.' She turned me over to them and then she basically disappeared. The male officer was still there, the two investigators introduced themselves to me. They said they had been updated on the basic situation and they wanted to question me. Then they both left. I was standing in the street with one or two officers. After about ten or fifteen minutes, the investigators came back and told me to go with them. I told them I wanted to go to my parents'. They asked me what I needed from the house, indicating the house would be closed for about a week. I said I needed my briefcase, phone, shoes, sweatpants, sweatshirt, keys, and medication. They obtained my shoes, shorts, phone, and briefcase. Investigators led me to their car. I was not handcuffed. I put my items in the backseat and then I rode in the front passenger seat. They asked me about my job. I'd asked them to go inside the house and pick up some of my files for the two or three cases I had the next day. I again indicated that I wanted to see my children. They told me that I was going to headquarters.

"At the sheriff's office, they parked and asked me to leave my stuff in the car. I followed them up to the sheriff's office on the second floor. We took the elevator. When I came in, they had to unlock doors. They let me use the men's room near the elevator; then we went into the office. I was not handcuffed. Up to that point, I had not been read my Miranda rights."

"Were you aware of the Miranda rule?" Speranza asked Kevin.

"Yes, about ten percent of my practice is general criminal defense," Kevin said.

Kevin testified that he'd arrived at the sheriff's office at about 4:00 A.M. He'd been taken to an office that contained two workstations. The investigators introduced themselves again and removed their jackets. Kevin noticed they were armed. They'd asked him if he was familiar with firearms and one of them showed Kevin his gun.

"At this point, what were the topics you were being questioned on?" Speranza asked.

"Same thing," Kevin said. "They wanted me to tell them what happened from Sunday afternoon till midnight. We discussed the events that led up to my nine-one-one call, and they asked me about our personal life."

"Were you starting to feel fatigued by this time?"

"Yes, I was."

"When was the last time you had slept?"

"I had been up since six in the morning on Sunday. I had been up for twenty-two hours without sleep."

Kevin testified that the investigators had asked him to describe the same events, only using different senses.

One time he would go through the previous evening's events describing only what he had heard. The next time it would be only what he had seen.

Kevin said that as the two investigators questioned him, there was usually a deputy in the room—but it wasn't always the same deputy. "They would rotate," Kevin said.

"Were you allowed to make any phone calls on your cell phone when in that office?"

"No, my cell phone was in my briefcase and I made no calls during that time period."

"Did you make any requests of the investigators while you were being questioned?"

"At least twice I asked if I could go home and check on my kids. I said, 'If there's any new pertinent information you need, I'll be glad to supply it. If not, I want to go home and check [on] my kids.'"

"And what did they say to that?" Speranza inquired.

"They said, 'No. Later. We'll see about it. I have a few more questions.'"

"They asked you who might be capable of such a violent act?"

"Yes, they did. I told them a few possibilities. He asked me for what I thought was a hypothetical situation in which someone might be capable of such a violent act," Kevin stated.

"And you did that?"

"Yes."

"What did you say?"

"I came up with a burglar who was confronted when trying to break into someone's home. You know, if that were the situation, then that sort of thing could happen."

Kevin described how the investigators had taken him to breakfast, and at about 8:00 A.M., they allowed him to stand on the sidewalk and take and make a few

Tabby at
age four.

Sam and Tabby on their bikes
during the summer of 1982.

Virginia Winebrenner's parents, Cyril and Clara Hentges. Clara passed away in 1991.

The Hentges family, all in one place. In the back row, from left to right, are Jerry, Russ, Roy, and Chuck. In the front row, from left to right, are Ginny, Denise, Clara, Cyril, Sue, and Sharon.

Sammy *(left)* is about 14 and Tabby 13, on one of the all-too-rare occasions when they visited Ginny.

The Winebrenners on Easter Sunday, 2000. From left to right: Chris, Ginny, Cleo, Cyril, and Cyril's wife, Patty.

A rare photo of Cyril and Tabby together. From left to right: Samantha, Cleo, Cyril, Tabby, and Ginny. It is November 25, 2001, the day after Chris's funeral.

Cleo and Ginny Winebrenner have been together for more than a quarter of a century, through the good times and the bad.

On the eve of her first wedding, Tabby gets a hug at the rehearsal.

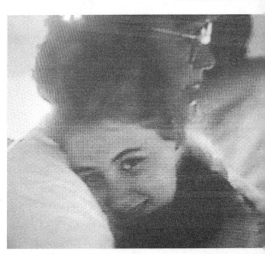

Tabby grins as she turns to face the groom while taking vows.

During the ceremony, Tabby snuck a quick, excited glance at her sister and her other bridesmaids.

It's official. Lawfully wed, Tabby heads for the reception line.

The bride had a hug and a kiss for every guest.

A candid moment as something catches Tabby's attention on the other side of the room.

Tabby unfurls her tongue for the cameraperson.

2:15PM
8/25/1996

Tabby stands in front of the Howard Community Center's concession stand, about to be led up the aisle by her father *(left)* and her grandfather *(right)*.

A studio portrait of Tabby not long after she moved to Rochester with her first husband.

Every year on Chris Winebrenner's birthday, a member of his family goes to the casino and pops a couple of quarters into a slot machine on his behalf. In 2004, Cyril's cousin Jamie *(pictured here)* did the job. "Chris didn't have any luck at all," Jamie reported.

Patty and "Little One," the family Cyril left behind.

Cyril's Aunt Becky. She says, "Don't let anyone tell you that Cyril is all bad, because he isn't."

Mug shot of Cyril Winebrenner, following his arrest for first-degree murder. He is still wearing the military-style haircut he first received when he enlisted in the army a few months before. Winebrenner said he killed his sister Tabby because her husband Kevin paid him $5,000. Kevin claimed it was because of an increasingly bitter sibling rivalry. *(Photo courtesy of the Monroe County Sheriff's Office)*

Mug shot of Cassidy Green. She met Kevin Bryant when she was attempting to start her own escort service. It was her gun that was used to shoot Tabatha Bryant. Following Tabby's murder, Cassidy drove the getaway car and helped dispose of evidence. *(Photo courtesy of the Monroe County Sheriff's Office)*

The house in Penfield, New York, where the murder took place. The house has undergone some changes since the time of the murder. There had been very tall evergreen trees lining the entire front yard. Those have been cut down. *(Photo by Amy Cavalier)*

The garage entrance to the Bryant home. According to Cyril Winebrenner, the initial attempt to enter the home on the night of the murder was made through the garage. But apparently the door from the garage to the inside of the home was locked. *(Photo by Amy Cavalier)*

Two years after Tabby's death the Bryant home remained empty. But Kevin's parents still saw to it that the lawn was mowed and the flower gardens weeded.

Cyril Winebrenner entered through the sliding glass doors atop the wooden deck at the rear of the Bryant home.

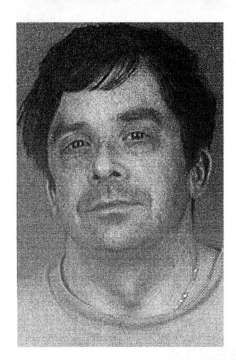

A police photo of
Kevin Bryant.
*(Courtesy Monroe
County Sheriff's Office)*

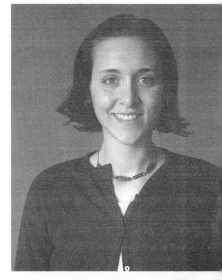

Rochester reporter
Amy Cavalier covered
Tabatha Bryant's
murder from the press
conference the
morning after until all
three defendants had
been sentenced.
(Photo by John D. Hanlon)

This is the strip joint—known in this book as Nookie's Tavern, and now under new management with a new name—where Kevin took his wife and where Tabby met her boyfriend Richard Oliver.
(Photo by Amy Cavalier)

The entrance to the Bloomdale Mobile Home Park, where Cyril Winebrenner and Cassidy Green moved after they were asked to leave the Bryant home by victim Tabatha Bryant.
(Photo by Amy Cavalier)

It was out of this mobile home that Cassidy Green planned to operate an "escort service" called Sunset Sensations. At one point Cassidy, Cyril Winebrenner, three other adults, and a dog lived in this trailer simultaneously. *(Photo by Amy Cavalier)*

The Monroe County Sheriff's Office in downtown Rochester where Kevin Bryant was questioned for hours on end by investigators during the first day of the investigation.

Kevin Bryant, Cyril Winebrenner, and Cassidy Green all met their fate in this building, the Monroe County Hall of Justice in downtown Rochester.

The Honorable Patricia D. Marks presided over almost all of the court hearings involving this case's three defendants. She presided over the trial of Kevin Bryant and sentenced all three of the accused.

Tabatha Bassett Bryant, 1976–2003.

calls on his cell phone. He said he couldn't get in touch with anyone and left messages.

Speranza asked what Kevin had eaten for breakfast and Kevin stated that he had not eaten. He'd ordered orange juice only and sipped at that while looking out the window as the investigators ate. He testified that breakfast lasted for about an hour. The investigators chitchatted about work between themselves and he paid no attention. Kevin said that while they were still at the breakfast restaurant, he began to get callbacks from the messages he had left. He spoke with the children's primary-care physician and a psychologist about how to break the news about their mother's death.

"The investigator has said that he read you your rights at the restaurant. Is that correct?" Speranza asked.

"No, that did not occur until after breakfast, about an hour or an hour and a half after we got back to the sheriff's office," Kevin said. "Then he said, 'You're an attorney, you know about your Miranda rights.' I said yes. That was all I heard him say."

"Were you ever read the five Miranda rights?"

"Not at all."

"Were you shown a piece of paper with your five Miranda rights written on it?"

"Not at all."

"Were you given a waiver-of-rights card?"

"No."

"From twelve-fifteen A.M. until five P.M. on July 14, was there any other discussion or reference to your Miranda rights?"

"No."

"Do you recall Investigator Siena asking you about stab wounds?"

"Yes, I do."

"When did that occur?"

"That was after we got back from breakfast, but before we went to lunch."

"About what time did Investigator Siena ask about knife wounds?"

"Noonish."

"And what did he say?" Speranza asked.

"He told me that he'd heard that there had been no gunshot wounds. He'd heard there were only stab wounds."

"What did you say to that?"

"I said could be, but I did not believe that to be the case. I told him I had never seen a gunshot wound or a stab wound before."

"Did you make a statement to Investigator Siena to the effect that you felt responsible for Tabatha's death?"

"I said in a sense I felt that way because if I had left her upstairs with the kids that night—if we had a better relationship and had been sleeping in the same bed—then this might not have happened."

The investigators said that they wanted to go to lunch soon after that. Kevin testified that he'd asked them if he could be taken home and they'd said they'd see about that after lunch.

"Do you take medication?"

"Yes. Blood pressure medication, a Xanax prescription, two or three heart medications. I was supposed to have taken my heart medicine three to four times that day, but I hadn't taken any since between ten and eleven P.M. on July 13. At the house I'd asked police to get the daily pill box on the counter in the bathroom upstairs, but they hadn't done that. After noon I started to feel the effects of not taking my medication."

"What were those effects?"

"I came down with a migraine headache," Kevin replied.

"What were the symptoms?"

"What happens to me, it's like I'm underwater, nothing's clear visually."

"What did you do?"

"I told them I didn't feel good."

"How did they respond to that?"

"They didn't respond. After lunch they returned me to their office, I asked them to take me home or I'd try to get a ride. At two or three o'clock in the afternoon, I called my father and someone else to see if I could get a ride. I said, 'Look, you're either going to arrest me right now or I'm going to leave. What are you going to do?'" Bryant testified. "He said, 'You're not under arrest.' That's when I left."

Speranza argued to Judge Marks that Bryant's statements were inadmissible because he was in custody and wasn't advised of his right to remain silent before he talked to investigators. Though Kevin did not confess to any crime during that initial interrogation, his statements included admissions that he and Tabatha were estranged and that she was having an affair—which became the basis for the investigators' theory of Kevin's motive.

Bryant said investigators made only a "passing reference" to his right to remain silent. Under cross-examination by Assistant District Attorney Joanne M. Winslow, however, Bryant said he wasn't aware that police were required to read that right to people in custody before they were interrogated.

After Kevin was through on the stand, Deputy Bridget Davis took the stand and told the court about statements Kevin Bryant had made during his initial interrogation during the hours following Tabatha's murder.

Deputy Davis said that Kevin spoke about a myriad of subjects, including the phase of the moon, his financial difficulties, how it was getting tougher and tougher just to cash a check, and how his wife had a boyfriend.

CHAPTER 52

The Sheriff's Scenario

On Thursday, August 5, 2004, in a statement released to the press, the Monroe County Sheriff's Office stated its theory as to how Tabatha met her demise: "Bryant shot his wife in the face with a twenty-two-caliber rifle while her half brother stabbed her repeatedly, causing her death." The sheriff, it was clear, was still buying into Cyril's version of the crime. The DA's office, on the other hand, would attempt to convince a jury of a very different scenario.

On Friday, August 27, 2004, Kevin's lawyers asked Judge Marks to order the U.S. Army to turn over Cyril Winebrenner's discharge records. They hoped that the records would adversely affect his credibility as a witness. Judge Marks refused on the grounds that Bryant's lawyers failed to show sufficient reason to believe that Winebrenner's records contained information that could be used to challenge Winebrenner's credibility. The judge stated that Winebrenner joined the army in March 2003 but was discharged after one month. Winebrenner's explanation for his brief military stint was that his asthma had prevented him from completing basic training.

Matthew Lembke handled this portion of the defense. He was younger and huskier than Speranza, with brown hair and a haggard appearance. Lembke stated that he believed that Winebrenner was lying when he placed the blame on a physical ailment. Lembke wanted to review the records to determine whether Winebrenner was discharged for psychiatric reasons.

"Winebrenner received two days of psychiatric treatment in October 2002," Lembke said. "His military service lasted thirty days, which is unusual, to say the least." Referring to Winebrenner, Lembke said, "This is an important witness in the case—perhaps the *most* important witness in the case. He's the perpetrator of the crime."

Although Judge Marks declined Lembke's request, she made it clear that questions regarding Winebrenner's military service would be allowed during cross-examination when Winebrenner testified.

On Wednesday, September 1, 2004, it was announced that Kevin's trial, which had been scheduled to begin on September 8, was postponed. According to Joseph Valentino, the law clerk for Judge Marks, the postponement was because John Speranza was ill. This was the second time proceedings had been delayed because of Speranza's health. He had been hospitalized in December 2003 for an undisclosed illness.

It was announced on Friday, September 10, that, with Speranza having recovered from his illness, the start of jury selection for Kevin's trial was rescheduled for Tuesday, September 28. At that time three hundred prospective jurors would be called to the Monroe County Hall of Justice for what was expected to be a three-day selection process.

At a court hearing held this day, Speranza asked that jury selection be held "behind closed doors."

Judge Marks denied the request but agreed that, if a potential juror indicated that they had been exposed to media coverage of the trial, they could be questioned further in a room separate from the other jurors and those in the courtroom.

CHAPTER 53

"Bad Acts"

At a pretrial hearing on Tuesday, September 21, 2004, Joanne Winslow introduced in court an eleven-page document that outlined "bad acts" allegedly committed by Kevin. These were acts that would, if allowed into evidence, help an eventual jury understand just what kind of character the defendant was. There were twenty-eight points made in the document, all derived from the statements of six witnesses.

There were two decisions to be made: Would the bad acts be made available through the press, to the public? Second, would the bad acts be allowed into evidence at Kevin's trial?

The first hearing, held in a court closed to the public, was presided over by state supreme court justice Kenneth Fisher. Kevin's defense attorney John F. Speranza asked that the courtroom be closed and information sealed so that uncharged bad acts, which the prosecution wanted to introduce into evidence, would not prejudice potential jurors.

Judge Marks, who presided over all other court

hearings involving the murder of Tabatha Bryant, was not at this one. "I wasn't there because the lawyer who represented the media had been active in my campaign for reelection. I wouldn't be able to have him appear before me, unless they waived the conflict, and they didn't, which was reasonable," Judge Marks explained later. A member of her campaign staff, it turned out, was also an employee of Rochester's *Democrat and Chronicle*.

Because this hearing had to do with whether or not Kevin's bad acts should be available to the press and public, Judge Marks thought it best if Judge Fisher took the bench in her stead. The courtroom was not closed and the information was not sealed as the parties next assembled in the courthouse that Friday.

Winslow outlined the evidence she hoped to introduce into evidence at the trial, the twenty-eight alleged bad acts, which would help jurors understand the defendant's character. The evidence presented showed that Kevin Bryant used drugs, including cocaine, and bought prostitutes and strippers. One allegation stated that Kevin tried to set up his wife on a bogus drug charge a month before she was murdered. Another stated that he had "frequently discussed" killing Tabatha's boyfriend, or having him killed, as a way of curing himself of his cuckold status.

Prosecutors said they wanted jurors to hear about how Kevin "frequently dallied with prostitutes on Tuesdays and Thursdays" at his law office, how he asked a man who drove one of the prostitutes to his office if he would kill Tabatha Bryant for $5,000, and how he bought cocaine from Winebrenner and said he was going to give it to a prostitute. Prosecutors wanted to show that Kevin talked with a person about launching several enterprises, including the purchase of cocaine in the South and resale of it in the Rochester area.

It was alleged: 1) in May and June of 2003, Kevin was

putting a lot of pressure on Cyril and Cassidy to kill Tabatha, and that Cyril suggested getting Tabatha arrested for cocaine with intent to sell so she would go to jail for a long time; 2) Kevin gave Cassidy approximately $1,500 to buy cocaine to set Tabatha up by putting the cocaine, packaged into small envelopes for sale, in her minivan.

A separate allegation stated that Kevin had tried to hire a client to injure or kill his wife and her boyfriend.

The papers alleged that Kevin used cocaine with strippers at a "hotel party" in Gates—a suburban town just west of the city of Rochester—and boasted about paying them for sex with drugs, instead of money; approached a person about his desire to open an escort service but as a "silent partner" so he wouldn't be disbarred; told a fellow Monroe County Jail inmate after his arrest, "I did it," when asked about his wife's death; later said he heard a noise and found his wife dead but intimated that he knew the killer and said that paying $5,000 for his wife's death was a bargain because "you're dealing with drug addicts and they work cheap"; tried to hire another inmate to kill Winebrenner in the Monroe County Jail so Winebrenner couldn't testify; asked an acquaintance with a background in criminal forensic work how a "clean kill" could be committed.

Witnesses said Winebrenner had been "hanging out" with Kevin for months—partying with him and prostitutes at hotels. This, prosecutors argued, explained why Bryant trusted Winebrenner enough to hire him as the hit man.

Witnesses said Kevin hired a private detective to spy on his wife's boyfriend, Richard Oliver, and wanted him killed.

Truth was, the defense team was thrilled by one aspect of the "Bad Acts" list. It contained evidence given by a jailhouse snitch. Historically, the use of jailhouse snitches is a sign of desperation in a prosecution. Jail-house snitches provide the worst kind of information, and are almost inevitably corrupt and untruthful in some way. They are often used by the prosecution only when the physical evidence against the defendant is weak or nonexistent. The prosecution had no slam dunk in the Bryant case, that was for sure. Their witness list was already heavy with criminals and deal making. They were going to have to put pimps, prostitutes, and other ne'er-do-wells on the stand and were going to have to get a jury to believe them, if there was any hope of convicting Kevin.

But Kevin's defense team wasn't happy with the fact that the prosecution was now resorting to a jailhouse snitch, one who said that Kevin had offered to pay him to bump off Cyril Winebrenner. The defense had a counteroffensive—one found distasteful by many, as it showed that the defense intended to "blame the victim."

Kevin's lawyers attempted to introduce bad acts by Tabatha to establish a motive in her murder. Included were statements by witnesses who said that Tabatha was having an affair—a fact that made her husband angry—and that she was a "partyer" and "an unfit mother." Evidence indicated that Tabatha had incurred the wrath of her husband further by using drugs and lap dancing at strip clubs.

The local paper referred to Tabatha as an "ama-teur lap dancer at the strip joint where she met her boyfriend."

"It was open and notorious that Tabatha Bryant was running around wildly," Speranza said.

Prosecutor Joanne Winslow said, "We feel it's impor-tant for a jury to be able to understand how this began: what was the beginning, the middle, and the end. We feel it's important for a jury to be able to understand how this evolved. Otherwise, you're taking the single and small portions of the act and asking the jury to understand the case from a narrow point of view. I think a full picture would be much easier to understand."

Defense attorney Speranza said the bad acts regarding Kevin were irrelevant, salacious, inflammatory, and useless: "All it will do is prejudice a jury," Speranza said. "It's the natural tendency for a fact finder or juror to use those things and give them undue weight."

Speranza said he was trying to get ahold of Winebrenner's military records, which would show that he spent time in a psychiatric ward and was mentally unstable.

In the end Judge Fisher denied Speranza's request. Fisher called the allegations "lurid stuff," but he said Speranza failed to prove that Bryant wouldn't receive a fair trial if the information was disclosed.

The highlight of the new alleged evidence came from the statements of an inmate who claimed that Kevin, while in the Monroe County Jail, wanted him to commit a new murder. The evidence suggested that Bryant asked an inmate to "get rid" of Cyril Winebrenner, now a prosecution witness. That inmate allegedly told Bryant he could fight Winebrenner in the shower, for a price, then break his neck.

About this evidence Winslow said, "My argument says it shows consciousness of his own guilt."

Speranza—who referred to some of the witnesses Winslow wanted to put on the stand as "drug users"— responded, "Look at [the] context in which it was made, it was a jailhouse snitch."

Referring to the inmate informant, Speranza said, "We don't know if this person got any prosecutorial consideration. We haven't had a fact-finding hearing, where persons have been subjected to cross-examination prior to the admissibility of these statements."

The press asked Winslow what was her case's single-most important witness or piece of evidence. She replied, "In a case like this, I don't know if there will be any particular thing. I would hope that all of the relevant evidence will be considered."

She then noted that showing a motive could be the most important factor in convincing a jury of Kevin's guilt.

At that point key witnesses for the prosecution were expected to be: Green and Winebrenner's neighbor from a Bloomfield trailer park, who was expected to testify that the couple were usually broke but had money and purchasing power after the murder; Tabatha Bryant's boyfriend was expected to verify medical evidence that he was intimate with her shortly before she was killed; and an acquaintance of Kevin Bryant who was expected to testify that Bryant said he wanted to buy a gun to kill his wife and handed over $500 for a .38-caliber pistol, which was never delivered.

Judge Marks took the weekend to think about the matter of the bad acts, and she made her decision regarding it on the following Monday morning, September 27.

Of the thirty alleged bad acts outlined by ADA Winslow, Judge Marks ruled that eleven would not be allowed at Kevin's trial because, she said, "they are not relevant to any pertinent issue in the case."

These eleven included expected testimony about hotel parties frequented by strippers and a party in Bryant's living room with dominatrix strippers. Another inadmissible allegation was the one that stated that Kevin frequently had discussed killing his wife's boyfriend or having him killed.

Judge Marks later commented on this decision: "It was a prior bad act that was too prejudicial to the case. The only bad acts that can come in are those that are material to the issue. Usually those that are deemed material to the issue go to motive or intent, method of operation, identification, or common scheme or plan.

Those are the most common areas. I ruled that when he said he was going to kill the boyfriend, it wasn't pertinent to his going to kill his wife. It was merely a bad act that would show propensity."

On the other hand, testimony that Bryant previously had planned to kill his wife, and had asked clients of his if they would be willing to accept payment to do the dirty work for him, would be allowed.

Judge Marks also ruled that jurors would be allowed to hear how Bryant had attempted to set up his wife to get arrested on cocaine charges by planting the drugs in her van. Also ruled allowable were allegations that Kevin, while in the Monroe County Jail, had talked to fellow inmates about having his alleged accomplice in his wife's murder—and the anticipated star prosecution witness, Cyril Winebrenner—killed. Another potential witness who regularly visited Bryant could testify, the judge ruled, but the fact the witness worked as a prostitute should be avoided.

Judge Marks also allowed testimony from an inmate housed with Bryant after his arrest, who claimed Bryant wanted to kill Winebrenner to prevent him from testifying. Marks said such conversations could be "indicative of a consciousness of guilt."

On Wednesday, September 29, 2004, jury selection began. When twelve jurors were seated, after less than a day of voir dire, there were more men than women and the ages of the jurors ranged from their twenties to their sixties. Once the panel was complete, Judge Marks announced that the trial would resume first thing Monday morning and court was adjourned.

PART IV

CHAPTER 54

"Murder for Cash"

On Friday, October 1, 2004, Kevin's trial began in the courtroom of the Honorable Patricia D. Marks in the Monroe County Hall of Justice, only yards from the Genesee River, the vein that provided the metropolitan Rochester area its lifeblood.

Before the jury was brought in, Judge Marks considered three applications. One of those came from the defense attorneys, requesting that a videotape showing undercover drug dealer Donny "Rocky" Sands speaking with the getaway driver, Cassidy Green, be admissible as evidence in the trial.

Prosecutors argued that the tape provided no relevant information. Supposedly, Cassidy and Rocky talked about a vehicle on the videotape. To those listening in the audience, this was the first reference to Rocky and how Cassidy's drug bust in Henrietta was connected to the murder.

During the court argument, those listening construed that Rocky's job on the videotape was to engage Cassidy in a conversation about the homicide and to sell Cassidy cocaine so she could be arrested—and subsequently questioned by the sheriff's office regarding Tabatha's murder.

The defense insisted that the tape would be useful in the context of the case. Judge Marks decided to rule on the admissibility of the videotape later on. Judge Marks never did have to rule on whether the videotapes were relevant to the murder charge against Kevin.

"The tape was never offered as evidence, so it was never shown in court. So, technically, I did not rule that it was not relevant," Judge Marks explained later.

When the preliminary arguments were finished, the jury was brought into the courtroom and Judge Marks called for the commencement of the opening arguments.

In the prosecution's opening statement, Assistant District Attorney Kristin D. Splain began by describing the victim. She was a beautiful young woman, full of life, with so much to look forward to. Splain said that Tabatha Bryant was a bank employee who lived in a nice suburban home with her husband and their two small boys. She also had a boyfriend, ADA Splain said, a fact that angered her husband and caused for him to arrange for her murder.

She told the jury that Kevin handed Cyril Winebrenner, who had confessed, an envelope full of cash just moments after Tabatha's murder.

"Murder for hire—that's what this case is all about. A brutal murder for cash," Splain told the jury.

The prosecution's opening statement was then continued by Joanne Winslow, the chief of the district attorney's office major felony bureau.

"The jury will have credible evidence that will prove beyond a reasonable doubt that Kevin Bryant is responsible for hiring Cyril Winebrenner to kill Tabatha Bryant," Winslow said to the jury.

The prosecution's murder scenario had evolved. They would not try to sell Cyril's version of Tabatha's murder—in essence, Kevin had taken part in the actual murder of his wife, rather than being merely a passive financier.

The jury would never hear Cyril's version of the murder: Kevin had shot Tabatha while Cyril stabbed her. Beyond Cyril's word, there was no evidence that Kevin had pulled the trigger on the rifle that night.

The prosecution felt they didn't need to portray Kevin as a triggerman in order to convict him of first-degree murder. They would show that he was, however, the master-mind behind his wife's death.

On the night of the murder, Winslow said, Cyril Wine-brenner's girlfriend drove him to the Bryants' home. Winebrenner entered the home, shot Tabatha Bryant in the eye with a .22-caliber rifle, then—after the rifle jammed and could not be fired again—stabbed her fourteen times with a knife he got from the kitchen.

Winebrenner then started up the stairs to where Kevin Bryant and the couple's two young sons, ages three and five, were sleeping. Bryant met Winebrenner on the staircase. Winebrenner got an envelope containing $5,000 cash from Kevin and left.

That concluded the prosecution's opening statement. The court took a break, and when Judge Marks's gavel again called proceedings to order, it was the defense's turn to give their opening statement.

The defense team's leader, John Speranza, delivered it. Compared to the concise opening statement by the prosecution, spectators found Speranza's statement a meandering affair. Speranza was not a man known for his economy of words. It was common knowledge, in and around the courtrooms of Monroe County, that Speranza had never made a point that he wasn't willing to belabor.

As the trial proceeded, it would become a recurring

theme that Judge Marks would try to get Speranza to make his point and move on, but her efforts did little good. Speranza was what he was, and was not about to change.

A little pestering wasn't going to alter his "tortoise style" into "hare style." When Judge Marks's comments had no effect, there was a dreary resignation in the courtroom that Speranza was going to finish the trial every bit as repetitively as he had started. But Speranza was effective when he pointed out the flaws, as he saw them, in the prosecution's case.

"You've heard what they (the prosecution) anticipate they're going to prove. We believe that the evidence will show something different," the defense attorney said.

Speranza said that he would concede that Kevin knew that his wife was having an affair, but the defense would offer to the jury eyewitness reports that Kevin and Tabatha Bryant were making attempts to keep their marriage intact.

It was true that Kevin had filled out preliminary papers to file for a divorce, but those papers had never been served to Tabatha. Instead, Kevin had made plans to go with his wife on a church camping trip on July 16, where he hoped to reconcile. A minister from the Bryants' church would show that.

As evidence that Kevin did plan to go on the camping trip, Speranza promised to show that the defendant had arranged to take time off from work and had purchased camping items at the local Home Depot.

Speranza said that he intended to prove that Winebrenner killed his half sister on his own after their relationship deteriorated. "It had nothing to do with Kevin Bryant," Speranza said. "Winebrenner continually and repeatedly threatened her."

Speranza, in fact, promised to prove that Winebrenner's estranged relationship with Tabatha led to the murder. He said Winebrenner could not be taken at his word because he was a "mentally unhinged loner," had twice changed his story, and had negotiated a lesser sentence for himself in exchange for his testimony against Kevin Bryant.

Speranza told the jury that Winebrenner had had a falling-out with his sister that had resulted in the murder. He described Winebrenner as a "wanderer," who had a history of mental instability, and who had abandoned a wife and child in Iowa.

Speranza told the jury how Winebrenner had come to live with the Bryants in 2002, how he had taken a job working in Kevin's law office, and how he had met Cassidy Green, a prostitute and drug dealer, of Bloomfield, New York.

The meeting between Winebrenner and Green, Speranza said, took place in December of that year when she had come to Kevin Bryant's office, having plucked his name at random out of the Yellow Pages of the phone book.

Cassidy Green needed the attorney to help her set up an escort service out of a trailer camp in her hometown. Speranza said that Winebrenner had left the Bryant house in March 2003 to join the army, but his stint in the service had only lasted a month, ending under mysterious circumstances.

Speranza told the jury that when Cyril Winebrenner returned to Penfield after his discharge, he had reunited with Green, toward whom his behavior had become increasingly violent. There were bruises on Cassidy Green's face on the night of the murder because of blows she had taken from Cyril.

Cassidy wasn't the only woman Cyril was having problems with after his failed attempt to become a soldier. Speranza said that the relationship between Winebrenner and his sister deteriorated that spring as well.

"Tabatha eventually tossed Cyril and Cassidy out of the Bryant home," Speranza told the jury. He said that he would introduce evidence to show that there was a "continued, spiraling deterioration" in Winebrenner's behavior and that he became increasingly violent, a trait that directly led to the murder of his sister.

Speranza attempted to discredit the prosecution's case by hammering away at the poor character of its witnesses. He characterized the prosecution witnesses as a series of "snitches" and "drug addicts," all of whom had something to gain by testifying against his client.

And he was done. It was a Friday, and the jury had been given an earful. With both opening statements concluded, Judge Marks informed the court that the first witnesses would be called by the prosecution the following Monday. She said that everyone should expect about a total of thirty witnesses to be called and that, if everything went as planned, the trial should last about a month.

Journalists would spend the weekend in speculation. Not only were there guesses about how the prosecution was going to go about presenting its case, but also about the role the media would have in the trial.

On Monday, Judge Marks was expected to rule whether television and newspaper cameras would be allowed in the courtroom. The TV program *48 Hours* and the *Democrat and Chronicle* both had applied for coverage.

There had been a state law allowing cameras in courtrooms until 1997, when it expired, but some judges were still allowing cameras as long as neither the prosecution nor the defense objected. ADA Winslow made it clear that the prosecution had no objection, but Speranza said he would talk with the defendant before making up his mind.

Outside of court Winslow was asked how the prosecution was going to begin its case the following Monday. "I imagine it will start with what happened that night," she said.

CHAPTER 55

The Boyfriend Takes the Stand

That October 4 wasn't just a normal Monday at the Monroe County Hall of Justice. Media trucks with satellite dishes mounted on the top were parked out on Exchange Boulevard. CBS was eager to learn whether its evening news magazine show would be allowed to put video cameras in the courtroom.

If the access was granted, they wanted to set up inside as quickly as possible. Not that there was any extra room in there for the tools of the electronic media. It was the first full day of testimony and all the seats were full.

Judge Marks had a large courtroom and it was not often full. Relatives from both the Bassett and the Bryant family were in attendance. Each family took up several rows of seats, visibly readying themselves for the ordeal.

The eager journalists inside and in front of the courthouse had their bubbles burst right off the bat. As soon as Judge Marks took the bench and called court to order, she made an announcement.

Despite requests from CBS and the Rochester *Democrat and Chronicle* newspaper, no cameras would be allowed in the courtroom. Although the prosecution had said that it had no objection to cameras being present, the defense did have an objection, and both sides had to agree in order for cameras to be allowed. The objection, she said, had originated with members of the defendant's family. Those familiar with the dynamics of the Bryant family read this as Vivian, Kevin's father, had said no.

As the day's proceedings began, the halls outside Judge Marks's courtroom were filled with the very camera crews that had not been allowed inside. It wasn't just CBS—newspaper photographers and videographers were there, along with camera people from the various local television stations.

The prosecution had said that it would start with what happened on the night of the murder, but that's not what they did. They began by establishing motive. Although it is not mandatory for the prosecution to prove why a crime was committed—only that it was committed and by whom—experienced prosecutors, like Joanne Winslow, know that it is a lot easier for a jury to bring back a guilty verdict in a murder case when they have been provided a believable motive.

In their opening statement the prosecution had said that the murder was a result of a love triangle. So, the first order of business was establishing the third corner of that triangle.

"The prosecution may call its first witness," Judge Marks said.

"The prosecution calls Richard Oliver," said ADA Kristin Splain. Tabatha's boyfriend, Richard Oliver, the factory worker with the shaved head, took the stand.

His testimony, the prosecution had told the jury during its opening statement, would be important in understanding how this crime came to be. The evidence would show, Winslow had said, that Tabatha and Kevin's marriage had fallen apart through a series of infidelities, both sanctioned and nonsanctioned.

Kevin had stated that he and Tabatha had gone together to a strip club. The implication was that they went there to have fun, to spice up their sex life, which had become boring. Although it wasn't stated out loud by the principals, the best theory was that the generational age difference between the husband and wife, along with the husband's poor health, were contributing factors to the marital boredom.

Then again, if the age difference had been such a contributing factor to Kevin and Tabby's marital woes, then why, when she took a boyfriend, did she choose a man who was even older, although healthier, than Kevin?

Perhaps it was the very fact that these men were older that appealed to Tabby. Her grandparents, after all, had raised her. She only had seen her father a handful of times when growing up, and certainly this had left a void in Tabby's life.

Kevin had said that Tabatha had engaged in "amateur lap dances" at the strip bar, that they had had a sexual threesome—Kevin, his wife, and a prostitute all in bed together.

Then Tabatha had met a man at the strip bar whom she liked. She had asked to have another sexual threesome, this time with Kevin and the man she had met. Kevin did not care for the idea.

He hired a private detective to find out what was going on with Tabatha and the boyfriend. The infidelity, as far as he was concerned, had shifted from sanctioned—acts that he approved of—to nonsanctioned—acts that he did not condone. He considered divorce.

For those outside of law enforcement who were trying to understand how Tabatha ended up dead,

Kevin's statements about the deterioration of their marriage did not stand up well on their own.

You cannot judge a victim solely on what her murderer has to say about her. Oliver's statements would be key because he could corroborate some of that.

What did Kevin mean by "amateur lap dancer?" Did Kevin take Tabby to a strip joint to watch her sit on other men's laps? Was that what she wanted, to get even because she knew he frequented prostitutes? Did she remove her top when she writhed over strangers? Lap dances, after all, usually begin with a striptease and the woman ends up wearing nothing but a G-string and pasties, or sometimes nothing at all—depending on the law of the land, the amount of light in the room, the size of the tip, and who might be watching.

Did she do this to please Kevin? To please herself? To please the stranger? And how did the women who worked there feel about all of this? Weren't they losing out on tips because this housewife was coming in with her husband and playing stripper with the customers?

Questioning Tabatha's boyfriend would be ADA Kristin Splain. Calling him a "boyfriend" stretched the meaning of the term, as this was hardly a boy. He was a middle-aged man.

Jurors noticed immediately that Tabatha had not been cheating on Kevin with a younger man, as one might expect when a wife was twenty years younger than her husband. In fact, they learned that Tabatha's boyfriend had been a couple of years older than Kevin. Answering Splain's questions, he stated that his name was Richard Oliver and he was forty-nine years old.

It is unknown if any of those jurors were interested in psychology, or if any made the connection between Tabatha's seeming penchant for older men and the fact that she was raised in a home without a father.

"What do you do for a living, Mr. Oliver?" Splain asked.

"I am a machine operator and setup man at Schlegel," Oliver replied.

"How long have you worked there?"

"Fourteen years."

Oliver said that he worked the night shift at the factory. His hours were 3:30 until 11:30 P.M. He worked five days a week, Monday through Friday.

"Did you ever use narcotics?" Splain asked.

"Yes, I was a cocaine addict," Oliver replied.

"Do you still use cocaine?"

"No, I have been drug-free for almost a year," he replied.

"You knew Tabatha Bryant?"

"Yes, she was my girlfriend."

"When did you meet her?"

"I met her early in January 2003."

Oliver testified that when their affair began, they met about once a week. But, after a time, they began meeting several times a week at his house for romantic trysts.

"Did you learn of her marital status?" Splain inquired.

"Yes, she was married at the time," Oliver replied.

"Did your knowledge of her marital status change the relationship?"

"It didn't change it; it just progressed slowly," Oliver explained. "She would come over on her days off, Tuesday and Thursday, she was a part-time teller at M and T Bank."

Things, he testified, became more serious on Valentine's Day of that year.

"I told her I was starting to fall in love with her," Oliver testified.

On Kevin's birthday—the day that Kevin had a birthday party at home featuring women in black leather corsets toting whips—Richard and Tabby went out to dinner.

The relationship, he said, cooled during June 2003, the month before the murder. He wanted her to leave her husband, but she remained with Kevin. He found this frustrating.

During the weeks leading up to her death, he did not see Tabatha as frequently, Oliver testified. They never stopped seeing each other completely, he testified.

Tabatha's presence in his life was not a secret kept from his own family, or from the Bryant children, Oliver said. He admitted to taking Tabatha to his nephew's graduation party and introducing her to his family there.

"Do you recall the date of your nephew's graduation?" Splain inquired.

"Yes, it took place on June 20, 2003," Oliver replied.

"There were members of your family at the graduation party?"

"Oh yes. There was a lot of my family there."

"How long were you and Tabby at the party, Mr. Oliver?"

"We were there from seven, seven-thirty, until about ten, ten-thirty."

"Was that the first time Tabby had met members of your family?"

"No, she had dinner with my father and I the night before the graduation."

"Could you describe your relationship with Tabatha during June and July of 2003?"

Oliver said that there were also occasions when they met at his place of work, or at hers. On those occasions they would go swimming, go for long walks in a park, or go out to lunch together.

"About how frequently were you seeing Tabby during that time?"

"I would spend four or five days a week with her."

"On the average, how long would those dates last?"

"Oh, about four hours during the day and a couple of hours in the evening."

"When did you become aware of the fact that Kevin and Tabatha Bryant had children?"

"I met the children, maybe at the end of February, maybe the beginning of March."

Splain asked how often he had met the children and he replied, "More than once."

He told the court that Tabatha's children had been with her, at least two times, when she brought him lunch at work. Once they all had dinner together.

"We did a lot of things together," he said.

Splain asked for an example.

"Once the kids visited my work during an open house where family members got to see what they did."

"How long did the boys stay at your work on that occasion?"

"They stayed about one or two hours."

"Had [you] been to the Bryant house?"

"Yes, I was."

"How many times were you there?"

"Maybe three times."

"Do you remember the occasion for those visits?" Splain inquired.

"Once when she was sick. Other times just for brief visits, you know, if I was in the area," Oliver replied.

"Did you ever meet Kevin Bryant?"

"No."

"But you knew of him?"

"Oh yes."

"Did you ever meet any other members of Tabatha's family?"

"None beyond her half brother Cyril and his girl-friend, Cassidy," Oliver answered.

"How often did you meet them?"

"We went out with them maybe three or four times. We went to breakfast together once, and once we went out to see a band."

"When did you and Tabatha Bryant first become sexually involved?" Splain asked.

"In the middle of February 2003."

"You say there came a time in July when you did not see Tabatha as frequently?"

"Yes."

"Did you still speak to her every day?"

"Yes. On the phone."

"About how often did you speak to her on the phone?"

"Four, five times a day."

Oliver testified that he and Tabatha last had sex on July 10, three days before she was killed. That was a Thursday. Oliver said that he saw her in the afternoon for a few hours and later in the evening for an hour or so.

According to Oliver, he last saw her on Saturday, July 12, 2003, about thirty-six hours before her death, when he visited the M &T Bank in Perinton, where Tabatha worked.

"Why did you visit her at that time?"

"I dropped off some cigarettes I had bought for her," Oliver answered.

He testified that, on Sunday, July 13, he spoke with Tabby in the late morning. "It was around eleven, eleven-thirty," Oliver recalled.

"Did you speak to her again that Sunday?"

"Yes. At about nine o'clock she called me. She was at home."

"Did you have another conversation after that?"

"Yes, at about eleven-fifteen, we had a brief conversation."

"About how long would you say that eleven-fifteen conversation lasted?"

"Maybe a minute or two."

"She was at home?"

"Yes."

"Did you hear any noise in the background during that conversation?"

"No, I did not."

The next morning, he said, he woke at 7:45 A.M. He saw on the news that someone had been killed on Pennicott Circle in Penfield. Concerned, he called Tabatha's cell phone.

"When she didn't answer, I got her voice mail and left a message. I asked for her to get in touch."

He said he continued watching the news and eventually they said that the murder had taken place at 2 Pennicott Circle.

When Oliver learned that the murder had taken place at his girlfriend's house, he immediately called 911 and was instructed to speak with sheriff's investigators, who came to his home the following day. Oliver voluntarily gave a detailed statement. Later, investigators visited him again and took DNA samples in the form of two oral swabs.

That concluded Kristin Splain's direct examination of Richard Oliver. John Speranza rose and began cross-examination.

"How many times have you gone over your testimony with the district attorney's office?" the defense attorney queried.

"Two times," Oliver replied.

"And how long did each of those rehearsals last?"

"One hour each time."

"And with whom did you speak during those practice sessions?"

"I don't remember their names. It was three women." Oliver said the women were not, to his knowledge, recording his statements, and he did not see anyone taking notes.

Speranza made Oliver repeat that he had been addicted to cocaine during his relationship to Tabatha. He made him repeat that he had carried on the relationship—despite his knowledge that she was a married mother of two.

"You indicated that you had met Cyril Winebrenner on one occasion?" Speranza asked.

"Yes, sir."

"Did Ms. Bryant express any fear of her brother?" Speranza asked.

"Objection, Your Honor," Splain interrupted.

"Sustained," said Judge Marks.

"How many times did you see Tabatha Bryant and Cyril Winebrenner together?"

"Three or four times." Oliver said that these were occasions when they went to "the club"—perhaps Nookie's.

"On Sunday, July thirteenth, you indicated you spoke to Tabatha Bryant at nine P.M. and Mr. Bryant was not home?"

"Yes, sir."

"You spoke to her again at eleven-fifteen P.M., and she didn't say if he was home or not?"

"That's right."

"Are you positive of the time of that call?"

"Yes, I know it was exactly eleven-fifteen because she called my cell, which shows the time."

CHAPTER 56

Getting the Children
Out of the House

Next on the stand was Edward W. Peets, the sheriff's deputy who was the first to respond to Kevin's 911 call and the first member of law enforcement to arrive at the scene of the crime. Peets stated his full name and that he was employed by the Monroe County Sheriff's Office. He apologized for his raggedy voice. "I'm fighting a cold," he said. He was questioned for the prosecution by Kristin Splain.

Peets said he was a road deputy and K-9 handler in what the office called "A Zone," an area encompassing Pittsford, Perinton, and Penfield. A fourteen-year veteran, Peets said that on the day of the murder, he was working First Platoon, a shift that usually ran from 10:00 P.M. to 6:00 A.M.

Shortly after midnight on July 14, 2003, he had reported to 2 Pennicott Circle in response to a call that someone had been shot. Peets was in Perinton, corner of Baird and Fairport, when he got the call. He arrived at the house in Penfield at about 12:07 A.M.

During the drive to the site, Peets learned through the dispatcher that the call had come from a husband who claimed his wife had been shot. He was not greeted by anyone when he arrived, and he told the dispatcher to call the complainant back on the phone.

When he arrived at the Bryant home, the garage door was up and the light in the garage was on. Peets had the dispatcher tell the complainant to step outside. Moments later, a man exited the house through the garage. Peets identified that man as the man in the courtroom wearing the blue suit, with maroon tie and glasses—the defendant, Kevin Bryant.

After setting up a quick cover position at the door that led from the garage to the inner house, Peets eventually entered the house through that door. He saw a woman, showing signs of injury, on a fold-out couch in the living room.

"She was lying on her back faceup," Peets testified. "She had obvious signs of trauma to her neck. There was a wound on her neck that was frothing and bloody. She appeared to be lifeless."

The basement was searched and found to be secure. Upstairs he found the Bryant boys in their room, both asleep. All possible entries to the house were checked for signs of forced entry, but none were found.

"Did you make any other observations in the other rooms or hallways of the first floor?" Splain asked.

"I observed and later photographed blood droplets on the linoleum floors in the kitchen and the hallway area leading from the house," Peets responded.

Splain then showed Peets a series of crime scene photos and asked him to establish that each was a fair and accurate representation of the scene it depicted. There were interiors and exteriors of the house, and photos of the victim. He then testified that medical personnel arrived at approximately 12:23 A.M. and that they stayed for only two minutes.

Deputy Peets was then told by a sergeant at the scene to remove the children from the second floor. "Deputy Hobbins and I went up to the second floor. We tried to determine how we were going to get the kids out of the house. We made a plan that we were going to go up, go get the children, and then walk them directly out of the front door. We went upstairs. I woke the child up who was sleeping on the top bunk bed. He was only dressed in a diaper. I took a blanket and covered him up, and covered his head, and carried him on my left side. When we walked down the stairs, each of us carrying one child, we were sure to take the blankets and put them over their heads, so as we walked out the front door they couldn't observe their mother in the family room." The deputies gave the children to their grandparents who were waiting outside the house.

That concluded Kristin Splain's direct examination. Matthew Lembke handled the cross-examination. He made the witness acknowledge that the defendant had no visible blood on him when he exited the house, and that no droplets of blood, such as those in the kitchen, were on the driveway outside the garage where Deputy Peets had observed Kevin walking.

Under cross-examination Deputy Peets said that the sliding glass doors that led from the kitchen to the deck at the back of the house were closed when he arrived. Those doors were covered by white vertical blinds. Peets saw no blood on the blinds.

In the living room he saw that blood had splattered during the attack onto the west wall. Lembke made Peets confirm that he had seen no blood in any locations other than those he had already noted. That concluded Lembke's cross. The witness was excused.

CHAPTER 57

The Private Eye

"Your Honor, the prosecution calls Louis Falvo to the stand."

Falvo approached the witness stand, took the oath, and sat.

Joanne Winslow, for the prosecution, asked the man to say and spell his name. He did, looking at the court reporter as he spelled his name, *F-A-L-V-O*. He made it clear that he was familiar with the process.

Falvo told Winslow that he was a New York State licensed investigator. She asked what type of investigations he did, and he said, "Private investigations, military and insurance investigations."

It was established that Falvo was an exemplary member of the community, and financially successful—a man of integrity, not the type that would be corrupted easily by money. Falvo had no criminal record. He had never filed for bankruptcy, nor had he ever had any financial problems.

"What was your first job as an investigator?" Winslow asked.

"I was in naval intelligence for fourteen years," Falvo replied.

Falvo had worked as a private investigator in Syracuse, New York, from 1972 through 1978. That year he moved his operation to Rochester and he had been an investigator there ever since.

Falvo established that he recognized and knew the defendant.

"When did you meet Kevin Bryant?" Winslow inquired.

"I met him in June 2003. At that time I entered into an agreement to be employed by him," Falvo said.

"What was the nature of the investigation the defendant wanted to hire you for?"

"He indicated to me his wife was having an affair and that he was concerned about the individual she was seeing. He hired me to conduct a background investigation on the individual," Falvo replied.

"And you did that, you checked into the background of the man his wife was seeing?"

"Yes, I did."

There would be no details forthcoming regarding the results of the background check on Richard Oliver. There was apparently nothing in Oliver's background that encouraged Kevin to pursue the matter further.

"When did you next meet with the defendant?"

"On June 13, I entered into an agreement with Kevin Bryant to begin surveillance of his wife and to document her actions for a child-custody matter," Falvo said.

"When did he want you to start?"

"He wanted me to begin that night."

"How did you go about the surveillance and the documentation?"

"I set up a surveillance at the bank when she left work. We commenced trailing her," Falvo answered.

"You were setting up your operation according to information provided by Kevin Bryant?"

"Yes, he told me where she lived and where she worked, and, as far as he knew, when she would be where."

"Tell me about Tabatha Bryant's movements on the first night that you tailed her?" Winslow inquired.

"I believe she went to the Outback restaurant. May I look at my notes from that night?"

Falvo's reports were marked as evidence, and then the witness was allowed to use them to refresh his recollection.

"'At four forty-five P.M. surveillance began at the M and T bank in Perinton," Falvo read aloud. "At five-fifteen P.M. she left and went to Mr. Oliver's residence. They left together and went to the Outback restaurant on Ridge Road. They left the restaurant and went back to Mr. Oliver's residence. After she left Mr. Oliver's residence, we discontinued surveillance.'"

Surveillance, Falvo said, was continued the following day around 9:30 A.M. He picked her up at home, followed her when she went in the early afternoon to Oliver's house.

"With her at his house on the afternoon of the second day, we began video documentation."

"Did the location of Richard Oliver's home affect your video documentation?" Winslow asked.

"Yes, it did. Oliver's home is in a rural area, so the surveillance had to be done from quite far away."

"Tabatha Bryant left Richard Oliver's house and returned to her own home that afternoon?"

"Yes, later that day, in the evening hours, I believe I went back to set up surveillance at the residence (Bryant's house). But Tabatha Bryant didn't leave that evening."

"When did you next tail Mrs. Bryant?"

"On Thursday, June nineteenth. We began surveillance

at her residence, but she was not present. She had apparently left the residence before we got there. We next located her vehicle just as she was arriving at Mr. Oliver's residence. She entered the house, spent several hours in there, and emerged late in the afternoon with Richard Oliver."

"What did they do?"

"They got in his car and she went with him. They went to the Chili Family Restaurant, on Buffalo Road," Falvo provided.

"They parked in the parking lot?"

"Yes. And outside the restaurant they met an elderly gentleman in his seventies. Tabatha and Richard went into the restaurant with the elderly man. After about an hour, all three—Tabatha, Richard, and the elderly man—exited the restaurant together. Mrs. Bryant and Mr. Oliver returned to his residence in his car. The elderly man went someplace else," Falvo said.

That evening, after Tabby had returned home, Falvo camped outside 2 Pennicott Circle to see if she would go back out, late. As it turned out, Tabby was in for the night.

On Friday, June 20, 2003, Falvo tailed Tabby to and from work at the bank. They watched her as she was out with her son K.C. in the early evening. That evening, without children, she went out again. Tabby met Richard Oliver at Topp's Plaza. They went to his residence, out near Hilton. After a time in the house, they left together. In her car they drove to a party on nearby Johnson Road.

"There appeared to be some party going on there. There were young people and cars parked along the street."

Keen-minded jurors, perhaps, made the connection that the elderly man had been Richard's father and this party was the graduation party for his nephew that Oliver had discussed taking Tabby to, in his earlier testimony.

Oliver had testified that it was at this party that he had introduced Tabby to members of his family.

After the party Tabby drove Richard back to Topp's Plaza, and there they parted ways.

Falvo testified that Mrs. Bryant was again tailed on Tuesday, June 24, 2003. On that date Falvo was able to videotape Richard visiting the Bryant home in Penfield, and later she and Richard going together to his house on the other side of the county.

Falvo said, "On Thursday, June twenty-sixth, in the morning hours, went to Mr. Oliver's residence. Mrs. Bryant was there. I don't recall what time she arrived. Later, when we left together, we had to discontinue the tail."

"Why was that?"

"They were driving so slow. There was no way to follow them without being obvious," Falvo said.

"So you let them go?"

"Right. Later, we went back to Oliver's house and Mrs. Bryant's car was in the driveway," Falvo said. "We stayed for a while; then we discontinued surveillance."

"When was the next surveillance?"

"On Tuesday, July first. In the morning."

"At that time, did you go to Mr. Oliver's residence and see Tabatha Bryant's vehicle?" Winslow asked.

"Yes, ma'am," Falvo replied.

The final day of surveillance, Falvo testified, had been July 2. On that date Mrs. Bryant was tailed, going from her residence to the Ridge-Mount Mall. Surveillance was again called off after the couple left the mall. Later, when the private investigator attempted to reestablish contact at Mr. Oliver's residence, he saw Oliver returning home alone.

"That was the last time we conducted surveillance," Falvo concluded.

Then they reviewed. Winslow took Falvo through it, step by step. On June 13, Falvo signed a contract for service, and he was in Kevin Bryant's employ until July 2. Falvo had been giving Kevin Bryant updates all along, usually just over the phone.

After the final day of surveillance, Falvo met with Kevin in person. He presented all of the evidence he had gathered, and they settled the bill.

"During your surveillance, did you see physical affection between Mr. Oliver and Tabatha Bryant?" Winslow asked.

"Yes, ma'am."

"Could you describe that physical affection, please?"

"Yes, I believe we secured a videotape of Oliver leaning into Mrs. Bryant's vehicle and another of the two of them holding hands."

Defense attorney John Speranza had nothing to accomplish with cross-examination. Falvo didn't hurt Kevin. Evidence of Tabby's infidelity did not harm his client. The victim had been stepping out. There was no telling what trouble she might have encountered out there in the wicked, wicked world. Mrs. Bryant, after all, was not known to hang out in the nicest places.

Speranza went through the motions of a cross-examination, even though his goals were nonexistent. He asked two or three questions, asking Falvo to basically reiterate something he had testified to under direct.

"Did you agree to work for my client as part of a marital dispute?"

"Yes, sir."

"Did my client tell you that the work was part of a custody battle?"

"Yes, he did."

Then Speranza, seeming bored, said he had no further questions and the witness was excused.

CHAPTER 58

Crime Scene Investigators

"Prosecution calls Marcia Bledsoe," said Kristin Splain.

Bledsoe took the stand and testified that she was a forensic biologist who had been employed by the Monroe County Public Safety Laboratory for more than nine years. She got her B.S. at Syracuse and her M.S. at Buffalo. She was a member of the American Academy of Forensic Sciences. She previously had testified forty times in court as a forensic expert.

Kristin Splain asked Bledsoe to describe her job and Marcia Bledsoe said, "I analyze various items that are brought into the laboratory. I check items to see if semen is present, if blood is present, or if saliva may be present. Depending on what I am trying to find, I will do presumptive tests to determine if a particular substance may be present. I also do confirmatory tests."

On July 31, 2003, Bledsoe testified, she'd performed tests related to the murder of Tabatha Bryant. She tested some blood that had been given to her from its storage space in the vault refrigerator. When she received it, the blood was inside a purple-topped tube, inside a sealed blue plastic bag.

Using the blood, she had created what she called a "bloodstain card."

"Could you tell the jury, please, what a bloodstain card is?" Kristin Splain inquired.

"It is a filter paper," Bledsoe replied. "The filter paper had four circled areas on it. A portion of blood was taken from the tube and placed into each of the four circled areas. The bloodstain card was then allowed to dry, and then it was packaged and put into the vault freezer."

The blood, it was later determined, had belonged to the victim.

Bledsoe testified that she also tested six cotton swabs that had been taken from Tabatha's body cavities. Two were oral, two vaginal, and two rectal. She gave one swab from each category a presumptive test, an acid phosphatase test, (a substance found in most seminal fluid).

"The vaginal swab and the rectal swab gave a positive phosphatase result, indicating that seminal fluid may have been present," Bledsoe testified. "I then decided to do further testing to find this out. I took a small amount of the vaginal swab and a small amount of the rectal swab."

She extracted the substance from the swabs by soaking them in water and then made slides. She then observed those slides under a microscope and determined that, though there were spermatozoa present on the vaginal slide, there were none on the rectum slide.

"How could the rectal slide test positive for sperm in the presumptive test, but negative in the confirmatory test?"

"Because there must have been a source other than seminal fluid for the phosphatase in her rectum," Bledsoe explained.

"On that same day, did you have occasion to test a cardboard box labeled 'bullet'?"

"On July 28, 2003, I tested Laboratory Item number seventeen, which was a box labeled 'bullet.'"

"What type of test did you do on that?"

"After observing the bullet, which had red/brown stains on it, I performed a presumptive test for blood. The first test was positive. On the confirmatory test, I got a negative result, showing that no blood was present."

"Was that a full bullet or a fragment?"

"A metal fragment."

"Do you also, on that approximate date, test a firearm?"

"Yes. A Marlin-Glenfield rifle."

After establishing the chain of evidence, Splain asked, "What did you do with the rifle?"

"I observed that the firearm had stains and some dust-like material. I put the rifle under a high-intensity lamp to see if I could see any bloodlike stains. After that, I chose ten areas in which to do further testing for blood. I got two positive presumptive results." She then returned the rifle to firearm examiner Bob Stanton.

On September 3, 2003, Bledsoe testified, she had tested a drop of blood that had been taken from the linoleum floor of the Bryant kitchen. It came in a box labeled "J—three to four feet from the dishwasher." Both a presumptive and confirmatory test indicated that the droplet from the linoleum floor was blood. A second droplet, this one labeled "kitchen near outside bedroom" also tested positively. It, too, was blood.

On August 25, 2003, Bledsoe performed tests on the front passenger-side car seat from the getaway car. The seat, Bledsoe testified, "was in a tape-sealed box that was labeled 'Item one.'" In the bag was a light blue car seat. She collected the trace material from the car seat. She observed the car seat under high-intensity light and found five stains that she felt deserved further investigation, four on the front and one on the back of the seat. The four stains found on the front of the seat tested negative for blood, but the one from the back of the seat tested positive.

She testified that she also had examined and tested the T-shirt with a dragon on it that had been found hanging from a tree on the grounds of Cassidy's uncle. She found no blood on the shirt. Splain asked her, if a shirt had blood on it, but then was washed, would she be able to determine if the blood had been there? Bledsoe said that it was a possibility, but a thorough washing could remove all traces of blood.

She also had tested Cyril's coat for blood. She'd found two stains, one on the right sleeve and another on the inner lining. Those spots tested positive. That concluded the direct examination. Matthew Lembke performed the cross.

Lembke forced Bledsoe to admit that she had tested the floorboard to the car and had found no blood—and the same result had occurred when she tested the car's door panel. No testing, Lembke established, had been performed on the Geo Prism that Cassidy and Cyril had driven in after her car had broken down.

Joanne Winslow said, "We call B.J. Holland."

Bernard Joseph "B.J." Holland III told the court that he had been an assistant pathologist at the Monroe County Medical Examiner's Office since September 2000. He worked as assistant to the pathologist. During autopsies his job was to make the incisions, remove or eviscerate the organs, assist with the collection of evidence during the autopsy, and establish a chain of custody for items that were received or taken during the autopsy.

Holland testified that he had worked in that capacity during the autopsy of Tabatha Bryant. He had taken

fluids and other items from Dr. Caroline Dignan, who
had performed the autopsy. Blood had been removed
from the chest cavity, for example. Blood samples were
placed in glass vials and sealed. When the autopsy was
finished, those items were transported to the toxicol-
ogy lab down the hall. A representative from the toxi-
cology lab had come over to the autopsy room for the
items and Holland had handed them over.

Other items Holland had handled included the
swabs from the sexual assault kit that Dr. Dignan had
taken from the victim's bodily cavities. Holland described how those swabs were taken. It was done with
a tool that looked like a Q-tip, which was inserted into
the body cavity, and then was handed immediately
over to Holland so that it could be sealed and labeled.
Holland testified that he himself, at a later date, July
17 to be exact, had delivered the items from the autopsy
to the Monroe County Public Safety Laboratory, where
they received further testing.

That concluded Winslow's examination. The defense had no questions and the witness was excused.

Karen Mahoney, a toxicologist with the medical examiner's office, testified next. She had an associate
degree in applied sciences (biological technologies)
from Monroe Community College. Her duties, she
testified, were to determine if there were any toxic
chemical substances, or street drugs, in samples taken
at autopsy, and to determine if those substances may
have contributed to the person's death.

She had received samples from the autopsy of
Tabatha Bryant at 4:10 P.M. on Monday, July 14, 2003,
only sixteen-plus hours after Tabatha's murder. She had
gone to the autopsy room to receive the items. Assistant pathologist B.J. Holland had given them to her.

She said she had performed an acid phosphatase test

on three swabs, taken from mouth, vagina, and rectum. The vaginal swab tested positive. The other two did not. She also had tested some blood samples. The samples were then taken to the Public Safety Laboratory "for typing and DNA" purposes.

Deputy Michael Burnside took the witness stand and testified that he'd been on the force for about ten years and described his duties as responding to crime scenes, motor vehicle accidents, and other police matters.

"I take photographs and collect evidence related to those incidents," Deputy Burnside said.

He was assigned to road patrol on July 14, 2003. He'd been off-duty, however, when his lieutenant called him in the middle of the night and told him to report to Pennicott Circle for a possible homicide. He stopped at headquarters to pick up cameras and other equipment and then reported to the crime scene, arriving at about 2:30 A.M.

He said the house was in "general disarray," and that the first things he noticed were the victim in the living room and the drops of blood on the floor in the kitchen. Burnside then walked around the house taking photographs of various locations from different angles. Burnside positively identified the photos he had taken that night as Kristin Splain introduced them into evidence.

Burnside testified that he used swabs to take samples of the blood droplets on the floor. These were sealed and labeled by the location where the blood droplet had been found. By the time he finished collecting these samples, he estimated, it was about 4:30 A.M.

When his job at the crime scene was done, he delivered the items he had gathered to the Technical Services Unit Laboratory, a facility that can be accessed only by technicians with the Monroe County Sheriff's Office.

Burnside said that he was still at the scene when the medical examiner's office arrived to take photos and to remove the body. With the body gone, it was Burnside's job to collect the pillow, sheet, blanket, and comforter that had been on the fold-out couch.

After delivering the gathered materials to their appropriate destinations, Burnside testified, he returned to the crime scene and gave the pullout couch another, more careful examination. At that time he found a hole in the upper-right-hand corner that appeared to have been put there by some sort of projectile. When he looked underneath that mattress, there appeared to be an exit area.

He moved the pullout couch and saw a hole in the red wall-to-wall carpet. Between a piece of carpet on the floor and the padding that ran between the carpet and the floor, Burnside found what appeared to be a projectile from a firearm. After some further searching, Burnside found a .22-caliber rimfire shell casing on the floor of the living room. The bullet and the casing were sealed and marked. By the time the casing was found, it was almost noon on July 14.

After he finished gathering evidence on the main floor, Burnside testified, he went upstairs to search the second floor. He thought he remembered three bedrooms up there. He searched but found nothing pertinent.

Kristin Splain then turned Deputy Burnside over to Matthew Lembke for cross-examination. Lembke got Burnside to admit that even though he flipped over the pullout couch's mattress to take a picture of the bullet's exit hole on the bottom, he did not recall where the entrance hole at the top of the mattress was. Burnside admitted that he had heard another bullet fragment was found in the bedding he had removed from the pullout couch, but that he had no firsthand knowledge of that fragment. The jury learned that near the pullout couch was a chair. On the chair were a pair of blue jeans, with a belt still attached, and a bloodstained piece of paper.

On redirect Splain had the witness explain why he had not found the bullet fragment that was in the bedding. He said that he had not shaken out the bedding because he did not want to lose any trace evidence that the bedding might contain.

Deputy Daniel Loffman testified that he was a technician for the sheriff's office, and had been on the force for about seven years. He described his duties as developing fingerprints, taking photographs, and helping other deputies gather evidence.

He stated that on March 29, 2004, nearly nine months after the murder, he had taken a DNA sample from Tabatha's boyfriend, Richard Oliver, in the form of an oral swab.

It was also Loffman who had picked up, on August 19, 2004, the bullet fragment that had shaken out of Tabatha's bedding. After picking it up from the district attorney's office, he repackaged it and sealed it inside a bag so that it could not be tampered with. He then submitted the fragment to the Public Safety Lab.

As she would for every day of the trial, Amy Cavalier, reporter for the *Penfield Post*, was seated in the courtroom.

"It was a very interesting experience for me, and having been the first murder I have ever had to cover, you can imagine it was a very big learning experience," she would say later.

"I personally do not know what life was like for Tabatha and Kevin Bryant or Cyril Winebrenner and Cassidy Green. There was much speculation surrounding this murder in the suburban town of Penfield. It is not my job to speculate," Cavalier would say as well. "That's not to say this murder did not touch me personally. I covered this story since the day it happened. I had been covering Penfield as my full-time beat for three months when Tabatha Bryant was killed. She was twenty-six, the same age as I was. Yet, here was this woman so different than me, married to an attorney with a beautiful home and two children."

She didn't have to travel very far to attend the trial. Cavalier lived right there in Downtown Rochester with her dog, Lucy.

CHAPTER 59

"I Picked His Name
Out of the Yellow Pages."

On Tuesday, October 5, 2004, Cassidy A. Green testified. Cassidy looked small on the witness stand. Cyril had described her as standing four foot ten and weighing seventy-six pounds. He had not been exaggerating how short she was, although she had put on weight since she had been in jail.

Her shoulder-length, dirty-blond hair had been tied into a ponytail. Spectators could see where a yellowy blond dye was growing out of her hair.

She seemed timid, almost scared, and fiddled nervously with her fingers as she spoke. At times her hands appeared to be shaking. Amy Cavalier described her as behaving like "a beaten dog, almost unsure, yet at the same time, cocky."

She was at her best when being examined by Joanne Winslow, whom she had gotten to know over the months since the murder. She was cooperative and projected vulnerability. She spoke softly—so softly that she was at times difficult to hear—but her answers always were straightforward. She testified for the remainder of the morning session and her testimony resumed after the break, at approximately 2:00 P.M. At that point her lawyer, Felix Lapine, who was in the courtroom throughout her testimony, waved to her and she smiled back at him.

She began her testimony by stating her name and age, and by identifying Kevin Bryant.

"How did you first meet the defendant?" Winslow asked.

Cassidy explained that she had wanted to set up an escort service and was seeking legal assistance.

"I needed DBA papers drawn up and some tax advice," Cassidy explained.

Cassidy testified that the escort service was to be called Sunset Sensations.

"What services did Sunset Sensations provide?" Winslow asked.

"It was an escort service, hot-oil rubs, lingerie modeling, and dances," Cassidy said.

"How did you get Kevin Bryant's name?"

"I picked his name out of the yellow pages."

"You picked his name at random?"

"That's right."

She told the court that it was in Bryant's law office that she met Cyril Winebrenner, Tabatha's half brother. Cyril, down on his luck, was working in Kevin's office and living in the Bryants' home.

"Did you develop a relationship with Cyril Winebrenner?"

"Yes, ma'am."

"What was that relationship?"

"We became boyfriend/girlfriend."

Cassidy explained that she had eventually moved in with Cyril Winebrenner.

"When did you move in with him?"

"I don't remember the exact date. Sometime around the end of January," Cassidy said.

"In 2003?"

"Yes, ma'am."

"Where was Cyril living when you moved in with him?" Winslow asked.

"He was living with the Bryants and their two children at the time," Cassidy replied.

"Do you remember the address there?"

"Two Pennicott Circle."

Cassidy testified that at the time she moved in with Winebrenner and the Bryant family, she was employed as an "escort," which is generally a euphemism for prostitute. She worked at an establishment called Whispers.

"Did you have any other source of income?" Winslow asked.

"I sold cocaine," Cassidy replied.

She explained that when she first moved into the house on Pennicott Circle, she was trying still to start up her own business, Sunset Sensations, and that Cyril was working still in Kevin's legal office.

"After I had been living there for a short time, Kevin gave me a job in his office, too," Cassidy said.

"Do you remember when you started working for the defendant?" Winslow asked.

"Not exactly. Maybe the beginning of February."

"What sort of work did you do for the defendant?"

"I did some filing, and I tried to learn some real-estate stuff."

"Did you work there full-time?"

"Part-time. I came in when I was needed."

"Did Cyril work there part-time as well?"

"No, ma'am. Cyril worked for Kevin full-time."

Cassidy said that in the spring of 2003, Cyril left the Pennicott Circle home to join the army.

"Did you move out as well when Cyril joined the army?" Winslow asked.

"No, ma'am. I stayed on with the Bryants," Cassidy said.

"About how long was Cyril gone?"

"About thirty days," Cassidy said.

"How would you describe the relationship between Kevin and Tabatha Bryant during the time you lived in the same house with them?" Winslow asked.

"They weren't screaming, but they were very argumentative with each other," Cassidy replied.

"Was Cyril different in any way after he returned from the army?" Winslow asked.

"Yes, he was."

"How so?"

"He became increasingly violent toward me. He threatened to kill me, and himself," Cassidy answered.

"And was the relationship between Cyril Winebrenner and Tabatha Bryant different as well, after he returned from the army?"

"Yes, it was."

"In what way?"

"That relationship deteriorated also."

"Did Cyril hate his sister?" Winslow asked.

"They got angry with each other," Cassidy said. "They had sibling rivalry, but he didn't hate her."

"Do you recall a pair of hotel parties that you attended during the last two weekends of March?"

"Yes, ma'am."

"Did Kevin Bryant go with you to those parties?"

"Yes, ma'am."

"Were those parties run by the escort service you worked for?"

"No, ma'am."

With that, the subject of the hotel parties was dropped.

"Was there a change in Kevin and Tabatha's relationship between March and May of 2003?"

"Yes, there was. They began to argue more frequently."

"Would it be fair to say that they were now arguing every day?"

Cassidy said it would. She then testified that she and Cyril moved out of the Bryant home at the end of May 2003. They moved into a trailer with friends in eastern Bloomfield. By mid-2003, the Bryants' marriage had tumbled farther downhill.

"Do you recall hearing a conversation in which the defendant spoke about what he wanted done to Tabatha Bryant?"

Cassidy replied that before she and Cyril moved out of the Bryants' house, there was an occasion when she, Cyril, and Kevin were driving home from Kevin's office.

"I heard Kevin say that he couldn't get ahold of Tabatha on her cell phone and that something had to be done."

"What did he say had to be done?"

"He didn't elaborate on it that day."

Cassidy testified that sometime after overhearing that comment, she learned that Tabatha had a boyfriend, whom she had met at an "establishment," and that this fact infuriated Kevin.

"Do you recall a conversation at the law office prior to you moving out of the house relating to what the defendant wanted done with Tabatha?"

"Yes, I do. Kevin wanted to know if five thousand dollars would be enough to get rid of a body."

"Any body in particular?"

"He indicated that it was Tabatha's body."

"What did you say when he asked you that?"

"I told him that I wasn't Cyril and I didn't know, because he wanted Cyril to do it."

Cassidy testified that Kevin asked Cyril and her whether they could help "get rid of" his wife.

"What did you do after that?"

"I went to Cyril and asked him the question. Then I went back to Kevin and told him that Cyril said it would be enough, but he'd have to look into it to see how it could be done."

"By the Fourth of July of 2003, you and Cyril were no longer living with the Bryants, is that correct?"

Cassidy said that it was and told the court that she and Cyril had moved into a trailer on Route 5 and 20 in West Bloomfield. The trailer belonged to a guy named Jeff Null, who was to be Cassidy's partner in Sunset Sensations. Also living in the trailer were Vinny and Emily, plus a dog.

"During the time you were living in Jeff Null's trailer, did you ever speak to Tabatha?"

"I spoke with her on the phone on a number of occasions," Cassidy replied. "We met somewhere to eat. On the Fourth of July, me and Cyril had dinner at the Bryants', with Kevin and Tabatha and the two boys."

"Who prepared dinner on that occasion?"

"I was supposed to, but I burned the spaghetti."

Kevin's parents and Cassidy's parents were also at the party, Cassidy noted.

"My mom saved me," Cassidy said. "She went out and bought some more spaghetti so she could remake the dinner."

"At that Fourth of July party, what was your personal observation of the relationship between Kevin and Tabatha?"

"He was very angry with her."

"Then, after dinner, were you upstairs with Tabatha and her two boys?"

"Yes. Tabby was getting dressed. She was going out. The boys were getting ready for bed. We came downstairs, to where Kevin and Cyril were. I was in front and Tabby was behind me," Cassidy called.

"Did you overhear any of Kevin and Cyril's conversation at that time?"

"All I heard was Kevin saying, 'It's got to be done. It's got to be done now,'" Cassidy said.

"Was there another get-together the following day, July 5, 2003?" Winslow asked.

"Yes, there was a cookout at Mendon Ponds." She said that the Bryants and Cassidy's parents were also there. Cyril, however, had stayed at the trailer in West Bloomfield.

"What, from your own personal observation, was the relationship like between Kevin and Tabatha at the Mendon Ponds cookout?"

"Very angry. Tabby was angry with Kevin because he'd forgot to pack the diapers." Cassidy testified that the Bryants had argued at the cookout. She said that she, Cyril, and Kevin had left the cookout together, leaving Tabatha with the children. Together they had driven to Cassidy's West Bloomfield home.

"I asked to borrow fifty dollars from Kevin and then went in the house and told Cyril that Kevin was outside and needed to talk to him. They walked around and talked outside the trailer for five minutes; then Cyril came back in the trailer," Cassidy testified.

"Do you recall being present when the defendant made a statement to the kids about whether Tabatha would be around anymore?"

"Yes, Kevin said they wouldn't have to worry about Mommy because it was a boys' world. He said Mommy wouldn't be around much longer."

"When did this statement occur?"

"It was in the car, sometime before Cyril and I moved out of the Bryants' house."

"On July thirteenth, a Sunday," Winslow said, referring

to the night of the murder, "did there come a time in the evening when you tried to contact the defendant?"

"I phoned him. I talked to him," Cassidy said.

"What time was that call?"

"About nine-thirty."

"What was the purpose of the call?"

"It was to relay a message. I called to tell him that Cyril wanted to get everything done," Cassidy said. "Kevin told me that he would be home and Tabby would be home and he said where the kids were. He said Tabby was on the couch and the boys were in bed and would be there the rest of the night. He said to call when we were on our way out."

"Did you call back?"

"Yes. We called just before we left the house."

Cassidy told the court how Cyril put rubber gloves in his pocket, and how he polished rifle bullets.

"He took the bullets out of the gun, polished them with his shirt, and then put them back in the gun," she said.

"Do you know where he got the rifle?" Winslow asked.

"I am under the impression that it was my rifle," Cassidy replied.

She testified that it was a rifle that she had gotten as a present from her father, and that she recognized it because her initials had been burned into the stock. It was the rifle she kept in the trunk of her car.

The jury and spectators in the courtroom received some insight into Cassidy's character when she cried only once while on the witness stand. Her tears did not come as she recalled the plotting and execution of Tabatha's murder—but rather when she was asked to identify a photo of her car, the pink mid-1980s Chevrolet Monte Carlo that served as the getaway car. The photo needed to be ID'd so that it could be submitted as evidence.

Asked to describe her car further, a still-emotional Cassidy said, "It was loud. . . . It had no exhaust. . . . The tailpipes were missing. . . . It had straight pipes and no Cadillac [catalytic] converter."

They drove directly to the Bryant house in her car. She drove. Cyril rode in the passenger seat in the front and the rifle was placed across the backseat.

"What happened when you arrived at the Bryants' house?" Winslow asked.

"Everything was locked. The overhead door was down. The sliding glass doors were locked. When we first got there, we both got out of the car. I went to the side garage door. The door was open. I went into the garage. I checked the other door going into the house, but it was locked. Then I looked for money that was supposed to be on top of the filing box. That's where Kevin had told me it would be on the phone. Cyril checked the door, too, and he said we were going to the Noco Station, on Browncroft and Creek."

"How far away was the Noco Station?"

"One or two minutes."

"Who drove?"

"I did," Cassidy said.

"What did you do when you got to the gas station?"

"I used their pay phone to call Kevin. I told him that everything was locked. He said come back and everything would be taken care of. He would open the doors. And he said to send Cyril up to talk to him when he was done," Green testified.

Phone records backed Cassidy Green's claim that she had called Kevin from the service station, when she said she had.

They then returned to the house and this time the doors were indeed open.

"Everything was open," Cassidy said. "The overhead door was open; the gate was open; the side door was open. Cyril took the keys out of the ignition of the car and put them in his pocket."

Cyril was not going to take the risk that Cassidy might get nervous and drive away while he was inside the house.

"Then he got the gun out of the backseat," Cassidy said. "I sat there in the car while he was in the house."

While Winebrenner was inside the house, Green testified, she heard a sound.

"It sounded like a small champagne cork, or a wine bottle, or whatever," she said.

Moments after she heard the sound, she testified, Winebrenner returned to the car.

"He was covered with blood. He put the gun in the backseat. He wrapped up his jacket and put it in the garbage bag I had in the car. I usually used the bag for litter."

Cyril, she explained, gave her back the car keys and she promptly started the car.

"What did Cyril say about what had occurred inside the house?" Winslow asked.

"He said he had just killed Tabby. He told me that he had shot her three times and that he had to cut her to make her stop breathing," she said.

With Cyril back in the car, following the murder, the first order of business was to get away from the crime scene, Cassidy testified. Cassidy hightailed it out of there. The escape got off to a shaky start, she testified.

"I got on the expressway going the wrong way," she said, referring to Interstate 590, smiling at the memory. When she got on the expressway, she mistakenly got on the northbound side rather than the southbound side, and didn't realize her error until she saw that an upcoming exit was in the town of Irondequoit, a northernmost suburb of Rochester that butted against Lake Ontario.

Eventually, she said, she got the car turned around and they headed toward home.

"Was the car running well?" Winslow asked.

"No."

"What was wrong with it?"

"She was kind of cranky," Cassidy said, using a feminine pronoun to refer to the automobile. "She liked to blow alternator belts. She's sort of sluggish when you try to get her up to normal speed. It was highway driving, so we drove around forty or forty-five miles per hour because of the car."

Cassidy explained that they stopped at three gas stations. At the first gas station, Cyril asked Cassidy to go inside and buy a pack of cigarettes. She told him she couldn't do it because she didn't have her identification. Because of her size, people always were asking her for ID before selling her cigarettes.

Cyril couldn't go in to get the cigarettes because he hadn't changed his clothes, so they left and he changed in the car.

"Cyril had a change of clothes in the car?" Winslow asked.

"I had brought along a change of clothes for both of us," Cassidy replied.

"What did Cyril do with the clothes he took off?"

"He put them in the garbage bag."

They pulled into a second gas station. No longer afraid of being seen in public, Cyril bought a twenty-four-ounce bottle of Corona, a popular Mexican beer, and cigarettes.

At the third gas station, they tried to call Kevin. They tried several of the numbers they had for him: his house, his office, his cell. But they could not reach him.

At this point the courtroom broke for lunch. During the afternoon session, Joanne Winslow resumed her direct examination.

"Did Cyril have any money on him before the two of you got to the Bryants' house?" Winslow asked.

"No, nothing to speak of."

"Did you?"

"Ten or fifteen dollars."

"Did Cyril have any money on him after you left the Bryants' house?" Winslow asked.

"When we got to the Hess station, Cyril pulled out an envelope of money and counted out five thousand dollars right there."

"After you stopped at the three gas stations, what happened next?"

"We got on Route sixty-five and headed south."

"Did anything happen while you were heading south on Route sixty-five?"

"Cyril took out a large kitchen knife, wiped it off, and flung it out the window, somewhere near Mendon Ponds."

According to Cassidy's testimony, she took Route 65, also known as Clover Road, "all the way out" to Bloomfield.

"Did you do anything else as you returned to the trailer where you lived?" Winslow asked.

"Cyril said that we had to get rid of the clothes. We threw away Cyril's shirt along Stetson Road," Cassidy said. Either accidentally or on purpose, the dragon shirt was thrown onto land belonging to Cassidy's uncle. She said she never saw that shirt again.

The rest of the incriminating evidence, she said, wasn't disposed of until after they had returned to their trailer. Cyril changed his clothes and bagged the bloody items.

"You once again took the Monte Carlo to dispose of the rest of Cyril's bloody clothes?" Winslow asked.

"No, ma'am. We started having trouble with the Monte Carlo about a mile from the trailer," Cassidy said.

"What was the problem?"

"The high beams started to cut out completely and the car started to lose power," Cassidy replied.

"So what did you do?"

"We borrowed a car from our friend [Emily Gibbs]."

"Did you personally ask to borrow the car?"

"No, Cyril did. He asked Emily and [Vinny] if we could use their car," Cassidy said.

"What kind of car did Emily and Vinny have?"

"It was a Geo."

They put the bag holding the bloody jeans and down-filled leather jacket—and the .22 rifle used in the murder—in Emily's car and headed southward on country roads for the Township of Bloomfield.

"What did you do next?"

"We got rid of the down-filled leather jacket in a tunnel on Wesley Road," Cassidy said. A map showed that Wesley Road was an east-west road about two miles south of the trailer where Cassidy and Cyril lived.

"Did you ever see that jacket again, Cassidy?"

"Yes, ma'am."

"When was that?"

"When I returned to the tunnel on Wesley Road with sheriff's deputies," Cassidy said.

Then they drove to a road called Silvernail Road, which ran north/south parallel to Stetson Road, and discarded the last bloody item, Cyril's jeans.

"He got rid of his pants in the bushes," she said.

Cassidy testified that she never saw the jeans again.

After that, Cassidy testified, they went to fill Emily's car with gas at the Hemlock Sugarcreek. They went to a bar and got a drink, then went to Clay Street, where Cyril put the gun in his car, a Pontiac parked in front of another bar.

"What did Cyril do with the rifle after that?" Winslow asked.

"I don't know," Cassidy replied. "I didn't see him do nothing with the rifle."

After that, they went back to the trailer.

"Cyril grabbed his black army bag with his clothes in it and left two thousand dollars on the bed."

"You say the money Cyril had was in an envelope?"

"Yes."

"What type of envelope was it?"

"Looked to be a bank envelope."

She also said that on the night before Tabatha was killed, she had told Cyril that she wanted him to move out. He had struck her in the face several times, although it was unclear if she told him to get out and this made him hit her or he hit her because she told him to get out. Whichever, the murder was the swan song of their relationship, the grand finale. After Tabby was dead and the evidence had been disposed of, there was nothing left for Cyril to do but pack his stuff and split.

That concluded Winslow's direct examination.

CHAPTER 60

"Selling Cocaine Was Your Job?"

Cassidy Green was then cross-examined by defense attorney Speranza. Judging from the shaking in her hands and the way she played with her fingers, she was even more nervous during cross-examination than she had been during her direct examination.

Speranza made Cassidy admit that she had made a deal with prosecutors in which she faced lesser charges for her role in Tabatha's murder—and had drug-selling charges dropped altogether—in exchange for her damning testimony against his client.

His tone clearly communicated that he thought Cassidy Green to be no more than a pathetic gutter-snipe, who, out of desperation, had cut a deal to rail-road his client.

"You are testifying here today under an agreement with the district attorney's office, is that right?" Speranza asked.

Cassidy said that it was.

"Isn't it true that you have entered into three different agreements with the district attorney's office in exchange for your testimony?"

"Yes, sir."

"Isn't it true that in this case you have been charged with murder in the first degree?"

"Yes, sir."

"And you know the penalty for that crime is either a lethal injection or life in prison without parole?"

Her voice was extremely quiet as she said, "Yes."

"So, as you sit there, you are indicted for murder one?"

"Yes, sir."

"And you know the penalty?"

"Yes."

"And you've made an agreement with the DA's office to try to avoid being convicted for murder in the first degree."

"Yes."

"Isn't it true that, on November 17, 2003, you were indicted for various counts of drug sales?"

"Yes, sir."

"Weren't there, in fact, three charges? You sold to Rocky. He was a government informant and he set you up on three buys of cocaine?"

"Yes, sir."

"And isn't it true that, if convicted, you could face one to three years, with a maximum of eight to twenty-four years?" There was a pause as Cassidy failed to answer right away.

"You knew that?" Speranza said.

"Yes, sir."

"You are testifying in part to benefit yourself, aren't you?" Speranza asked the diminutive witness.

"I'm here to tell the truth," she replied.

"You're also here to benefit yourself," Speranza said.

"You could say that," Cassidy Green responded.

Speranza, in the form of cross-examination, reviewed in a deliberate fashion, item by item, Cassidy's criminal record—a record common to drug addicts. He wanted the jury to understand fully the type of woman who was testifying against his client.

"You've been convicted of petit larceny?"

"I have."

"That case involved you signing a withdrawal slip for a bank account belonging to someone else? You were tried in a court in Victor, New York?" Speranza asked. Cassidy said yes.

The defense attorney would state the different crimes that Cassidy had committed, and then ask her to agree or disagree with the truthfulness of what he was saying. Cassidy, of course, was forced to agree.

Still, Speranza did not stop, and he forced Cassidy to delve deeper into her drug history.

"In your direct testimony, you indicated you sold cocaine—that that was your job?"

"Yes, sir."

"You began selling cocaine before you moved to the trailer in Bloomfield?"

"I lived in Bloomfield my whole life."

"You sold cocaine prior to moving into the trailer?"

"Yes, sir."

"You sold *a lot* of cocaine?"

"Yes, sir."

"At the trailer, you were selling at least a couple ounces a week, about eight or nine ounces a month?"

"Yes, sir."

"You were making about two thousand to eight thousand a month selling cocaine, is that correct?"

"That is correct."

"You never paid income tax on any of the income you made from selling cocaine?"

"No."

"The DA's office hasn't charged you for those sales or for income tax fraud, has it?"

"No."

The defense attorney subsequently made the young woman admit that her testimony that day differed from statements she had made earlier. He showed Cassidy copies of her written statements. He asked her to verify that it was her signature on the documents, and she did.

"You were aware that if you lied in those statements and then signed your name to them, that you would be committing a crime?" Speranza asked.

Cassidy said she knew.

Cassidy had made two statements on July 30. They had been transcribed and she had signed them. Each statement indicated that it included everything she knew about the murder of Tabatha Bryant.

She'd made a statement on August 2, 2003, and then another one four days later. The latter was an oral statement she had made under an agreement with the district attorney's office.

Speranza had copies of each of Cassidy's statements handy as he questioned her. If he asked her about a specific statement she made on a specific date, and she said that she did not recall, he would pull out the appropriate document.

He would hand her the paper and ask her to read it, and then to confirm for the court whether or not she had said it. Each instance that he brought up helped to illustrate his main point: the more Cassidy had to gain from her statements, the more damaging her statements were to Kevin Bryant.

"In the statements you made for the district attorney's office in August 2003, you agreed to tell prosecutors everything you knew about the murder of Tabatha Bryant?"

"Yes."

"In this statement, you indicated to police that you

and Cyril Winebrenner were in the drug-selling business?"

"Yes, sir."

"You and Cyril Winebrenner were cocaine addicts?" Speranza asked.

"I was selling cocaine," Cassidy replied. "I don't know what Cyril was doing."

"The proceeds of the drug sales you made were both yours and Cyril's?"

Cassidy admitted that this was true. They had shared the profits.

"You worked for Kevin Bryant's law office temporarily, is that correct?"

Cassidy said it was true, but she only worked there twice after she moved out of the Bryant home.

"So, you basically made your living selling cocaine, isn't that correct?"

"Yes, sir."

"Did you indicate in that statement that Cyril and Tabatha had problems, that they argued a lot, that there was bad blood between them?"

"Yes, sir."

"Did you indicate that Cyril Winebrenner changed his cell phone number because he didn't want his sister calling him?"

"Yes."

"You said Cyril often talked about hurting Tabatha and that Cyril said he was going to, and I quote, 'fucking snap' and that he was gonna kill her, is that right?"

Cassidy was forced to admit that she had said that during one of her first statements to prosecutors.

"You said that Cyril and Tabatha got angry with each other, is that correct?"

"They had sibling rivalry, but he didn't hate her, he never threatened her to her face."

"He made comments to you about her?"

"He made comments to me about a lot of people."

"He threatened to hurt her?"

"He threatened to hurt several people."

"You knew Cyril Winebrenner had a nervous break-down? You knew he was in a mental institution in Iowa before coming to New York?"

"Yes, I knew he was violent," Cassidy replied.

"He hit you?"

"Yes."

"He choked you?"

"Yes."

"Hit you with a belt?"

"Yes."

"Pulled a blade on you?"

"Yes."

"Threatened to kill you?"

"Yes—me and him." By "him," she meant that Cyril had threatened to kill her and then himself.

"In July, you told [Peter Murray] (pseudonym), your boyfriend now, what Cyril had done?"

"Yes, sir."

"After Cyril came back from the army, he'd changed, he was more violent?"

"Yes. He was never physical with me before he went into the army."

Speranza made Cassidy confirm that the rifle used in the crime had been hers; that in her initial statement to police, she had said that the rifle had been in her car, with no ammunition for it, either in her car or in her trailer; that the last she knew, the gun was in the trunk of a car on Clay Street. Cassidy confirmed that this was what she had said.

"In your July thirtieth statement, the first statement you made to police, you referred to what had oc-curred on Saturday, July twelfth, and Sunday, July thir-teenth. You swore you'd stayed up most of Sunday night doing dope, is that correct?"

"Yes."

"You said on July thirtieth that the day before Tabatha was murdered, you stayed in the house because you didn't want people to see the marks on your face from where Cyril had hit you?"

"Yes, sir."

"You said during that same statement that between nine and nine-thirty on the evening of the murder, Cyril Winebrenner made two calls from the trailer, is that correct?"

"Yes, I did say it."

"But you did not say to whom those calls were made?"

"I believe I said I didn't know who he called."

"During another statement, didn't you say that it was you who called the Bryant house between nine and nine-thirty, but that no one answered the phone, and you did not leave a message?"

"Yes."

"You testified at this trial that you made a couple of calls to Kevin Bryant on Sunday, July thirteenth, around nine or nine-thirty. During those conversations Kevin Bryant told you the kids were going to bed and that Tabatha Bryant was downstairs on the pullout bed."

Cassidy admitted that that was the gist of her testimony under direct examination.

"In your statements on July thirtieth, the first statement, you make no mention of a call to Kevin Bryant. In your second statement, which you made that same day, you did not say anything about the call between nine and nine-thirty, is that correct?"

"Correct."

"When you were filling out these sworn statements, you swore you were telling them everything you knew about the murder of Tabatha Bryant? You promised to tell the truth—yet you said nothing about calling Kevin Bryant between nine and nine-thirty?"

"Yes."

"Under direct testimony, you testified about a call to

Kevin Bryant. He said he was putting the kids to bed upstairs and Tabby was downstairs on the couch. In your first statement on July thirtieth, you indicated that Cyril Winebrenner had made two calls, but you didn't know who he'd called. At nine-thirty you wrote you left the trailer to settle up with Rocky. At some point you are not telling the truth, correct?"

"Correct."

"You indicated you left with Cyril and you didn't know that he'd made an appointment with Rocky."

"I did say that."

"So, going to see Rocky wasn't true and Cyril making two phone calls wasn't true."

"Yes."

"Cyril had keys to Kevin Bryant's house and office?" Speranza asked.

"He had a key to the house—yes, sir."

In an earlier statement to police, for example, Cassidy had said that she did not return to the Bryant home with Winebrenner after calling Kevin Bryant on the phone, but rather she stayed at the service station.

It was revealed that she also had changed her story regarding where she saw Winebrenner load the rifle, where he got rid of his jacket, whether she or Winebrenner called Bryant before the homicide, and which door Winebrenner used to enter the home.

"Incidentally," Speranza said, "when you got up in the morning or night, and you went out to sell drugs, you knew you were committing a crime?"

"Yes."

"So, every time you sold or possessed cocaine, you knew it was illegal, isn't that correct?"

"Yes."

"You probably committed hundreds of crimes selling cocaine, right?"

"Yes."

Speranza then attacked the different versions Cassidy had told of how the evidence was disposed of. In her earlier statements, she had said that Cyril ditched his leather jacket when they stopped at the Noco gas station for fifteen minutes. She had said that he had been wearing it when he got out of the car, but wasn't wearing it when he returned—and that she had not seen the jacket since.

"But this morning you testified to a different scenario, didn't you?" Speranza asked.

She admitted that she had.

"When your story changes like this, at some point you are not telling the truth?" Speranza asked.

"Correct," she replied.

"In one of your earlier statements, you said you got back to the trailer at twelve forty-five P.M. and that you had to go back out to deliver a bag of dope. Your statements this morning are much different than those in these statements," Speranza pointed out.

Speranza then reiterated that, in essence, she was being paid for the testimony she gave against Kevin Bryant. For her testimony, her drug charges would be dropped. If her testimony served to convict Kevin, ten years would be chopped off her sentence.

"So, in a very real sense, you are here to serve yourself—to save your own neck, isn't that correct?" he said, in conclusion.

"I have no idea," Cassidy replied.

In an early statement, Speranza noted, Cassidy said that she had not gone back to the Bryant house the second time on the night of the murder. She had said that she had stayed at the Noco station. Cyril went to the Bryant house the second time alone and afterward he came and picked her up at the Noco station. After that, she had said, they went to the Sugarcreek in Hemlock to fill Emily's car with gas. Even the car they were in at the time of the murder had changed, depending on which story was believed.

"You said once you got back to the trailer, there was money in one-hundred and twenty-dollar bills. You didn't know where the money came from, but Cyril said it was mostly dope money."

"That's true," Cassidy admitted. Speranza was referring to the same money that Cassidy now said came from the envelope Cyril had received from Kevin Bryant, payment for killing his wife.

"That's different than what you said this morning."

"Yes, sir."

The weekend before the murder, Speranza pointed out, Cassidy had said in her earlier statements that she had gone to a small party for another of her boyfriends, a guy named Tito.

This was the first public mention of Tito, but it came as a shock to no one that Cassidy's relationship with Cyril had not been monogamous. She told Cyril that she had been to see Tito, and that she loved Tito.

It was this revelation that led to Cyril striking Cassidy and leaving the bruises on her face that she bore on the night of the murder. After hitting her, he smashed a computer in her room.

Cassidy agreed with Speranza that indeed she had said all of those things in an earlier statement. That established, Speranza hammered at the source of the money Cyril and Cassidy acquired on the night of the murder. It didn't come from Kevin Bryant at all—that would be his point.

"You knew Tabatha Bryant had five to ten thousand dollars on her at any given time. You knew that?"

"Yes."

The jurors and spectators must have been thinking that this was a lot of money for a woman to carry around with her "at any given time," especially a woman who had to work two jobs to make ends meet.

"Did you discuss that with Cyril on several occasions, that Tabatha had large amounts of money on hand?"

Cassidy agreed that she had.

"On Saturday, July 13, 2003, according to your testimony, Cyril didn't have any money and you had about fifteen dollars. You said that?"

"Yes."

"So basically you were both broke?"

"Correct," Cassidy said.

"On July 13, 2003, you testified you and Cyril had broken up?"

"Correct."

"You wanted Cyril Winebrenner out of the house that day?"

"Correct."

"And that's when he got physical?"

"Yes."

Now Speranza moved to the Independence Day gathering at the Bryants' house, during which Cassidy claimed she had heard Kevin make incriminating remarks.

"You testified this morning about a Fourth of July party. And you claim to have heard Kevin say, 'It's definitely got to be done.' You didn't hear a response from Cyril?"

"Correct."

"You testified that there was a conversation that allegedly took place between you and Kevin Bryant having to do with some payment that was allegedly to come from Mr. Bryant?"

"Correct."

"In your prior statements from July thirtieth, there's no mention of payment though, is there?"

"Correct."

"So, sometime between these sworn statements and your testimony this morning, the issue of payment by Kevin Bryant came up."

Since no question had been asked, Cassidy did not respond to that, and Speranza continued.

"In your July thirtieth statement, you make no mention of a conversation with Kevin Bryant about 'five thousand dollars would be enough,' is that correct?"

"Correct."

"That's different than what you testified this morning, correct?"

"Correct."

"This morning you testified about rubber gloves. You testified that Cyril put the gloves in his pocket."

"Yes, I did."

"Where did he get the gloves?"

"I got them out of the desk. I handed him the box and he pulled them out. I believe he grabbed two or three out of there."

"How did Cyril get into the Bryant home on the night of the murder?"

"I don't know how he got into the house. I wasn't paying attention to how he got in there."

"You testified that all the doors were open, correct?"

"They were."

Speranza then made Cassidy admit to changing her story during her various sworn statements regarding where the rifle was and where the ammunition for it was kept.

In one version of her story, she had said that the gun had been kept at her parents' house and that they had gone there to get it. In another statement she said the gun was already in the trunk of her car.

Speranza noted the changes in her story regarding whether or not there was supposed to be an envelope of money on top of the filing cabinet in the Bryants' garage on the night of the murder.

The implication was that the envelope had been an invention of Cassidy's later designed to make Kevin look guilty—that, as he had shown, the money had actually come from Tabby, who carried thousands of dollars around with her at all times, apparently even when she slept.

Speranza asked whether she had been telling the truth when she said during her August 2 statement that Cyril had entered the Bryant house through the rear glass doors because the gate had been left open. He pointed out that there had been no mention of Cyril entering through the glass doors because the gate was left open during her July 30 statement, and no mention of money on the filing cabinet during that first sworn statement.

It had been a long day for Cassidy Green. She was exhausted. Judge Marks decided that she had had enough and adjourned court for the day. First thing the following morning, Cassidy would be back on the stand and Speranza would continue his relentless cross-examination.

Starting up where he had left off, Speranza noted, Cassidy Green never told the same story twice. It was always changing, always pushing in the direction of his client's guilt.

Speranza then returned to the issue of the envelope of money, which was, of course, key to his defense. The prosecution had decided not to try to show that Kevin had actually participated in the murder, as had been stated in Cyril's confession.

Because of that, proving Kevin's guilt was dependent on making the jury believe that he had 1) tried to recruit others into killing Tabatha for money and 2) had paid Cyril after the murder for doing the job.

Speranza noted that during her testimony at the trial Cassidy had said that Cyril counted the money out at one of the gas stations.

"Were you telling the truth when you said that?" he asked.

"Yes, I was," Cassidy replied.

"Yet, in your July thirtieth versions," Speranza said, "you mentioned nothing about the money, you said nothing of the money. In your August second statement, you said it was near Mendon Ponds that Cyril Winebrenner took out the money and showed it to you in an envelope."

Even the envelope itself had changed. It went from not existing at all to being a regular envelope to being a bank envelope, in its final version during her trial testimony.

Speranza asked Cassidy if she had any explanation for the changes in her story. She said that during her earlier statements, she had not said that it was a bank envelope because she didn't remember. She replied, "Over a year, and having time to think about things, details have come."

"When did you remember that the money came in a bank envelope? Was it over the past three weeks?"

"It was before three weeks ago."

Having thoroughly established the fact that Cassidy's story had evolved over time, Speranza shifted gears. He sought now to demonstrate for the jury that those changes had not at all been a matter of details coming to her over time.

Speranza sought to demonstrate that the changes were *purposeful,* inserted into her story by a prosecution that was eager for a conviction. He established that in addition to the three sworn statements she had given to the prosecution before her direct testimony at the trial, she had spent three weeks with prosecutors rehearsing what she was going to say on the stand.

"Did you review the questions and answers with Ms. Winslow and Ms. Splain for three weeks?" he asked.

"We went over my statements and what questions I would be asked," she replied.

"Were you videotaped?"

"Not to my knowledge."

"Were Joanne Winslow and Kristin Splain taking notes?"

"No, sir."

"Were your answers recorded?"

"Not to my knowledge."

Forcing Cassidy to confirm each of his statements, Speranza reiterated that there was no mention of an envelope or the counting of money before she testified before the grand jury; that before the grand jury she had said that she had asked Cyril Winebrenner, even before Cyril discarded the knife near Mendon Ponds, whether or not he had "gotten the money he was supposed to"; that the first time she mentioned the counting of the $5,000 and that it was in a bank envelope was during her previous day's testimony while being questioned by the prosecutor.

"You testified you'd been getting prepared for the past three weeks, meeting with your lawyers and the state's lawyers, getting ready to testify," Speranza said.

"That's true," Cassidy said.

"And we determined yesterday that you are here to benefit yourself with your testimony."

"That's correct."

Speranza then refreshed the jury's memory that her sentence would be determined on a ten-year sliding scale, dependent on her testimony.

Cassidy again confirmed his statement and Speranza said, "No further questions," causing Cassidy to breathe a visible sigh of relief.

"I have a few questions to ask on redirect," said Joanne Winslow. "Mr. Speranza asked you about a sliding scale. In your final agreement, your sentence ranges from fifteen to twenty-five years and there's a recommendation from the people that the judge will determine your sentence?"

"Yes, ma'am," Cassidy replied.

"On July thirtieth, were you charged with anything relating to the drug possession charge?"

"I don't believe so."

"Were you jailed?"

"No, ma'am."

"On August second, were you charged in the Bryant homicide at that point?"

"Yes, ma'am."

"Was that murder in the third degree?"

"I believe so."

"It wasn't until you went before the grand jury that that was upgraded?"

"Yes, ma'am."

"No further questions," Winslow said.

"A couple of questions on recross," Speranza said, rising to his feet. "Isn't it true that, under your agreement with the prosecution, you were given the option of pleading guilty to manslaughter in the first degree? And you were not to be charged with the drug charges, the state and federal tax violations, and the hundreds of cocaine deals and other crimes you could have been charged with?"

"Yes."

"And so," Speranza said in his "let me get this straight" tone, "in exchange for your testimony, you will be allowed to plead to manslaughter in the first degree and to be sentenced to the lowest end of that range based on the prosecutor's recommendation to the court?"

"Correct."

"No further questions."

And with that, Cassidy Green, who if possible had shrunk even smaller during her time testifying, was allowed to leave the witness stand.

* * *

In court for every day of the trial, of course, were the court reporters Anthony DiMartino and Judy Ging. On a special machine, they took down every word that was spoken in the court. At the end of each day, they would transcribe the day's proceedings. On the bottom of each day's transcript they would sign the following statement: "I, [name], do hereby certify that I am an Official Court Reporter of the Seventh Judicial District, at Rochester, County of Monroe, State of New York, duly appointed; That on the —th day of October, 2004, before the Honorable Patricia D. Marks, County Court Judge, I reported in machine shorthand the proceeding had in the County Court, in the matter of the People of the State of New York v. KEVIN BRYANT, Defendant; And that the transcript, herewith numbered pages 1 through — inclusive, is a true, accurate, correct and complete record of those machine shorthand notes."

CHAPTER 61

A Black T-Shirt
With a Dragon on It

Also testifying that Wednesday were Cassidy Green's uncle James and aunt Roberta Green. James took the stand first. It was established that James was Cassidy's uncle by adoption.

"Could you please explain what you mean by that?"

"She's my stepniece. My brother married her mom and adopted her."

"Do you have a close relationship with Cassidy?"

"No, ma'am. It has been at least four years since I have seen her," James Green said.

James Green said he and his wife had lived in West Bloomfield for about thirty-eight years; his house and property were on Stetson Road in that town. Sharp-eared spectators recognized the name of that road. They had heard it the day before during Cassidy's testimony. Some piece of evidence had been dumped there. The shirt, that was it. Stetson Road had been one of the roads in the Township of Bloomfield that Cyril and Cassidy had cruised down in the borrowed Geo while looking for appropriate places to ditch murder evidence.

"Please describe your property in relation to Stetson Road, Mr. Green," Winslow said.

"I own five acres of property, four on the side of the road that our house is located on and one acre on the other," he testified.

He said his land was in an L-shape, on the bend of a road. He said about one-and-a-half acres of the land is yard and the rest is woods, rocks, and brush.

"I have some trails going through there that I maintain with a riding mower," he testified.

James testified that sometime after Tabatha's murder, probably in late July or early August 2003, a few weeks after the murder, he had been riding his tractor around his grounds when he discovered a bloody T-shirt on their grounds.

"Can you describe the shirt you found?" Winslow asked.

"It was a cotton T-shirt, black in color, with a decal of a dragon on it," Green replied.

Was this shirt "with a decal of a dragon on it" the same "shirt with a dragon on it" that Tabby had given Chris Winebrenner for his eighteenth birthday? Had Cyril taken the shirt after Chris's death and worn it on the night of Tabby's death? Or was it just a coincidence that Tabby's gift to Chris—the one his mother could never find after he died—and the shirt Cyril threw away both had dragons on them?

"How did you come about finding the shirt?" Winslow queried.

"I was riding my tractor along the trails in the woods I keep cleared, and I come across it," James Green replied.

"Where exactly did you find the shirt?"

"It was about a quarter of a mile from the house on a trail. It was stuck on a thorn on a bush off the trail."

Winslow showed Cyril's T-shirt to Green and asked him to identify it, which he did.

"What did you do with this T-shirt after you found it?" Winslow asked.

"I put it on my tractor and took it back to the house," James said.

"What happened to the shirt then?"

"I eventually asked my kids if anyone recognized it. They didn't. And my wife took it and washed it in case someone claimed it."

Soon thereafter, he said, a sheriff's deputy came to the door and asked if anyone had found an article of clothing on the grounds. James and his wife showed the T-shirt to the deputy, who then took it without explaining why it was important.

On cross-examination Speranza asked James Green for more details regarding the discovery of the shirt.

"How far from the road was the shirt when you found it?" the defense attorney asked.

"I would estimate about twenty-five to thirty feet," James replied.

"Does the road that passes by have a curb?"

"No curb."

"There is a shoulder to the road?"

"Yes, sir."

"Is the shoulder wide enough for a car to park?"

"Yes, sir."

"Why did you decide to keep the T-shirt?" Speranza asked.

"I thought it might have belonged to a friend of one of my three kids," James said. "There had been a graduation party for my youngest daughter around the Fourth of July. Also a week later, my wife and I went on vacation and I knew that my kids had had friends over, so I thought the shirt might belong to one of them."

Roberta Green then took the stand and corroborated her husband's story: "The shirt was left in the kitchen for a week or so before I took it and washed it. Once it was cleaned and dried, I put it in one of my daughters' rooms. That's where it stayed until sheriff's deputies came for it. They took it and I never saw it again."

CHAPTER 62

The Testimony of Vinny Bennett

As it turned out, Cassidy Green was not the only prosecution witness who was testifying against Kevin Bryant as a direct result of being set up by a drug sting operation. The next witness was twenty-two-year-old Vinny Bennett, who told jurors that he had lived with Cassidy and Cyril in a trailer in Bloomfield at the time of the murder. He said that he was under the impression that Cyril and Cassidy had borrowed his car, a Geo, on the night of the murder and were not driving her car at the time of the crime, as she had testified.

Bennett testified that sometime after 11:00 P.M. Cassidy and Cyril had asked if they could borrow his car. He said he didn't hear Green's noisy Monte Carlo leave the trailer park that evening, although he didn't go outside at all to check and see if it was gone.

Bennett also testified that he had gone to see Kevin Bryant about hiring him for an assault case a couple months before Tabatha's death. Bennett said Bryant was agitated and showed him pictures and papers documenting an affair Tabatha was having.

On cross-examination defense attorney Matthew Lembke got Bennett to admit that, as was the case with Cassidy Green, he had been arrested for selling drugs to an undercover informant named Rocky.

Bennett, it was revealed, was arrested on August 14, 2003, and charged with selling cocaine and marijuana.

"Isn't it true that, on August 25, 2003, you entered into an agreement with the district attorney's office to avoid jail time and instead receive five years' probation in exchange for your testimony at this trial?" Lembke asked.

"Yes, sir," Bennett conceded.

Lembke then tried to make the most out of the discrepancy between Bennett and Green's testimony. Not only did Cassidy say that she and Cyril had gone to the murder scene in her Monte Carlo, but one eyewitness, a woman, had said that she saw the Monte Carlo pull up to the Bryants' house twice during the late evening of July 13. All of this would be thrown into question if Cyril and Cassidy had been driving a Geo that night.

On rebuttal the prosecution had Bennett repeat the fact that he had not heard Cassidy's Monte Carlo pull away from the trailer on the night of the murder and that it was a loud car.

It was again Speranza's turn: "You say you didn't hear the Monte Carlo leave on the night of the murder?"

"Yes, sir."

"And it was a loud car?"

"Yes, sir."

"Louder than your Geo?"

"About the same."

Speranza pretended that he hadn't quite heard that properly: "About the same, you say?"

"Yes, sir."

"The Geo was just as loud as the Monte Carlo?"

"Yes, sir."

"Since the Geo was so loud, did you hear the Geo leaving the trailer park that night?"

"No, sir."

"No further questions, Your Honor," Speranza said, and Bennett was excused from the witness stand.

Since Cassidy did testify that after the murder her car broke down and that she and Cyril were forced to borrow a friend's car in order to dispose of his bloody shirt, pants, and jacket, the best interpretation regarding the discrepancy was that Bennett's memory of the evening—since he was not the one committing a murder and stayed in his trailer all night—was imprecise.

Vinny Bennett, it could be theorized, had merely confused the time at which his car was borrowed. After all, he had no reason to keep his timeline straight. Even if the matter weren't this easily explained, the point was moot. All indications were that Cassidy and Cyril did what they said they did, so it really made little difference which car they drove to and from the crime scene.

CHAPTER 63

The Testimony of Tim Hunter and Jennifer Larch

Next on the stand was a redheaded thirty-one-year-old paroled convict named Tim Hunter, who testified that on July 8, 2003, he and a lady friend accompanied Kevin Bryant to his office in Greece, where Bryant offered him money to murder his wife.

"He asked what I did," Hunter said. "I told him I did construction. He asked me if I did demolition work. He asked me if I could terminate his wife."

Hunter said that Bryant had pulled out his wallet and showed a photo of his family: Kevin, Tabatha, and the two boys.

Hunter said, "I asked him why he was gonna kill his kids' mother. He said, 'She crossed me and I couldn't deal with that.'"

Hunter turned the offer down. Five days later, Tabatha was killed. Hunter testified that Bryant gave him $500 to kill his wife and promised $5,000 more after he did it. He said he took the $500, but never committed the crime.

On cross-examination Hunter detailed his long criminal career.

On Thursday, October 7, 2004, jurors viewed a graphic videotape of the crime scene. The tape showed images of Tabatha faceup on the bed in the Bryant home living room. Clearly visible were the gaping knife wound in her neck and the bullet wound in her right eye. The camera panned around the room to show the extent of the blood splatter caused by the attack. There was blood on the walls, the ceiling, on the blades of a ceiling fan, and on the shade to a small nearby table lamp.

Following the tape, twenty-nine-year-old Jennifer Larch testified. Although the importance of Jennifer's role in the case was not emphasized during Kevin Bryant's trial, it is clear that Jennifer's phone call to the local sheriff's office after she recognized Tabby's picture in the newspaper did more than anything else to break this case. Before Jennifer gave her deposition four days after Tabby's murder, the Monroe County Sheriff's Office had a theory. After Jennifer's deposition the sheriff had a case. By taking the stand at Bryant's trial, she was finishing the job she had started on July 18, 2003, when she knew the man with the scars on his chest had killed his wife. She recalled the revulsion she had felt in Kevin's office when he talked about killing the woman in the picture on the wall, and she held her chin high as she testified.

Bryant was dressed in his usual neat but not necessarily tailored attire, that day in a blue blazer and a blue shirt.

Judge Marks had ruled previously that Larch could testify only if it was agreed that the fact that she was a prostitute was not to be mentioned. Now the judge told the nervous woman to speak up, and to speak into the microphone so that everyone would be able to hear her.

The judge told her that there might be objections to some of the questions she was asked, and that if there was, she was to wait until Judge Marks had ruled on the objection before answering.

Winslow then began her questioning. It was determined that Jennifer lived in Lakeville with her mother and her four-month-old son, a new development in her life since the days when she was selling her body to Kevin Bryant.

Jennifer correctly identified Bryant as the man sitting in the middle, between his counsel, at the defendant's table. Jennifer testified that she first met Kevin in 2003. Asked which month, she said "Februaryish." Jennifer said she had seen Kevin on July 1 of that year at about 8:00 P.M. She and her boyfriend, Tim Hunter, had gone to Kevin's law office on West Ridge Road in the town of Greece. At that time, she said, Kevin angrily told her that his wife had been cheating on him. Kevin had said that his wife was meeting her boyfriend every Tuesday and Thursday. His anger had been such that he'd become red-faced. She testified that she had gone again to Kevin's office. At first, Tim stayed in the car and she went into the office alone. Kevin asked her who the dude was. She said he was her bouncer. He asked her where Tim worked and she said Buckley Movers. Kevin said he was looking for a guy who could get rid of someone. She asked him who he needed to get rid of and he had smiled, nodded, and said, "My wife."

Jennifer testified that she told Kevin he was crazy, but that he had said he knew how to get away with it. Kevin asked point-blank if she thought Tim would be willing to do the job. He offered $500 to get a gun. He offered $4,500 to be paid after the job was done.

The woman left the office at that point and talked to Tim in the car for a moment. Then Kevin came out and Jennifer split. Kevin and Tim talked in the car. She said that when she got back in the car, after Kevin had gone back inside, Tim had $500.

Winslow asked if there had come a time when Jennifer saw an article that caught her attention in the *Democrat and Chronicle.* Jennifer said she had. She had been sleeping in the front seat of the car when Tim had slammed the article against the car window, waking her up.

Right away she saw Tabatha's picture and the word "murder" and she knew what had happened. The article had been in the Thursday, July 17th edition. Jennifer then recounted how she had realized she had information that could help solve a murder, so she asked a friend what to do. Eventually she was instructed as to what to do, and she made a deposition for the sheriff's office. Jennifer learned that her deposition was in evidence, under its new name, "People's Exhibit #86."

"Do you know a person by the name of Cyril Winebrenner?" Winslow inquired.

"I heard his name now," Jennifer replied.

"Before this incident?"

"No."

"Did you know that name?"

"No."

"And did you know a person by the name of Cassidy Green?"

"No."

"Thank you," Winslow said, signifying that she had finished questioning the witness.

"Cross-examine," Judge Marks said.

Speranza began his questioning by inquiring how many sworn statements she had made previous to this day's testimony. She said twice, her deposition and her testimony before the grand jury. She said that at least twice she had met with Winslow and Splain to discuss her testimony, but that the women had not, to her recollection, taken notes during those interviews or taped them. Speranza made her admit that at the time the incident she described had taken place, she had a "strong" crack addiction.

Speranza then handed Jennifer a copy of her deposition and asked her to read it. He made her admit that nowhere in the deposition, had she said she heard Kevin Bryant say that he would "get away with it." He made her reiterate that Kevin Bryant and Tim Hunter had been complete strangers up until the moment Kevin allegedly asked the "bouncer" to kill his wife and gave him a $500 advance with which to buy a gun. She said that was true. Speranza then made Jennifer admit that Tim had been on parole at the time of the alleged incident and was currently in jail because of a parole violation. She said that that was true.

The defense attorney made the witness admit that she had been charged with burglary stemming from an incident that took place only two days before Tabby's murder. She admitted that she had broken into a friend's home in Scottsville and had taken $3,200 worth of items, including a TV, a computer, and a guitar. It was established that she had been given a court-appointed lawyer and was facing trial in November 2004. Speranza tried to establish that the DA's office had been lenient on Jennifer because of her cooperation testifying against Kevin Bryant. Although various objections from the prosecution stymied him to some extent, he did manage to establish that Jennifer had ended up being charged with a misdemeanor despite the severity of the burglary. He tried to get Jennifer to admit that she knew the same prosecutor's office involved in this murder case was the one responsible for prosecuting her regarding the burglary. Jennifer said that she hadn't realized that. She'd thought that the prosecution in her burglary case had been a small-town DA's office.

"I thought it was the Wheatland DA," she said—
Wheatland being the township that contained the Village of Scottsville.

Speranza reminded her that Wheatland was in
Monroe County, and she said she'd never put two and
two together. He then made her admit that her testimony at this trial and her deposition did not agree on
a number of points. She had switched which day she
had seen Tabby's photo in the newspaper.

"I was high when I made the deposition."

"You were high on crack cocaine?"

"Yes, but I'm completely sober now and have been
for over a year."

"So, essentially, when you told the police under oath
that Mr. Bryant had asked you, according to your testimony today, whether your boyfriend did side work,
you told him Buckley Movers, you were high on cocaine?"

"Yes, I was, but that doesn't change the facts."

"Doesn't change the facts. Okay. When you told
him that Kevin said, 'That's not what I mean, Jennifer,' you were high on cocaine?"

"Yes."

"And so in your mental state of being high on cocaine is when you swore to this supporting deposition, affirmed under oath that it was true, and basically
laid out the story that you told today, correct?"

"Yes."

He then made her admit that she had changed the
day she'd seen the photo in the paper because the prosecution had shown her the article and it had "refreshed her memory."

But then Speranza lost ground. It was a miracle he
didn't visibly wince when Jennifer then blurted out,
"You're making it sound like I lied about it. I didn't lie
at all. It's the same things that happened. It happened
in the same order. I just didn't know the exact date."

Speranza tried to regain the offensive by getting Jennifer to admit that she was still guessing about what day she had seen Tabby's photo in the *Democrat and Chronicle.* Judge Marks scolded Speranza for cutting the witness off in the middle of her sentences, destroying the momentum.

Speranza was in the judge's doghouse. Judge Marks said on the record, "I asked you not to, and you chose to argue with me. I think it was inappropriate, Mr. Speranza, and I'm going to ask you show me more courtesy than you have in that context."

Speranza apologized and Judge Marks declared a recess. After the brief break, Speranza immediately began a strong stretch of cross-examination. He painstakingly established that yes, Jennifer must have seen the photo in the paper on Thursday, and she gave the deposition the next day, on Friday evening. Then he hit her with this:

"All right. Now, you swore under oath, and you said, 'I recognized her picture in the paper as being the same woman I had seen pictures of on Kevin's office wall. I could not believe it. I got sick to my stomach. I've been throwing up for three days.'"

"Right."

"So that was all made up?"

Again Jennifer held her ground, giving Speranza more information than he wanted.

"No, it wasn't made up," she said. "I had miscarried a pregnancy on Monday, and I had been throwing up from being sick, and I guess it just all kind of got jumbled together in my mind."

He made her reiterate that three days had elapsed between her seeing the photo and contacting authorities. In her current version, it was only one day. She agreed that was true. He finally managed to get her to ramble like someone might if fabricating a story, something she hadn't done before.

Jennifer said, "So it was approximately a full twenty-four-hour period, at which time I was smoking crack around the clock, and I was using—I, as far as I—it felt like three days, must be." Speranza must have suppressed a grin at the words "must be." She might as well have said, "Yeah, that's the ticket."

Speranza then established that Jennifer had said she and Tim had used the money from Kevin Bryant to get an apartment. Jennifer insisted that the apartment had been rented after Kevin gave Tim the money, but before she saw Tabby's picture in the paper. In other words, she had not known that it was blood money.

Speranza made Jennifer admit that there had been an attempt to make a deal to help Tim with his legal situation because he was cooperating with Joanne Winslow. In a sidebar Winslow said she'd refused to make a deal with Tim Hunter for this simple reason: "If Tim Hunter had reported what he knew immediately, Tabatha Bryant might still be alive today."

In the long run, however, with the exception of irregularities in Jennifer's timeline, Speranza did nothing to shake Jennifer from her story that the defendant had paid her boyfriend $500 to buy a gun to shoot his wife.

CHAPTER 64

The Deputy in the Driveway

"Prosecution calls Deputy Bridget Davis." Deputy Davis was one of the first to arrive at the murder scene.

Davis told the court that she was a radio patrol deputy for the Monroe County Sheriff's Office. She was a six-year veteran of the force. She described her job duties as "patrol the streets, respond to calls, take reports." She was responsible for Penfield, Perinton, and Pittsford. She said that on the early morning of July 14, 2003, she had been patrolling Penfield when she responded to a call, woman shot, at 2 Pennicott Circle. She'd arrived at the house and was assigned to stand guard outside, at the northeast corner of the house. Later she was moved from the outer perimeter to a new spot to guard near the garage. From there, she was assigned to stand in the driveway with another deputy, Deputy Morency, and Kevin Bryant was also standing there. Deputy Davis then correctly identified Bryant in the courtroom. She said that Bryant was still wearing the clothes he'd been to bed in, and he had a cordless phone in his hand. She'd stood near the two men and had taken notes regarding their conversation.

"What was Kevin Bryant saying when you first began to listen to the conversation?" Winslow asked.

"He was talking about a phone call he had just received from MCI, about ten minutes before the shooting. He was stating he didn't know who was on the other end of the phone. He stated to me he did not know who was on the other end of the phone, and when we asked if it was a woman or a male, he said it was a female."

She testified that Bryant had said that the person on the phone hadn't said anything, but he knew that it was a female. Deputy Morency wanted to know how he could tell it was a woman if she hadn't said anything.

"Because they said 'hello.'"

"Did he say what happened about ten minutes after he received that call?"

"He said he heard shots."

Winslow asked if Deputy Davis had observed Kevin's demeanor as he stood in the driveway. She said she had, and he was calm.

"Did there come a point in time where he had some type of a physical reaction or made some type of physical motion?"

"After speaking of the phone call, he, like, turned to the side of the driveway and dry heaved."

"Now, how long did that last?"

"About three to five seconds."

"Did he actually throw up?"

"No." She said she'd asked him if he was okay and he'd said he was.

Deputy Davis testified that Kevin had said he'd been planning a camping trip, a church retreat for the next weekend. He said that he'd had a good weekend with his wife, but they had been having their problems.

"What did he say was the reason for those problems?"

"All she wanted to do was play, and he had to work all the time."

Deputy Davis heard Bryant say that he'd hired a private investigator to follow his wife, and he'd learned that she was having an affair with a totally bald man by the name of Richard Oliver. He'd told in some detail how he'd gone about getting the private investigator and how the private eye had delivered his final report in a multimedia fashion. There had been pictures and a video. He'd said that he'd asked Tabatha to quit her boyfriend, so they could concentrate on repairing their torn marriage, but she'd declined. Kevin said while standing on the driveway in his T-shirt and shorts that he'd been contemplating divorce proceedings and that he was an attorney. Kevin had been asked if Tabatha knew about his plans to get a divorce and he said yes, they had discussed separation. He'd said that the marital difficulties had commenced in November, December, and January 2002/2003. He'd first become aware of Richard Oliver during the last week of April 2003 through a list of phone calls he had seen. He'd then attempted to call his parents on the cordless phone he still held. Deputy Morency held his flashlight so Kevin would be able to read the numbers on the phone. In the light Davis could see that there was blood covering the tip of Kevin's thumb, pointer finger, and the two middle fingers. Kevin failed to make the call. He was too far from the house and he couldn't get a signal, so he asked for assistance. The deputies saw to it that Kevin's parents were contacted and they came over to pick up the kids. Before his parents arrived, Bryant described what had happened in the house that night.

Deputy Davis said, "He stated that he was upstairs, and he heard a shot or maybe two shots, and he heard Tabatha scream, 'Oh, my God,' and he said he had never heard her screaming like that before, and then he said she shot her once, and then—"

"Did he say once or at least once?"

"At least once. Then he said he was 'running up.' He paused, and then he said, 'no, downstairs.' And then he just paused and said, 'or the girl that called the house'—'or the girl that called,' and he was referring to 'shot her just once.' It was evident he was referring to maybe she shot her just once."

Deputy Davis said that when sheriff's deputies had arrived at the scene, they noticed that the garage door was open, with the family's motor vehicle inside the garage. Had the Bryants left the garage door open, or had it been opened by (possibly for) the killer or killers? Deputy Morency asked Bryant why the garage door was open and Kevin said that he must have forgotten to close it after the last time he'd taken out the garbage. Kevin said he had gone out briefly that evening, to work, and then to get a cup of coffee. He returned home at 10:30 P.M. and took out the garbage soon after. The garage door, he figured, must have been open from that point on.

It must have occurred to the deputies that a thing like that might be enough to attract a burglar. Everything inside the garage would be easy pickings. The burglar's only concern would have been the homeowner, a concern that could have been diminished if the burglars had gotten a look at Kevin Bryant.

Deputy Morency had asked if Tabatha had had any problems with her customers at the bank, and Kevin had said no. He said he'd worked earlier in the evening at his office, from about 8:30 until 10:00.

Deputy Davis testified, "He said he finished putting out the trash, and then he went upstairs and woke Tabatha up because she was sleeping with Stephen, and said, 'Why don't you come to bed?' And Tabatha ended up going downstairs and sleeping on the pullout couch. He said he received a phone call about ten minutes later. He said about ten minutes after that, he heard the shots."

Deputy Davis testified that Bryant had told her that they hadn't slept in the same bed for about a week. Describing what he did after he heard the shots and the screaming coming from downstairs, Kevin had said he went immediately to Tabatha's body to see if she was alive. She wasn't breathing. There were just bubbles. He said he'd put his hand on her chest, under her breast. She'd been lying on her back. He had also touched her on both arms. He said he couldn't remember hearing any car doors or house doors opening or closing. He then had reiterated that Tabatha just wanted to be free. She just wanted to have fun. She'd felt that she'd never had an opportunity to be young and free.

In Deputy Davis's presence, Bryant had said that he'd found notes from Richard Oliver to his wife. In those notes, Kevin claimed, Richard had talked about the men he had killed in Vietnam.

Deputy Davis testified, "He was, like, 'I can't handle him hanging out with her.'"

Bryant griped that he'd discovered that Tabatha and Richard were speaking to one another on the phone 150 times a month. He mentioned that Tabatha's brother Cyril and his girlfriend, Cassidy, had been staying with them in the past. Kevin was laid-back about them staying in his house, but they stressed Tabatha out. She had wanted to charge them more money as rent, so they split.

"Did he talk to you about guns at all?" Winslow asked Deputy Davis.

"Yes, he said neither him nor Tabatha owned a firearm, but guns are easy to get, and anyone can get one."

Deputy Davis testified that Kevin had said he felt like

he was in a horrible dream and he wondered when he would wake up from it. Would it be today? Tomorrow?

She described him looking at the full moon and talking about how it could make people crazy. Those who were on edge were most apt to go insane, he'd added.

Deputy Davis said that Kevin had not been as calm when discussing Richard Oliver as he had been when describing Tabatha's murder. At no time did he ask if he could leave with his parents and children.

"He was mumbling a lot to himself, and, like, he just had his arms crossed and was shaking his head, was rubbing his mouth, just seemed more irritated, maybe," Deputy Davis said. Before the children were picked up by his parents, at no time did he ask if he could go in the house and check on the kids. Other than the dry heaving, he'd not made any health complaints. Even though he was barefoot, in his shirt and shorts, he never requested an opportunity to put something else on, or to put something on his feet. She said the weather that night had been typical of July in Rochester. Warm and dry. There was certainly nothing inclement about the weather. He never asked for an attorney. No one threatened him. No promises were made to induce statements. No physical force was used on him. At no point did he say that he desired to stop talking. He never asked for access to any medicine. He never was told that he had to stand at some particular place. At no time did he request access to a drink or to a bathroom.

She said that the interview on the driveway lasted until about 3:00 A.M., when investigators arrived and took Kevin Bryant in.

At that point in the trial, 4:17 P.M., Judge Marks called for the court to be recessed. They would resume the next morning at 9:30, with Speranza's cross-examination of Deputy Davis.

* * *

After trading cordial "good mornings," Speranza began to grill Deputy Davis. He asked her if during the three-hour questioning in the driveway, if Bryant would have been allowed inside the house.

"I don't believe they would let him in, but—" Deputy Davis started to say.

Speranza interrupted her by saying, "You know they won't let him in. Why are you hedging?"

Winslow objected that Speranza was arguing with the witness and Judge Marks sustained. Speranza then got Deputy Davis to admit that she, at no time, heard anyone advising Kevin of his rights. Speranza quizzed her about the quality of her notes. She said she thought her note-taking abilities were pretty good. He made her admit that her testimony had implied that Kevin had talked about his marital difficulties just after his parents had come to pick up the kids, when she now acknowledged that Kevin's statement of "I can't handle him hanging out with her" actually came well after his parents had left with the boys.

Davis also admitted under cross-examination that she had not reviewed her notes before testifying. She had read her written report, but not the notes she took as Kevin was being questioned in the driveway.

Speranza tried to win points with the jury by pointing out that Deputy Davis had proclaimed Kevin's demeanor at first "calm," despite the fact that she was not a trained medical professional. It is doubtful that the jury bought into this. The jury must have figured that Deputy Davis knew "calm" when she saw it.

In time Speranza got around to his point, that Kevin was not calm at all when talking to the deputies in the driveway, but rather was somnambulant because of the prescription medications he was on.

She reiterated that Kevin had said that he and Tabby were planning on going to a church retreat that Wednesday. He said he had filled out his divorce papers, but was going to give his wife one last chance at reconciliation before serving her with the papers after they returned from the retreat.

Speranza asked her if Kevin had mentioned hearing a loud car and she said he had. Speranza then pointed out that she had mentioned nothing about the loud car during her direct examination and she pointed out that she had not been asked. He then pointed out that there was a reference to the "loud car" comment in Deputy Davis's written report, but no reference to the comment in her contemporaneous notes. She replied that she originally had not written the quote down because it stood out so much, she knew she would remember it.

The other quote that had appeared in her written report—but not in her notes—was Bryant discussing how he felt as if he were in a bad dream and wondered how long he would have to wait to wake up from it.

Speranza got Deputy Davis to say that Kevin responded to questions about his marital difficulties "without hesitation." This was, Speranza implied, not the behavior of a man who was trying to cover up the crime he had just committed.

In a bit of a switch, Speranza then got Deputy Davis to notice that in her notes she had written that Kevin had gone to the Noco station for coffee, whereas in her written report she did not specify where Kevin said he had gotten his coffee.

One could wonder if Speranza's dwelling on the Noco station really was doing his client any good, even if he was successfully showing glitches in the methods Davis used to record information. The Noco station, of course, was part of Cassidy's story as well. Kevin, Cyril, and Cassidy had all been to the Noco station during the hours and minutes before Tabatha's murder—he for coffee, they to make a phone call—a fact that Speranza did not want the jury contemplating.

On redirect Winslow returned to Speranza's implication

that Deputy Davis couldn't tell calm from somnambulant. Davis said that Bryant never mentioned taking any drugs, and that he never seemed dizzy or drowsy. At no time, she said, did he seem like he had anything but a clear head. At no time did he seem as if he were having trouble understanding or answering the questions. With that, Deputy Davis was allowed to leave the witness stand.

CHAPTER 65

911

On Friday, October 8, 2004, jurors heard a tape of Kevin's ten-minute call to the 911 operator reporting the murder of his wife, just after midnight on July 14, 2003. This October day would have been Tabatha's twenty-eighth birthday. To commemorate the date, friends and family in the courtroom wore red ribbons with roses in the center.

The Reverend Terry Smith, Tabatha's uncle, told reporters outside the courthouse that he and the rest of Tabatha's family wanted to make sure the community understood the proceedings were about Tabatha's life, not just about her death.

"Tabatha didn't do anything in a small way. She was always up for any kind of adventure and really loved to have a good time," said Smith.

Samantha, Tabatha's sister, tearfully told a reporter the story of how Tabby had worn red shoes at her wedding because someone told her she couldn't. If Sam remembered who the someone was, she didn't mention it to the reporter.

The victim's cousin Becky McCaffery recalled, "We did our hair together, and we did dance routines together, and she loved to sing and we'd sing songs. You know, she was one of my best friends, and I miss her very much."

CHAPTER 66

The Lead Investigator

"Prosecution calls Paul T. Siena," said Joanne Winslow on the morning of Friday, October 8, and the lead investigator in the case took the stand. He said he was an investigator in the Major Crimes Unit for the Monroe County Sheriff's Office. He had been with the department for sixteen years.

His job description: "I investigate crimes that I'm assigned to, homicide investigations, robberies, rapes, things of that nature."

He said he'd been called in to duty during the early hours of July 14, 2003, because of a homicide in Penfield. He arrived at 2 Pennicott Circle at 1:45 A.M. He was quickly briefed on the situation.

Investigator Siena said, "When I first went into the home, we had gone in through the garage, and I went to the area of where the room where Tabatha Bryant was located. I didn't go into the room, but I did look in there. I saw a woman lying on her back on a [fold-out] sofa bed. There was blood in and around the area of her body. There was also blood on the walls, the ceiling."

Siena began interrogating Kevin Bryant at approximately 3:05 A.M., a little more than three hours after the murder. He introduced himself and his partner, David Vaughn, to Kevin before the questioning began. He gave Kevin a quick scan. He did not appear to have any blood on him.

Siena testified, "We explained to him who we were. We also explained that we would like to speak with him, and we asked him if he would come back to our office so we could have that conversation there."

The investigator stated that the interrogation began at that point and continued until 4:05 P.M., thirteen hours later. Kevin Bryant was calm and friendly while being questioned. When asked to go to the sheriff's office, Kevin said he was ready when they were and made no objection.

Before they left, Bryant asked to retrieve a few items from the house. According to Siena's testimony, those items were a pair of black shorts, brown leather shoes, his cell phone, and a red briefcase. Once the briefcase was retrieved for him, Siena had expressed some concerns to him about the briefcase's contents.

"Officer safety issues," Investigator Siena testified. "When we transport anything, you know, we are concerned with the contents of the briefcase or of the items that we transport. He smiled at us and basically said he wasn't much of a threat to us. There were no concerns about weapons or anything inside the briefcase, and he explained that there were files in the briefcase."

They left Pennicott Circle at 3:30 P.M. in Investigator Vaughn's unmarked Ford Taurus. Vaughn drove. Bryant took the front passenger seat and Siena got in the back. Kevin was not handcuffed. On the way to the station, they stopped at the Mobil On the Run, on Empire Boulevard, to get gas. They bought Kevin a

Coke, which he drank. They arrived at the sheriff's office headquarters at 4:05 P.M.

After making a quick stop at the rest room, Kevin and the two investigators went to Siena and Vaughn's office, which Siena described as "a corner office. It is about eleven by seventeen, eleven feet by seventeen feet. There are two large desks in there for us, L-shaped desks. There are seven chairs. There's a typewriter station. There's a four-drawer file cabinet. There are three large windows, bookshelf. It is a pretty nice office."

There were two desks, he said. "There's a number of chairs that are in front of the desks, so I sat behind my desk. Investigator Vaughn sat behind his desk, and Mr. Bryant sat in one of the chairs that is on the opposite side of the room in front of those desks.

"We began to discuss the incident," Siena said. "Basically, I had explained to him, again, our role in the investigation, that we were investigators. We were going to be investigating this and trying to determine what happened. There were additional people who were at the scene still, who were going to be continuing their work there. The technicians, our technicians staff, that they would be collecting evidence and going through the home. I asked him, at some point, if he needed anything out of the house and he said he didn't need anything. At some point there, I actually offered to get any special toys that the kids might want or [the] kids' clothing, and he said that the children were with his parents and that they would be fine for a few days.

"He asked me who was responsible for cleaning up, and I didn't understand his question, so I asked to clarify it. And he asked me once the body is gone, who cleans up the house? And I basically explained that it was up to the homeowner to do that, but that there were agencies who did provide that type of cleanup as-

sistance, biohazard cleanup, and that—I actually retrieved a card that I had for one such agency, and I gave
it to him, and he took it."

Joanne Winslow asked, "Did you begin to ask him
what led him to call the nine-one-one operator the
evening—early-morning hours of July 14, 2003?"

"Yes, we did."

"And what did he say?"

"He said that he had heard two shots, and then he
heard some screaming, and then a third shot, and
that he had gone downstairs and found his wife had
been shot, and then he called nine-one-one."

"Did you ask him anything further about the shots
that he had heard?"

"We did. I asked him to describe the shots, and he
had explained they were more like pops." Kevin then
told the investigators that the only experience he'd had
with firearms was firing a .22 rifle on a farm, but he
wasn't clear on who owned the farm.

Kevin then described his work schedule. He'd explained that he worked during the day and that often
he would go back to his office at night.

"Did he talk to you about his wife and how she felt
about his work hours?" Joanne Winslow asked.

"He did. He told us it became a point of contention
within their marriage, because she was upset. She
thought he was working too much, and that—that it
did become an issue in their marriage. There was additional conversation at some point regarding the fact
that he would go back to work in the evenings often,
but then when he would come home, she might want
to go out, and he didn't want to go out, so that became
another point of marital contention." Kevin told his interrogators that he and his wife had been sleeping apart
for about ten days.

"After putting the garbage out to the curb," Siena
continued, "he had gone to get a cup of coffee at the

Noco station, which is, I believe, on Browncroft and Blossom, and he had gone to get a cup of coffee, but when he got there, the Noco was closed, so he came home."

The nearby Noco station was the same location where Cyril Winebrenner and Cassidy Green called Kevin after their first visit to the house that night, when they had found all of the entrances to the house still locked.

Kevin told the investigators that when he got in from his attempt to get coffee, Tabatha was already asleep on the pullout couch. At that point he gathered the garbage from the upstairs bath and the children's rooms and took that out to the curb. Then he'd prepared for bed.

"He said that between eleven-thirty and midnight he'd picked up the phone and it was an automated MCI operator explaining that there was a collect call. He did take the call and that he said the voice was muddled on the other end of the phone, and he really couldn't determine what the person was saying. He asked if he could help the person, but he couldn't determine the response, so at some point shortly thereafter, he hung up."

Bryant then detailed the moment of the crime, how he had heard two shots, his wife screaming, and then a third shot. He had gone downstairs immediately and had discovered his wife dead. There was no sign of the killer or killers. He immediately called 911.

Joanne Winslow said, "Let me ask you a question, when you were at 2 Pennicott Circle, before going down to your headquarters office, did you have occasion to observe the position of vehicles in the driveway?"

"I did, yes. There were two vehicles in the driveway. One was a 2000 Hyundai; the other was a '99 Plymouth Voyager minivan. The minivan was on the right side of the driveway as you're looking at it from the street, looking toward the house, and it was on the right side of the driveway, but it was only parked about halfway up the driveway, not as close to the garage as the Hyundai. The Hyundai was parked on the left side of the driveway, but it was pulled all the way up to the garage."

"When you had an opportunity to talk to him in the early-morning hours, did you ask him about the position of the vehicles in the driveway?"

"I did, yes. He explained that the minivan was pulled back to allow the children the opportunity to play, and at some point he had taken the Hyundai to the Noco station so—and had gone back to work, and then that night later, and when he came back, finally he came back to the home that evening, he had parked all the way up toward the garage."

Bryant gave the investigators permission to search his house, and then went through a timeline of the evening of the murder in greater detail. At 5:30 A.M., Kevin had asked for and had been given permission to again use the rest room. The investigators offered him a food and drink break at that time as well, but Kevin declined. Around this time Investigator Siena learned that stab wounds had been discovered on the victim's body.

Then they talked about Tabby's boyfriend, Richard Oliver. Kevin knew a lot about him. Knew his address. Knew where he worked, what time he got off the night shift, the fact that he had a roommate. Kevin had done his homework when it came to Tabby's boyfriend. Kevin told them about the private investigator he'd hired. He said he'd given his wife an ultimatum: *Him or me? What's it gonna be?* She'd told him not to do that, because he would lose.

Investigator Siena testified, "He explained that there was a digital recording that he had actually made regarding a conversation that they had had, which was to show her demeanor during the conversation. It had been a tape of his wife calling Richard Oliver on his birthday."

Bryant said that when he went into the office during the evenings, he would sometimes return home and find that his wife had left. She would stay out late.

"How did he characterize her drinking when describing these late nights his wife spent away from home?" Winslow inquired.

"At first he said she drank, but not a lot. Later, he described her as 'staying out all night drinking.'"

Winslow asked if Kevin expressed his feelings regarding Tabatha's boyfriend. "He was not happy about it," Siena said. "He had to get up in the morning and take care of his kids."

"Did you ask him whether or not he was aware of anyone who would want to see harm come to Tabatha?"

"Yes, I did. He couldn't think of anyone specifically, although he did bring up a name of someone that he knew that carried guns. He gave the name of Rocky, and he explained that this person who he knew, Rocky, did carry a gun, but to his knowledge, that Rocky had never been to his house."

The investigators had asked if the house appeared ransacked to him, or if he had noticed anything missing. Kevin said no.

Siena said, "I had asked him if he had seen anything else anywhere in the home that was out of the ordinary. He explained he saw a drop of blood on the kitchen floor and he described to me exactly where that was, and at some point I actually gave him a small yellow pad and asked him to draw a diagram for me as to where this drop of blood was located in the kitchen, and he did do that for me."

At 6:35 A.M., they had taken another break, and this time Kevin had used his cell phone. Kevin had another soda. After the break Siena asked Kevin if anyone else lived or had lived in his house. Kevin said, yes, there had been. His wife's brother and his girlfriend.

"Did he describe to you the relationship between his wife and her brother?" Winslow queried.

"Yes, he did," Siena replied. "He explained that it was like any other brother or sister relationship, initially, but then he had gone afterward to say [that] after a period of time of living together, that some bad blood had arisen between the two, and he had actually become very close to Cyril—Kevin had become close to Cyril, and he kind of looked at Cyril like a brother, and he felt that he was closer with Cyril than he was with his own wife. He said he got along with Cassidy Green as well."

"Did he talk about Tabatha's role in the family?"

"He did, as far as children or home life, there were a number of issues that he had actually discussed. With regard to the children, that Tabatha was actually the primary caregiver for the children, and that she provided the emotional support and cuddling, I think is the term he used, for the children, and that, again, she provided the emotional support for the children. He had also mentioned at some point her role in the family, how they pay their bills, things like that."

"Did he tell you that she would take the checks and cash them and have cash on her?"

"He said it wasn't unusual for her to have in excess of five thousand dollars, because she would actually pay the bills."

It went unmentioned that Kevin's statement about the amount of cash Tabby had on hand at any given time did not make much sense. Adults in America tend to pay their bills by check. If, for one reason or another, they did not have a checkbook, they went to the post office and purchased a money order. Who paid their bills in cash?

Investigator Siena then testified that Kevin had said

that Cyril had been over to the house recently, but he did not recall the occasion. He described how both Cyril and Cassy had worked at his office. Cyril actually was taking on the role, somewhat, of a paralegal, and that Cassidy was an office assistant, basically, and that she answered phones, filed paperwork, things like that. Kevin told the men about his wife's two jobs, as secretary in his office and as a teller in the bank.

In the morning, at about 8:40, Kevin and the investigators had taken a breakfast break. They'd gone to the Maplewood Diner, on Lake Avenue. Before entering the diner, they made a quick stop at the grocery store across the street so that Siena could pick up some cold medication.

Over breakfast Kevin told the men about his practice. Kevin said he was a "general practice attorney, handling divorces, some DWI, some criminal work." Kevin bragged that he had worked on a murder case once, but then admitted that this was before he'd actually passed the bar, meaning his role during the murder case was as a paralegal.

Siena testified, "We asked him who he thought might be capable of something like this. He said, 'We are all capable.'" He expounded on the point, stating that anybody could kill, given the right set of circumstances. As an example he cited a burglar who was interrupted by a homeowner.

Siena said that Kevin's demeanor changed when he started talking about the ability to kill. He had increasing trouble making eye contact with his interrogators. He was tapping his fingers on the table.

They'd asked him again if he could think of anyone in particular who might have done this to his wife, and again Rocky was the only name Kevin could come up with, but he added that he couldn't think of anyone who would constitute a "credible threat to my family."

Investigator Siena testified that it was at this point that

he'd discussed the Miranda rights with Kevin. That is, his right to remain silent and the fact that anything he said could be used against him in a court of law. Siena had recited the rights by memory and asked Kevin if he understood. Kevin had said he did.

Investigator Siena then admitted to the court that never before had he recited the Miranda rights to a suspect—and Kevin Bryant officially had become a suspect as far as Siena was concerned when he pointed out that everybody had the capacity to kill if the circumstances were right. Siena admitted that he had gone by the rules and read a prepared Miranda form to every previous suspect.

Siena said, "I told him that he had a right to remain silent. Anything that he said could and would be used against him in a court of law; that he had a right to an attorney and to have him present for any questioning, and certainly that if you [choose] to answer questions now, he could stop answering one at any time."

After the discussion of the Miranda rights, still in the diner, Siena had asked Kevin about the book he had been reading when the attack took place. Siena wanted to know who wrote it, what it was called, what it was about, and how much of it Kevin had read that night before he was interrupted. Kevin had said it was a Tom Clancy novel, but he couldn't remember the title or what it was about. Siena asked if Kevin had checked on the children before he went downstairs and Bryant said he hadn't.

Siena returned the questioning to Tabatha's body. He asked Kevin to describe the wounds. Kevin did. He said that her throat had been open, as if a knife had been used. As he described it, he pounded a clenched fist rhythmically against the diner table. Siena thought the motion resembled a stabbing motion.

"Had you made any mention to him of stab wounds or stabbing of any kind, up to this point?" Winslow asked.

"No, we had not," Siena replied.

"Had he said anything prior to this point about stabbing or stab wounds?"

"He had not, no."

At that point Judge Marks recessed the court for the weekend. She reminded the jurors that the following Monday was the celebration of Columbus Day and was a court holiday. Court would be adjourned on Tuesday morning.

So Joanne Winslow's direct examination of Investigator Siena resumed on Tuesday morning, following the three-day holiday weekend.

"Did the subject of shooting versus stabbing come up?" the assistant district attorney asked.

"Yes, he said he thought the throat wound looked like a stab wound, but he didn't know that much about it and couldn't be sure. After that, I told him that I didn't think he was telling me everything."

"What did he say to that?"

"He said he felt responsible. His hands were shaking. His eyes began to tear. His feet were tapping. He ran his fingers through his hair. I pointed out that he seemed nervous and wondered if that meant he wasn't being totally candid."

"Did you ask him what he meant by 'I feel responsible'?"

"Yes. He said there had been times when he wanted to [be] rid of her. If he couldn't be with her, he wanted her out of his life. He told us that he had filled out the paperwork to file for a divorce, but he had not done it. He began to mutter, 'If I had been a better husband . . .' And, 'If I had slept with her . . .' And 'If I'd let her sleep with my son . . .' I told him he shouldn't beat himself up like that, taking blame for it. We asked him if he could further clarify what he meant and he said, 'Let's just say I'm responsible.' We asked him if he were admitting involvement. He said he was admitting nothing, that he wasn't saying anything. He was very sullen as this was going on, and his eyes were still tearing."

Winslow asked if Siena had asked the defendant about his wife's personality and Siena said that he had. "He explained that Tabatha had the ability to get under someone's skin," Siena said, "that she was the type of person that would pick an argument or pick a fight when it really wasn't warranted. He had preferred to walk away from those types of arguments, but she was the type of person that would get more upset if he didn't argue."

Siena had asked Kevin if anyone had witnessed Tabatha's anger toward him. Kevin said that his parents had. He specifically mentioned the Mendon Ponds argument on July 5 after he had forgotten the diapers.

Siena then asked Kevin for more details on how he had determined that his wife was having an affair. There were the late nights away, and then there were the phone bills, Kevin said. They were huge.

"We asked him if he had killed his wife and he said he had not. We asked him if he thought he was a suspect and he told us that everyone was a suspect. At eleven-twenty A.M., we left the Maplewood Diner and returned to headquarters," Siena said.

During the 911 call with operator Jacqueline Sanabria, Kevin had said that he had heard a car with a loud muffler leaving, and he had assumed that this was the getaway car. They had asked him if he could tell which way the car was going. Kevin had said that he thought the car headed southbound on Five Mile Line Road, but that he could not be sure.

"Did you ask him if he knew anyone who had a car with a loud muffler?" Winslow asked.

"Yes, but he said he couldn't think of anyone who owned a car like that," Siena said. "I asked him if it was routine for him to check to see if the doors were locked before retiring. He said it was, but that he couldn't be sure he had done it the previous night. He explained that after he had found Tabatha dead, that he had found the door from the kitchen into the garage area open, and also the exterior door from the garage into the yard was also open."

The house was uniquely vulnerable at the moment of attack, the investigators noted.

Siena said that Kevin told him he didn't think he got any blood on him during the moments after the attack. Siena then testified that he personally at no time saw any blood on the defendant.

At 12:35 P.M., on July 14, Kevin said that he was again hungry. Siena got the numbers to all of Kevin's phones—home, office, and cell—and then they went to Rubino's Sub Shop on Mount Hope Avenue for lunch. During lunch the men did not discuss the crime.

Instead, the topics lightened. They talked about kids and sports. Bryant ate a ham sandwich. They left the sandwich shop at 1:35 P.M. and returned to headquarters. They left Kevin alone for a time, and when they returned to him, he produced a digital recorder and played for them the recording he had made of Tabatha calling Richard Oliver on his birthday.

Just after 2:30 P.M., the topic turned to Kevin's dad. He said he'd called his dad and he was coming downtown to see him. Siena left Kevin with Vaughn at that point and went out to look for Kevin's dad. He didn't find him and returned.

The recording of Tabatha on the phone with her boyfriend was played yet again. Each time Kevin became more sullen. They again asked him point-blank if he had killed his wife. Kevin had responded that he couldn't answer that. They asked if he couldn't or he wouldn't. Kevin had begun to cry then.

"I told him that we would get to the bottom of it. It would be okay. He said that we better, or he'd 'f-ing' kill me. I say f-ing, but he used the actual term."

As it approached 4:00 P.M., Kevin indicated that he wanted to leave. He asked if he was free to leave.

"I told him he was not," Siena said. "He told us that he knew what we wanted him to say and that he wasn't going to say it. Investigator Vaughn then asked him if he was willing to roll the dice on his life at that point. He said he had to roll the dice." At that point Investigators Siena and Vaughn discontinued the interrogation of Kevin Bryant and he was released.

The subject then switched to Siena's role in the apprehension of Cyril Winebrenner. On July 31, he and Vaughn had traveled to Osceola, Iowa, to talk to Tabatha's half brother. They questioned him there. He confessed to killing Tabatha. They'd had Cyril brought back to Monroe County. The investigators and Cyril, Siena pointed out, had not returned to New York State in the same vehicle. On August 2, Siena had interrogated Cassidy Green, who admitted a peripheral involvement in the crime. Siena again stated that Kevin Bryant never complained of illness, or requested any medicine. He was clearly sober. He never asked for an attorney. That concluded Winslow's direct examination.

After a ten-minute break, Speranza began his cross. In cross-examination Speranza tried to discredit the case's lead detective by finding inconsistencies in his statements over time. The defense attorney spent hours poring over Detective Siena's notebook, reviewing the notes that Siena had taken during Kevin's initial fourteen-hour interrogation—not counting the three hours Kevin had spent standing in the driveway with the sheriff's deputies.

About his note taking, Siena said, "On a break I would fill my notes in, so they were not necessarily always contemporaneous, but at some points they were."

Speranza returned to Kevin's Miranda rights, when he had been "Mirandized," and if he had been "Mirandized properly."

Speranza attempted to show that many of the items that made it into Siena's final reports weren't consistent with what he had in his notebooks. And some statements made during Siena's direct testimony, such as the friendly and cordial demeanor of the defendant during the early hours of the interview, were not supported by his notes. Speranza tried to show that Siena's notes were incomplete and that he made leaps and took statements out of context when compiling his final reports.

None of this changed the fact that Siena had been a very damaging witness to the defense. Kevin Bryant, according to the lead investigator, had appeared on the verge of confession during his initial interrogation, and Speranza's lengthy and snooze-inducing cross-examination did little to alter the effect Siena's direct testimony had on the jury.

CHAPTER 67

Cyril Reneges

On Tuesday, October 12, 2004, Cyril Winebrenner was scheduled to take the stand and testify against Kevin Bryant. However, before this could happen, he rejected the plea agreement he had made with prosecutors and refused to testify.

Prosecutors had offered Winebrenner a sentence of from twenty years to life in exchange for his testimony, but after rejecting the deal, he was scheduled to stand trial in 2005 for first-degree murder.

The original deal had been made with the understanding that the prosecution would seek the death penalty for Winebrenner if he did not agree to cooperate. However, with the New York State Court of Appeals having ruled that the death penalty was unconstitutional—on the grounds that it was "cruel and unusual" punishment—Winebrenner's legal team wanted to hold out for a better deal.

According to the DA, Winebrenner refused the deal because he believed himself to be an unlikely candidate for parole and feared he would serve the complete sentence. He was hoping that a shorter sentence would be offered, or that a shorter sentence would be the result of his trial.

"When he entered into the agreement, there was still a viable death penalty, so at that time, he was sparing himself the death penalty as a potential sentence," Winslow said later. "He felt, given the circumstances of this case and how brutal the killing was, that parole would not allow him to get out anytime close to early in his life."

According to ADA Winslow, to begin with, Winebrenner had not been particularly happy with the agreement. Winebrenner wanted a determinate sentence, meaning that he would get out of prison and that there would be no parole when he got out.

"We flat out told him no, we were not willing to do that," Winslow said. Then Winebrenner said he'd be willing to plead to second-degree murder with a sentence of fifteen years to life.

"Our original deal was the only deal we were willing to go along with," Winslow said. "This was a particularly brutal and vicious murder and he just didn't deserve anything better."

After Winebrenner's stunning change of heart, Winslow was asked by the press how she thought this would affect the case against Kevin Bryant.

"I think our case will be fine. We're probably going to bring this to a jury at the end of the week and we have the testimony of Cassidy Green and other witnesses in the case who support that testimony and other proof which corroborates her testimony. We think we're going to be able to argue to this jury beyond a reasonable doubt that Kevin Bryant is guilty of murder," said Winslow.

According to the law, Speranza argued, his client had the right to confront every witness against him. In this case, however, that right was being denied. Winebrenner's story, he said, had been entered into evidence in large part through the testimony of Cassidy Green. Then Winebrenner himself had refused to testify.

"Cassidy Green testified extensively as to what Cyril Winebrenner allegedly told her and what he allegedly said constituting the elements of the crime, and now Winebrenner is not here for purposes of confrontation," he said.

In addition to losing Winebrenner, the prosecution also decided to drop another witness. They decided not to put Donny Sands, also known as Rocky, on the stand. He was the drug dealer who had turned down Kevin's offer to kill Tabatha for money, but had offered to plant cocaine on Tabatha in order to discredit her in divorce proceedings. It was Rocky who had helped sheriff's investigators find Cyril, and who had worn a wire while setting up Cassidy in a drug deal. Although Rocky had been, along with Jennifer Larch, responsible for breaking the case, prosecutors no longer felt it was necessary for him to testify.

CHAPTER 68

"One in Twenty Quadrillion."

Wednesday, October 13, 2004, was the ninth and final day of prosecution testimony. The first witness to take the stand that morning was a supervisor from Frontier, the local phone company, who testified that phone records corroborated Cassidy Green's testimony that she and Cyril Winebrenner had called Kevin Bryant several times before and after the murder.

Then an expert from the Monroe County crime lab took the stand and testified that DNA from bloodstains taken from Winebrenner's leather jacket and his seat in the getaway car matched Tabatha Bryant's DNA.

"What is the probability that the blood found on the jacket and the car seat could belong to someone other than Tabatha Bryant?" Winslow asked.

The witness replied, "One in twenty quadrillion."

"Thank you. No further questions," Winslow said.

Kevin's legal team had no questions in cross-examination.

The most memorable witness of the day was forensic pathologist and Monroe County medical examiner Dr.

Caroline Dignan, who showed jurors graphic photos of
Tabatha's wounds. Dr. Dignan testified that Tabatha
weighed only ninety-nine pounds at the time of her
death. She said that multiple stab wounds to many of the
victim's internal organs, rather than the gunshot wound
to her face, was the cause of death. She did, however, say
that the gunshot wound was a "significant contributing
factor" to Tabatha's death. Tabatha, the doctor reported,
had been stabbed five times in the neck and twice in the
shoulder. The other seven stab wounds had been in the
torso. Six stab wounds on Tabatha's back were so severe
they pierced her heart and injured her liver and spleen.
Dr. Dignan testified that Tabatha was shot in the right eye.
The .22-caliber bullet broke in two and exited her head
in two places. Based upon gunpowder residue found
around the gunshot wound, the muzzle of the .22 was
held several inches to several feet away from Tabatha's
face when fired, the doctor said. The stab wounds were
mainly in the neck and back. The victim suffered wounds
to two blood vessels to her brain, as well as damage to her
trachea, esophagus, lungs, heart, aorta, liver, spleen,
and stomach.

Prosecutor Joanne Winslow apologized to the jury
for the graphic nature of the day's evidence, but she
explained that it was necessary. "The nature of the
wounds oftentimes we use as part of our argument
there was intent to kill. Certainly the number of those
wounds and where they were and what organs they go
through all go to the issue of intent to kill," Winslow
said. Dr. Dignan was the prosecution's final witness.

After court, defense attorney Lembke told the press
that the defense team was still undecided as to whether
to put Kevin Bryant on the stand in his own defense.
He said they would attempt to introduce evidence
that he was trying to reconcile with his wife at the
time of the murder.

CHAPTER 69

The Defense and Closing Arguments

The case for the defense was like the landmarks of Greenwood, blink and it might be missed. Kevin's legal team not only managed to present their entire case in one day, there was time left over for closing arguments, the charging of the jury, and the beginning of deliberation.

It was Thursday, October 14, 2004. There were a total of four defense witnesses. Two of the defense witnesses were eyewitnesses to the murderers' getaway, claiming that the car was blue. (Cassidy's car was maroon.)

Another witness was the Bryants' minister, who said the couple had put their divorce on hold and were trying to reconcile by making plans to attend a church retreat together. The defense rested.

In closing argument prosecutor Joanne Winslow said there were three people involved in the conspiracy: Bryant, Winebrenner, and Green.

"Cassidy Green did testify that Kevin Bryant asked her whether five thousand dollars would be enough to get rid of his wife's dead body. She took that to Cyril Winebrenner and he told her that it would, but he would have to check out the details—meaning, find a gun," said Winslow. She said that the agreement between Bryant and Winebrenner was implied by Cassidy Green's testimony and was backed up by the testimony of other witnesses.

She added that there were at least two men who said that Bryant tried to hire them to kill his wife.

The prosecution's summation concluded with the playing of the 911 tape, Kevin Bryant calmly reporting his wife's murder. Winslow told the jury that they should focus on five areas of testimony and evidence. One of those areas was the 911 call Kevin made only minutes after the murder.

She said, "Mr. Speranza says Kevin Bryant called nine-one-one immediately after he heard the gunshots. Where's the proof of that? There are two phones in the room, one to the left, one to the right. He didn't have to move, he could have had the phone in his hand dialing. He had fourteen chances while she was being stabbed to call nine-one-one. He didn't do that.

"The point is, he didn't really want there to be help for her. That wasn't the plan. Did he check on his children? No. When he goes into the room where Tabatha Bryant is, does he check on the kids then? No.

"The reason is, he knows they are not going to be hurt. He didn't contract for their death. In the nine-one-one call, he shows not one sign of being upset. Listen to his words, those are the truest things you've got. If the choking sounds are real, that's because of all the blood. There was enough to make him gag. It was more than he bargained for probably.

"A man shows more emotion when he orders pizza

on the telephone than he did," Winslow said. "The jury has to listen to all the evidence and take it in its sum total. All of this supports that there was a conspiracy and, in fact, an agreement.

"'Someone's been shot'? How about, 'My wife needs help. Send an ambulance, police.' Is that the voice of a loving husband who wants to reconcile with his wife? A person shows more emotions when they order pizza over the telephone. Can you feel anything? Nope. Just like that. There's no evidence the Kevin Bryant touched Tabby's chest. Listen to what he says and how he says it. If you listen carefully when he says he took out the trash, you can hear him yawn. He's sitting next to his wife in this bloody, vile mess, and you can hear him yawn. It was no shock. It was what he paid for, what he expected."

Winslow conceded that Cassidy Green lied during her initial statements to police.

"She couldn't tell the police about the money on July thirtieth, because she wanted to go home, and she knew if she told them the truth, she wasn't going home," Winslow said, referring to Green.

Winslow reminded the jury that other witnesses—such as Tim Hunter and Jennifer Larch—had presented evidence that corroborated Cassidy's claim that this had been a murder for hire. Kevin had offered Hill and Larch $5,000 to murder his wife as well, she noted.

She added that the biggest flaw in the defense's theory of the crime was in the phone records. If Cyril had wanted to kill his sister without Kevin's knowledge, he would not have called ahead of time to alert the house that he was coming. And phone records showed that there was a collect call, about a minute long, to the Bryant house from a nearby gas station. If this phone call was not to Kevin from Cyril asking that he unlock the doors to the house so that they could get in, the defendant had failed to give an alternative explanation.

When the prosecutor's closing statement finished, defense attorney Speranza moved that the charges against his client be dropped on the grounds that the prosecution's star witness, Cyril Winebrenner, had refused to testify at the last minute. The judge denied the request.

Speranza, in his three-and-a-half-hour closing statement, did not say whether or not Bryant wanted to testify on his own behalf, but only that it had been the defense team's decision not to let him testify. Speranza told the jury that Winebrenner killed Tabatha on his own, that Winebrenner was a drug addict, and that the crime followed a series of escalating threats that Winebrenner had made to his half sister.

He said that logic was on his client's side: "Would you have hatched this as an alleged murder-for-hire scheme where the person you claim to have wanted to be dead is found in your living room and within minutes of discovery you call nine-one-one? None of it makes sense."

He said that the prosecution had failed to prove within a reasonable doubt that Bryant had entered into an agreement with Winebrenner to kill his wife.

Speranza said, "The evidence (against Bryant) came in through a person (Winebrenner) who did not appear at trial, who was not subject to cross-examination and . . . failed to establish necessary elements of the crime."

The defense said that without Winebrenner's testimony, there was no way really to know what agreement, if any, was made to kill Tabatha. Of course, Speranza had to deal with the testimony of Cassidy Green: "This is a case that rises and falls on the credibility of Cassidy Green," he said.

Speranza added that the woman's claims had no merit and pointed out that there were discrepancies between her testimony and the testimony of others. "Her testimony is extraordinarily inconsistent," he said. "It was self-interested and self-motivated because clearly she's getting a prosecutorial benefit to testify. She gave four or five different sworn statements, all of them different and all of them different from her testimony in court."

Those sworn statements included statements to investigators and grand jury testimony.

He noted that Cassidy had said that the getaway car was pink, while two eyewitnesses had described the car as blue.

"It boils down to Cassidy Green. Do you believe her? Is she consistent in her testimony? Is she worthy of belief?" Speranza asked. "Cassidy Green has no moral compass, bearing, or restraint. When it comes down to the messenger, can you trust her?"

In rebuttal Winslow argued that eyewitnesses might have disagreed about the color of the getaway car, but not about its muffler.

She said, "The car was a loud car by all accounts, including Kevin Bryant's. We certainly know where Tabatha Bryant's blood was found. The car is not an issue."

Tabatha's blood, Winslow noted, was found on Cyril's leather jacket.

Judge Marks gave the jury its instructions. She explained circumstantial evidence and how jurors must treat it.

"Circumstantial evidence," she said, "is evidence that doesn't directly establish guilt but can lead to a reasonable inference of guilt, if it passes a two-part test: One) Is the evidence credible? Two) Do the facts logically compel a conclusion of guilt, despite the absence of direct evidence?"

Marks then explained the three legal rules about circumstantial evidence: 1) jurors must not base an inference of guilt on guess, surmise, or suspicion; 2) circumstantial facts must be consistent with guilt beyond a reasonable doubt and inconsistent with innocence; 3) the facts must exclude every reasonable hypothesis except guilt.

Judge Marks then announced that the jury would be sequestered, which meant they would have to stay nights in a hotel until there was a verdict.

The defense had requested that the jury be allowed to consider a lesser charge, a "compromise" charge, somewhere between not guilty and guilty of first-degree murder. Judge Marks refused to allow this. She decided that the jury would have only two options, guilty of first-degree murder or not guilty. There would be no compromise option, such as guilty of second-degree murder, or guilty of manslaughter. This was because, according to Judge Marks, first-degree murder was the only charge that fit the crime Kevin was accused of committing.

CHAPTER 70

Four and a Half Hours

On Friday, October 15, 2004, the jury needed only four-and-a-half hours of deliberation to find Kevin guilty of first-degree murder. Sentencing was scheduled for October 29.

"We're pleased that the jury evaluated the evidence carefully and found him responsible for a brutal and cowardly killing," District Attorney Michael Green commented.

Kevin's family was outraged. Following the verdict, they continued to publicly stand by his innocence.

"Everyone who knows Kevin knows that violence is not part of his personality," said Matthew Bryant, Kevin's brother.

"That isn't how Kevin deals with his problems," added Kevin's father, Vivian Bryant. The father then added: "As any neutral observer could tell you about this case, there have been serious problems with the way it has been handled. For this reason, we expect a very different verdict for Kevin when this has been appealed."

Bryant's defense said an appeal would be considered.

Regarding his client's reaction to the verdict, Speranza told reporters, "He (Bryant) took it in stride. Obviously, he's disappointed as well."

District Attorney Michael C. Green said his office would ask for the maximum penalty of life imprisonment without parole.

"He (Bryant) doesn't deserve to see the light of day," the DA said, noting that the crimes were made even more heinous by the fact that they were committed while the victim's young children were asleep in the house.

But Kevin's verdict didn't mean an end to court proceedings regarding Tabby's murder. Because he rejected the plea agreement he had made, Cyril Winebrenner was now scheduled to stand trial for Tabatha's murder—and, in exchange for her testimony, Cassidy Green was expected to plead guilty to first-degree manslaughter and, as per her agreement with the prosecution, receive a prison term of fifteen to twenty-five years.

No, it wasn't the end of court activity, but after Kevin's verdict, there was a two-week break.

PART V

CHAPTER 71

Impact Statements

On Friday, October 29, 2004, at Kevin's sentencing hearing, friends and relatives were allowed to read previously prepared impact statements, telling the judge what impact Tabby's death had had on their lives. In theory, the judge was supposed to take these impact statements into consideration when she laid down her sentence, but it was strongly suspected that Judge Marks already had made up her mind on that point.

Samantha Bassett's impact statement was first. She read, "'Honorable Patricia Marks, I wanted to let you know who Tabatha Bryant was to all of our family and me. She was my little sister. All of my cousins looked after us (Tabby and I) as if we were sisters to all of them. Our Grandparents raised us from the time I was three and Tabby was two. Our Aunts and Uncles were like Moms and Dads to us and our cousins were like brothers and sisters. Everyone in our family has been affected by Tabby's death. Tabby loved people. She was always very friendly. A room full of strangers would not stay that way for long. She could go up to someone, introduce herself and within a few minutes they would be friends. She could make friends instantly with anyone. When Tabatha had her children she matured. She loved them completely. They meant everything to her. I lived with her, Kevin and the boys for a month when I was having a bad time in my life. When we went to the store after work we took the boys. Kevin was home and we could have left them with him but Tabby wanted to be with her sons. Even when we could have been done in half the time and we were in a hurry, we always took the boys. Tabby came to Greenwood often. She brought the boys for weekends. Grandma loved Tabby like her own daughter. The boys were grandsons to her. Grandma and Tab liked to dress alike. Grandma looked forward to those weekends. She also liked going to Rochester to see Tabatha and the boys. Tabby was always there for the people she loved. When I was having a rough spot in my life she offered her house open to me. I went and lived with her and watched the boys. When one of my stepsisters (Heidi) was at Strong Memorial with her daughter, Tabby heard about it and went to be with her. Heidi wasn't expecting her and was surprised to see Tabby. When one of my cousins need a change of pace, Tabby was there for her too. Tabby was always there for everyone when they needed her. Every time I wanted to talk, she was there. I miss her every day. For months after her murder, I wanted to call her to talk. Then I would remember that she was gone and I would never be able to talk to, or see her again. I wish I could turn back the clock and do something to change history. That won't happen either. I'm not going to try to explain away her boyfriend or any other "bad acts." She wasn't perfect. No one is. Tabby didn't deserve to be killed. No one does. All I ask is for you to make the best decision you can and for Justice to be served. Thank you, Samantha Bassett.'"

Tabitha's uncle Richard P. Warriner was next. He told the court that he had faith in the American justice system and that he "totally wanted" Kevin to be found guilty. He said his life, and the lives of the families involved, had been "disrupted beyond comprehension" by Tabby's murder. He pointed out that Tabby was a generous person who would comfort the homeless, who used her beautiful singing voice to brighten every occasion. With her gone, he said, there was a hole in the hearts of her family. He said he prayed that time would help heal the wounds felt by the families, and help remove the wedge that Tabatha's murder had driven between the Bassetts and the Bryants.

Warriner concluded, "'May two little boys growing up and learning, as they will, of these tragic events, be able to find hope, love and peace of their own. I want them to be able to trust their families and to be able to trust humanity as a whole.'"

Terry Smith, another of Tabatha's uncles, the minister who had delivered the eulogy at Tabatha's funeral, made an appeal to Kevin to confess to hiring Tabatha's murderers. A confession, Smith pointed out, would help start the healing process for the two families that had been so seriously harmed emotionally by Tabatha's murder.

"'He, and only he, knows if he's guilty,'" Smith told Judge Marks. "'If he'll admit his guilt, he'll release two families from the burden that his silence has caused.'"

ADA Winslow said, "It's easy to say, 'That was Cyril Winebrenner. . . .' But there would be no Cyril Winebrenner, but for the defendant and his starting the ball rolling."

Winslow termed the crime cold, calculated, and despicable. She added: "You can't call it anything else. To know what happened to Tabatha Bryant—how she was killed—and he knew the kids would be sleeping upstairs when this happened."

Judge Marks asked Kevin Bryant if he wanted to make a last statement before the sentence was read.

"I've asserted my innocence and continue to do so," Bryant said. "The verdict and sentence does not change that simple truth."

Referring to the murder, Judge Marks said, "It's probably the worst of the worst." Calling Kevin's actions "a cold, calculated, horrific crime," Judge Marks sentenced Kevin Bryant to life in prison without parole.

Outside the courthouse, after the hearing, Joanne Winslow and her boss, DA Michael C. Green, told reporters that Bryant's sentence was justified.

Moments later, defense attorney Speranza reiterated that he intended to appeal his client's conviction. Speranza said, "He says he's innocent. He grieves for his wife . . . and he's concerned about his two children." The lawyer said that Kevin was looking into getting visiting arrangements with his children.

CHAPTER 72

The Death Card

The friends and family who were frequently in the courtroom when the matter of Tabby's murder was being discussed got to take the month of November off. For a whole month they could go about their normal lives, without hearing about motions and objections and cross-examination.

But then December came and the vacation from Judge Marks's courtroom was over. The judge remained the same, the prosecution team remained the same, but the defendant and the defense team had changed. Now it was Cyril Winebrenner on the hot seat.

During a court appearance on Friday, December 3, 2004, Cyril attempted to plead guilty to first-degree murder. He told the judge that he was willing to accept life in prison without parole in exchange for his plea. But the plea was not accepted by Judge Marks—the same judge who had presided over Kevin Bryant's trial—because the district attorney was seeking the death penalty in this case.

One of Winebrenner's attorneys, Peter J. Pullano,

said, "Our position is there's no bar to his pleading guilty. There's no death penalty in the state of New York. The court of appeals has said that. So our position remains he can enter the plea. It's a (death) notice without teeth. Mr. Winebrenner has the same right to plead guilty as any other criminal defendant in New York."

Following the decision, ADA Joanne Winslow said she wanted to be sure that, once convicted, Winebrenner received the harshest possible sentence.

She said, "The family deserves closure, and we don't want there to be any legal maneuverings that cause us to believe the case is complete and [then] have it come back later and not be complete. The family deserves better."

Judge Marks said that she would reserve a decision.

"I am ordering both parties to submit written arguments by December fifteenth," Judge Marks said.

The judge called the uncertainty surrounding the death penalty statute in New York State "unique" and "challenging," and told the court that she would hear oral arguments on December 17.

"I need briefs in order to make a decision as to whether to accept the plea of guilt," Judge Marks added.

The oral arguments of December 17 never took place, however; they didn't have to. On Thursday, December 16, 2004, the prosecution conceded the point, rendering those oral arguments unnecessary.

For Cyril Winebrenner, the death card came off the table. Prosecutors withdrew their intention to seek the death penalty against Winebrenner in papers filed in the Monroe County Clerk of Court's Office. DA Green said the charge of first-degree murder stood, and, if convicted, Winebrenner would serve a maximum prison term of life without the possibility of parole. The move was a necessity if the prosecution was going to try Winebrenner on schedule.

"We looked at the situation we're in now," Green said outside the courtroom. "The courts have held the statute unconstitutional. The legislature has failed to act on it, and we really don't have a death penalty here."

The state court of appeals had thrown out New York's death penalty, and ruled that defendants charged with first-degree murder can go to trial only if the stiffest penalty they face is life imprisonment.

According to WHEC-TV, Mike Green had hoped the legislature would reinstate the death penalty before this case went to trial. About his decision, Green said, "We want to make sure that we're not back here seven years later, whether he pleads guilty or we have a trial, we want it to be over and done with, and we want to give this family some finality."

Winebrenner previously wanted to plead guilty, but Judge Marks wouldn't accept the plea while the question about the death penalty existed.

One of Winebrenner's lawyers, Peter Pullano, was asked if Winebrenner would still want to plead guilty.

"Obviously, the whole landscape changes," Pullano said. "We basically start from the beginning. We want the opportunity to talk with him. At this point, obviously things change dramatically for Mr. Winebrenner. We've got to talk to him about [what] his options are, when the judge has scheduled a trial. There may be something resolved in the mean time, [or] there may not."

About the matter of Cyril's attempt to plead guilty and the questionable death penalty in New York State, Judge Marks said later, "You can't plead guilty to the death penalty. The plea would have been accepted if Winebrenner had made a deal with the prosecution ahead of time. The plea would have been accepted if

the prosecution had withdrawn the notice seeking
the death penalty. I think, strategically, the reason
they did it was to get the DA to withdraw the death
notice. Not because he necessarily wanted to plead at
that point—although he did ultimately plead. He just
wanted to press the matter as far as the death penalty
was concerned, because of all the cases that had effec-
tively eviscerated the death penalty. Even if a valid
death penalty law was in effect at the time, he still
would not have been allowed to plead guilty, because
you can't plead guilty to death."

On December 30, the appellate division of the New
York State Supreme Court, Fourth Department, voted
to disbar Kevin Bryant and to strike his name from the
"roll of attorneys." Bryant previously had had his license
to practice law suspended, but now it was official—he
was no longer an attorney. The reason was simple:
lawyers are not allowed to be convicted of first-degree
murder.

CHAPTER 73

Cyril's Turn

There had been hints about the details of Cyril Winebrenner's original confession, the thirteen-page statement he had signed after being picked up at his mom's trailer in Osceola. Several times the sheriff's office had made reference to the press of their theory as to what happened on the night of Tabatha's death, and the theory was that Kevin had fired the rifle while Cyril wielded the knife.

That came from Cyril's written statement, which, up until this day, had not been available to the public. A pretrial hearing for Cyril Winebrenner, now twenty-four years old, was held in the Monroe County Hall of Justice. It occurred on Wednesday, February 9, 2005, about a month before Winebrenner's trial was scheduled to start. The hearing was to determine if Cyril's written confession could be introduced into evidence at his upcoming trial.

Joanne Winslow represented the prosecution, while the spokesman for the defense team was Donald M. Thompson. On the bench was Judge Marks. Testifying for the prosecution was Investigator Paul Siena, who had done the bulk of the initial interrogation of both Bryant and Winebrenner. Siena testified that the Monroe County Sheriff's Office was looking for Winebrenner because he had been implicated in Tabatha's murder by his girlfriend, Cassidy A. Green.

Green had told the sheriff's investigators that her boyfriend had left the Rochester area after the crime, and he had returned to the town in Iowa where he had grown up. Investigators quickly located Winebrenner and began to question him about his half sister's murder, which had occurred about two weeks before.

"How was Winebrenner's demeanor when you first started questioning him?" Winslow asked.

"He was friendly and upbeat," Siena replied.

"Did his demeanor stay that way?"

"No, it did not."

"What made it change?"

"I informed him that his girlfriend, Cassidy Green, had been charged in the murder of Tabatha Bryant," Siena said.

"Please tell the court how Winebrenner's demeanor changed when he heard this news."

"His hands were shaking, his lips were quivering, he began to sob, his feet began tapping, and he swallowed very hard when he took a sip of his soda," Siena testified.

Siena went on to say that Winebrenner confessed soon thereafter. Within hours investigators had prepared the thirteen-page statement, and Winebrenner had signed it.

"What was in the statement?" Winslow asked.

"There was a description of the slaying," Siena replied.

The investigator told the court that Winebrenner had also drawn a picture of the knife he had used to stab his half sister fourteen times, until she was dead.

"He also told us where we could find the car he drove in that night," Siena added.

Cyril's statement remained sealed. Cyril had not consulted with a lawyer before he signed it.

The prosecution argued that Winebrenner had "voluntarily waived his right to a lawyer before he talked with investigators."

"Were any threats used to force Winebrenner to sign the statement?" Winslow asked.

"No, there were not."

"Was Winebrenner under the influence of drugs or alcohol when he gave his statement?"

"He didn't appear to be."

In cross-examination Donald Thompson got Siena to admit that Winebrenner had told investigators that he had a severe cocaine habit, until late May or early June 2003, and that the defendant was undergoing withdrawal and was incapable of waiving his right to a lawyer.

Thompson said, "Obviously, if he is in a cocaine withdrawal situation or if he's in a cocaine use situation, that plays into the voluntariness [*sic*] question. How voluntary really are his actions at that point or what's he trying to do so he can go to sleep . . . get away from the police officer or be left alone."

Winslow said, "My position is that the statement was voluntary and therefore should be allowed because that's the issue before the court, whether it was voluntarily given or not."

Judge Marks had the option of allowing some, but not all, of the signed statement into evidence. She announced her decision at the subsequent hearing on Thursday, February 10, 2005. Cyril's thirteen-page statement was released to the public. Stories about the contents of the statement appeared on the local TV news that night, and the next day in the daily newspapers.

The city heard for the first time Cyril's version of what

happened on the night of July 13, 2003: how Kevin had offered him $5,000, plus a portion of Tabatha's life insurance policy, if he killed her; and how Kevin tried to find alternatives to killing Tabatha, none of which worked out. These alternatives included setting her up to get arrested with cocaine and putting pills in her drink so she would test positive for drugs at the hospital. Those plans fell through, however.

Kevin's next scheme, which he first spoke to Cyril about in the beginning of July 2003, was even more drastic: murder. Many newspapers quoted Cyril's comment on Kevin's viciousness: "Kevin said that the situation had gotten out of hand and that something had to be done immediately. If I didn't take care of it, then myself and Cassy would be a liability that he couldn't deal with."

But the part of the statement that received the most publicity was the passage regarding the actual murder. Winebrenner said that he and Cassidy drove to the Bryant home that night with the intention of shooting his half sister to death with the .22-caliber rifle he had brought along. They had to stop and call to make sure the doors were unlocked, he said. Cyril claimed that he entered the house through the sliding glass doors at the back that led to the deck. When Cyril got inside the house and saw Tabby asleep on the pullout sofa in the living room, he discovered that he didn't have the nerve to do it. He wrote about seeing Tabby's face and realizing she was his sister. Kevin was at his side and impatient for Cyril to kill Tabby. Cyril said he couldn't do it, so Kevin grabbed the .22 rifle and shot Tabby in the eye. The gunshot horribly wounded her, but did not kill her. She began to scream, and so Cyril became desperate to take her out of her misery. He grabbed a big butcher knife from a kitchen rack and returned to the living room, where he put the knife's blade into his sister's neck and upper torso so many times he couldn't count.

Cyril had written: "I freaked out. . . . I remember stabbing her in the throat, and how she started rolling around on the bed. I was stabbing her as she rolled and kept going until she stopped moving and stopped screaming."

Cyril's statement maintained that he had little to do with the planning of the murder, which he said Kevin wanted done because he had discovered Tabatha was having an affair. Kevin, according to Cyril, had said that Tabatha was "out of control" in her affair with Richard Oliver, the Parma man she had met at a strip joint. Cyril had written that after the murder, "Kevin stuffed an M & T bank envelope of money in my back pants pocket." When he counted it, Winebrenner wrote, "there was $5,000." Though he admitted that he received $5,000 from Kevin Bryant on the night of the murder, he claimed that it was actually his girlfriend, Cassidy Green, who had been calling the shots.

In the statement Cyril admitted that he understood what he was doing when he stabbed Tabatha: "I want to tell everyone that I am not trying to get out of this or the guilt associated with it. I fully understand the severity of my actions and I'm prepared to take the punishment what ever is deemed fit by my peers."

Within eight hours of the murder, Cyril was fleeing the area, heading back to Iowa.

The written statement disagreed with the testimony of Cassidy Green at Kevin's murder trial in a number of ways. Although both stories agreed that the girl had stayed outside while Cyril went into the Bryant home, Cassidy had testified that, according to Cyril's statement made only a couple of minutes after the murder, it was Cyril who had both shot and stabbed his sister. Kevin, in Cassidy's version of the story, had only come downstairs after the murder was complete in order to give Cyril an envelope full of cash.

Although Judge Marks had released Cyril's written statement to the public, she still had not ruled on whether it could be introduced into evidence by the prosecution at Cyril's trial. Cyril's defense team had argued that the statement should not be allowed in because their client had not waived voluntarily his right to a lawyer before the statement was made.

It was difficult for some onlookers to fathom what Cyril's defense team had in mind. The DA's office originally had offered Cyril leniency in exchange for his testimony against Kevin, and that deal had been accepted originally. However, just days before he was to testify, Cyril had balked and had refused to testify against his brother-in-law. The only explanation was that his lawyers must have believed that they could do better for their client by fighting the charges in court than they could by making a deal with the prosecution. Did they hope to get a jury to acquit Cyril? Did they plan to defend Cyril on the grounds that he was not guilty due to insanity—perhaps because of his "mini-breakdown" and his severe drug addiction?

CHAPTER 74

Mark Hare's Column

On February 15, 2005, Mark Hare, a graduate of St. John Fisher College and the State University at Brockport, had been a local columnist for the *Democrat and Chronicle* since 1997. Before that, he was editorial page editor for the afternoon *Times-Union,* and before that, deputy editorial page editor for the *Democrat and Chronicle.* A native of Owego, Tioga County, he began his career there as a reporter in 1984. He was a high-school teacher for six years before switching to journalism. On the day after Valentine's Day, 2005, Hare wrote a column about Cyril Winebrenner in which he asked the profound question: "What if Cyril Winebrenner had listened to the little voice in his head, walked out the door with the .22-caliber rifle, and drove away with his girlfriend? What if?"

Cyril, in his thirteen-page written statement, had stated that there was a moment when he had the .22-caliber rifle in his hand and he looked down at his sister's face as she slept and he knew he couldn't go through with it.

About that moment, Hare wrote:

> What if, in that moment of awareness, he had made another choice? What if, as the idea of killing his sister stopped him in his tracks, he had decided to make sure she lived?

He could have taken the gun and walked out the door and out of Kevin Bryant's life forever. Better yet, he could have awakened his sister, told her she was in danger, taken her, the Bryants' children and the gun and left Kevin Bryant with his own murderous intentions.

It would not have been easy. There would not have been a truly happy ending. The Bryants' marriage was allegedly in shambles. Winebrenner admits in his statement to using and selling drugs. These were people who apparently had lost their way in life, who were no longer grounded in the kind of relationships that sustain people in times of trouble.

But there are always turning points—like the moment of hesitation Winebrenner describes. There is a voice coming from that reservoir of humanity inside each of us, no matter how we have depleted it with our selfish choices. Listen to that voice. It is calling you back from the edge, back from disaster, and toward a new beginning.

CHAPTER 75

Which Version to Believe?

With the reemergence of Cyril's version of events on the night of Tabatha's murder, a debate developed. Which version to believe? Did Kevin shoot his wife, and then Cyril finished the job with a knife?

Or, did Cyril do the whole job while Kevin remained upstairs, only becoming involved when it came time to hand over the envelope full of money to the hit man? Is the truth a combination of the two scenarios?

Or, is Kevin telling the truth when he says that Cyril killed Tabatha on his own, and that there never was any payoff? He had implied that the $5,000 Cyril took out of the house had been Tabby's money and not his.

Reporter Amy Cavalier opined, "I don't really know what to think about Cyril's testimony, since he could have been high on cocaine when he made it (the defense's argument for not wanting the testimony to be used in court) or trying to reduce his involvement in the murder to save his own neck. I find Kevin's version of the night of the murder hard to believe, but I also find it very odd that the prosecution did not once allude to the fact that

Kevin could have shot the gun, as Cyril says in his testimony, during Kevin Bryant's trial. . . . Was this because they didn't have enough evidence to support that claim, or was it because they know it was a lie on Cyril's part? . . . That's something I don't have the answer to yet. If it were the truth, then I don't see why the defense wouldn't want that testimony to be used in trial to try and prove Cyril had a lesser involvement than he is accused of having, unless it is a lie and could be used against Cyril in court, like the defense used Cassidy Green's multiple versions of what happened in the months and days preceding and following the murder to discredit the accuracy of her testimony in Kevin's trial."

It is Kevin's story that spawns the most skepticism. It defies credibility that a killer could break into a man's home, shoot his wife in the living room, and then, unable to complete the job with the gun, run to the kitchen, find a knife, return to the living room, and stab the victim fourteen times—all while the husband sleepily puts down his Tom Clancy novel and walks hesitantly to the stairs, arriving at the main level only in time to hear the killer's muffler-less peeling out down the road. How long does it take to get from the master bedroom to the living room? One has to believe that if Kevin reacted to the emergency with anything approaching urgency, and had called out to see what was wrong, he would have interacted with the killer in some way.

There, of course, is the possibility that neither the story told by Kevin nor Cyril's tale represents anything closer than approximate truth. Both scenarios present problems.

When Kevin spoke with Cassidy or Cyril during the evening before the murder, he said that Tabatha was asleep on the pullout couch in the living room and that she would be asleep for the night. How could he know this?

How could he know that Tabatha would not wake up and need to go to the bathroom at 11:30 P.M. and then turn on the TV set? How could he know that she would sleep through Cyril jiggling the doorknobs of locked doors? How could he predict that she would sleep through the entry into the living room of a man, carrying a rifle, who would have an argument over her sleeping body about who would pull the trigger?

And here's the toughest question to answer of all. If Richard Oliver is correct that Tabatha called him at 11:15 on the night of the murder—he knows because the call came through his cell phone, which displayed the time when he opened it to answer—and they spoke for two minutes, Tabatha would have hung up only forty-three minutes before Kevin called 911 to report her death. How could Kevin possibly know that she would be back asleep in time for the home invasion and remain docile for her demise?

By 11:15 P.M., Cyril and Cassidy already may have been on their way from Bloomfield to Penfield, assured by Kevin that Tabatha was asleep for the night. It doesn't make sense.

If Kevin had drugged Tabatha so that she wasn't about to wake up, then how could she have talked to her boyfriend when he called her forty-five minutes before the murder?

The other factor that few want to think about is that Cyril, Tabatha, and Kevin were not alone in the house on the night of the murder. There were also two small boys. In one early version of the crime, Kevin said that one of his sons came into the bedroom to say that there was a commotion downstairs.

This is also difficult to imagine: "Dad, I think I heard gunshots downstairs, maybe you should find your bookmark, place it in your book, and go downstairs to see what's up?"

More likely, it was something like, "Dad, someone downstairs is hurting Mom. Why are you just lying there?"

No one wants to consider what those little boys heard or saw that night, but it can't be ruled out that there are witnesses to the crime who, as of yet, have not made public statements—and probably never will.

CHAPTER 76

The Big "Why?"

The other bothersome question is one of motive: the big "Why?" Why did Kevin, Cyril, and Cassidy do what they did? Most of us have a difficult time conceiving of taking a human life under any circumstances. Or, at least, only under the most dire circumstances: self-defense, defense of family, wartime. But murder . . .

What would drive the trio to commit murder? The prosecution in the case against Kevin Bryant told the jury that Kevin wanted his wife dead because he was jealous. But does this jibe with the lifestyle the couple had been living?

Kevin must have lived under an absolute double standard. It was okay for him to cheat on Tabatha whenever he wanted. Paying prostitutes for sex, and having sex parties was part of Kevin's lifestyle.

Maybe he didn't consider this cheating, because there was no romance involved. It wasn't like he had a girlfriend and was taking his affection elsewhere. He had sex with other women, who were professionals, and perhaps, in his own mind, this made all the difference in the world.

Tabatha was cheating on him because she had a boyfriend, a man with whom she went for walks and held hands. When Kevin cheated, it was in his office or in a hotel room, giving lines of cocaine and money to a prostitute, who may or may not have been wearing a leather corset and carrying a riding crop.

The stories from Cyril and Cassidy are consistent on one point. Kevin said that Tabatha had to be "taken care of." Something "had to be done." At one point he might have believed that getting a divorce would solve his problem, but he evidently came to the conclusion that divorce was an inadequate solution to his problems before he had an opportunity to serve the papers.

Kevin and Tabatha had told their minister at the Pittsford Community of Christ Church that they would be willing to go away together on a church trip in an attempt to heal their marriage. Were either of them sincere when they told the man of the cloth their desire to reconcile?

After all, sworn testimony indicates that Kevin was already making plans to kill Tabatha at that point, and the semen on Tabatha's body at the time of her death—which apparently belonged to neither her husband nor her boyfriend—might have been an indication that she, too, was not giving her marriage an opportunity to heal, as she claimed.

Maybe Kevin did feel that he was protecting his family—that is, his boys—when he paid to have their mother killed. Maybe the flaw with his divorce plan was that he feared he would not get custody of the boys. K.C. and Steven, he might have feared, would have gone with his mother, maybe back to Greenwood, or maybe to Parma to live with Tabatha and Richard. Maybe he could not deal with the thought of life without his sons.

But how did Kevin think he would get away with it? If everyone who testified under oath at the trial was telling the truth, then Kevin repeatedly asked members of Monroe County's drug-and-sex underworld if they would accept cash in exchange for bumping off his wife.

Didn't he realize that he was creating witnesses to his intent when he made these offers?

Perhaps he saw members of the underworld as the least likely to talk to law enforcement about anything, not realizing that those same people were vulnerable to police pressure and would sing opera to the members of the sheriff's office the second they were threatened with the consequences of silence.

How could he not see that the people he tried to hire, and the people he eventually hired, were not functioning on an even strain? They were drug addicts, prone toward poor judgment and would be quick to panic.

Some of them—in particular Cyril and Cassidy with their eight-ball-a-day habit—could not think clearly for very long before their preoccupation returned to where and when they were going to snort their next line of coke.

And as it turns out, when someone gets killed, it's not like in the urban myth, all witnesses looking the other way, not wanting to get involved. As it turns out, when someone gets killed, even the underworld is filled with conscience.

It would have taken probably only one squealer, but in this case there turned out to be two. First, Jennifer Larch, and then Rocky. Cassidy and Cyril's mode of deception collapsed quickly enough under the direct gaze of an expert interrogator. Consciences of the underworld most likely had secured Kevin's place in prison forever.

How often will Kevin get to see his children while

behind bars? Not as often as he would like, although he has seen to it that the boys are with his parents and not with the Bassetts.

There is a writer named James Ellroy, who is well-known for his hard-boiled police fiction. But in recent years, he wrote a nonfiction book called *My Dark Places*, in which he traveled with a cold-case squad for a fresh investigation of the murder of his own mother, which occurred when he was a small boy. Although the investigation bore little fruit, Ellroy did learn a lesson. Men kill women, and they don't need a heck of a lot of reason to do so.

Describing the lessons learned by a homicide detective over years on the job, Ellroy wrote: "He learned that men killed with less provocation than women. Men killed because they were drunk, stoned and pissed off. Men killed for money. Men killed because other men made them feel like sissies. Men killed to impress other men. Men killed so they could talk about it. Men killed because they were weak and lazy. Murder sated their lust of the moment and narrowed down their options to a comprehensible few. Men killed women for capitulation. The bitch wouldn't give them head or give them her money. The bitch overcooked the steak. The bitch threw a fit when they traded in her food stamps for dope."

So, maybe troubling over the motive for too long is a waste of time. Hardened homicide detectives will tell you: "It could have been anything."

Would a man who admitted to introducing his wife to group sex sentence her to death because she took a boyfriend? Sure.

Although Kevin Bryant knew that he would not be able to get away with claiming that his marriage was going well—there was the matter of the divorce papers and the private detective, who had tailed his wife and her boyfriend, to consider—Kevin did not want law enforcement to believe that he and Tabatha were in each other's faces screaming their brains out, so loudly that the neighbors noticed, only hours before she was killed. And yet there had been a loud row only hours before Tabby's murder. Had she returned from her last sexual fling only to be confronted angrily by a jealous husband? Was that the final straw? The reason why the deed had to be done right then and there? Kevin had to have realized that that level of hostility overheard by neighbors on the evening of July 13, 2003—so close to the woman's demise—would point a finger of suspicion at him.

CHAPTER 77

Preserving the Psychological Issues

On March 3, 2005, Judge Marks, while talking to an out-of-town writer, gave out strong hints that there was not going to be a Cyril Winebrenner trial. She told the writer, who had planned to attend Cyril's trial, that she had made her decision regarding the suppression of Winebrenner's thirteen-page confession, and that, if she were him, she wouldn't make any travel plans.

The implication was clear: she had ruled that the statement was admissible as evidence and that, as a result, she expected Winebrenner to plead guilty. Asked if the trial was still scheduled to begin on March 7, she said that if there was to be a trial, jury selection would begin on March 7, but opening statements would not occur until March 15 because she had to be out of town for a couple of days. Her decision regarding the admissibility of the statement, she said, would be announced at a court hearing at 3:00 the following afternoon.

So, by midafternoon, Friday, March 4, 2005, all of the parties had gathered in Judge Marks's courtroom in the Monroe County Hall of Justice. Assistant district attorney Joanne Winslow was there representing the prosecution. Winebrenner was there with lawyer Donald Thompson.

Everyone rose as Judge Marks entered the courtroom and took the bench. Judge Marks announced that she had ruled Winebrenner's confession, made to homicide investigators in the hours after his arrest, admissible as evidence. Winebrenner then pleaded guilty to the charge of first-degree murder.

Judge Marks told Winebrenner that despite his guilty plea, she could make no sentence promise and said she reserved the right to impose the maximum penalty of life imprisonment without parole. One of her options was to charge Winebrenner to life in prison without a chance at parole, the same sentence that had been meted out to Kevin Bryant. On the other hand, she could "reward" Winebrenner for pleading guilty and saving the county the cost of a jury trial, by imposing a sentence as low as twenty years to life.

Judge Marks scheduled sentencing for Winebrenner for March 28. Cassidy Green, who already had cut a deal with prosecutors to plead guilty to manslaughter in exchange for her cooperation in the cases of Kevin and Cyril, was scheduled to be sentenced on the same day. While many thought Cyril might receive the maximum sentence allowed, it was expected that Cassidy would receive a sentence of no more than twenty years because of her cooperation.

From the time Winebrenner was led into the courtroom in handcuffs until he was escorted out a guilty man, less than ten minutes had elapsed. He had spoken only to give one-word answers to yes-or-no questions.

After the hearing concluded, defense attorney

Donald M. Thompson implied to the press that family considerations outweighed the inevitability of a conviction when it came to his client's decision to plead guilty.

"Sometimes it's more important not to pursue the legal issues you have to preserve some of the psychological issues," Thompson said. Referring to the fact that Cyril and the victim were half siblings, the lawyer added, "His family's going through it on both sides of the coin. That frankly weighed heavily into his decision. He wanted to spare his family any further pain—which is also the victim's family—so all of that weighed into the decision as to whether to go to trial."

Thompson did acknowledge that Judge Marks's decision to allow Cyril's confession into evidence also influenced their thinking. The attorney added that he intended to ask Judge Marks for leniency, but he did not specify why.

Joanne Winslow told the press that the district attorney's office had done its part in influencing Winebrenner to plead guilty. Winslow said that during her meetings with Winebrenner, she had laid out the damning evidence they had against him.

"It was pretty damaging evidence, yes, and he told us more as well. As you know, he met with us many times in preparation for the Kevin Bryant trial and he made further statements to us and those, too, would have been admissible," Winslow said, adding, "We had a very strong case and I'm confident it would have been the same outcome after trial."

Reporter Amy Cavalier asked Winslow if there had been any reconciliation between the stories told by Kevin Bryant and that told by Cyril Winebrenner as to how Tabatha's murder happened. Bryant said that Winebrenner committed the murder by himself while he was upstairs reading; Winebrenner, however, stated that it was Bryant who had shot his wife just before

Winebrenner had finished her off with a knife taken from the kitchen.

"Winebrenner later admitted he was lying," Winslow said. "What he admitted to us was that it was he who fired the rifle and that he stabbed her and that he simply didn't want to admit everything at the time. He also told us that the gun jammed and that's why he had to stab her, to finish the job."

The assistant district attorney added that the point was moot. The question of whether or not Kevin Bryant fired the gun did not affect in the slightest the fact that he was guilty of murder.

"But for Kevin Bryant, none of this would have happened," she said. "If it wasn't for Kevin Bryant, I doubt that Tabatha Bryant would be dead today."

As for Winebrenner, Winslow saw no reason why Judge Marks should be lenient.

"The evidence showed that he shot her, then stabbed her when she started screaming," Winslow said. "I can't think of anything more horrific."

Cavalier then asked if Winebrenner's plea would alter the deal the prosecution had with Cassidy Green.

"No," Winslow said. "Green will be allowed to enter a plea after Winebrenner is sentenced. Her agreement was that she would testify in any proceedings related to this case. If the only testimony required was in Kevin Bryant's case, then she's met her agreement."

CHAPTER 78

Two Down, One to Go

Only Cassidy Green's case remained unresolved, and the Monroe County justice system wasted no time getting the driver of the getaway car into Judge Marks's courtroom.

Less than a week later, on March 9, 2005, Cassidy and her lawyer, Felix V. Lapine, stood before Judge Marks. ADA Joanne Winslow told Judge Marks that Cassidy had held up her end of the bargain by cooperating with the prosecution, and by truthfully testifying at Kevin's trial.

Winslow noted that Cassidy's testimony at Kevin's trial was particularly important because Cyril Winebrenner, who had previously agreed to cooperate with the prosecution and testify against Kevin, had backed out of his deal at the last second. "She cooperated with us, she met with us on numerous occasions, and she testified at great length in that (Bryant) trial. Essentially, without her testimony, I don't think we would have been able to convict Kevin Bryant for his role in his wife's murder, particularly since Cyril Winebrenner backed out on his agreement to testify," Winslow said.

In addition to providing the gun that was used to shoot Tabatha, driving the getaway car, and helping to stash the murder weapons, Cassidy admitted that it was she who had negotiated the deal with Kevin Bryant to kill Tabby. She pleaded guilty to first-degree manslaughter. According to the deal that had been cut, Cassidy was expected to get fifteen years in prison. Formal sentencing would take place March 30, same day as Cyril's sentencing. Judge Marks scheduled it this way for the sake of the families. Family members only would have to come to court once more.

Cassidy's original agreement with the prosecution had stated that she would receive twenty-five years in prison, but it was expected that Judge Marks would show additional leniency.

Felix Lapine, the defense attorney, said that the leniency in Cassidy's case was warranted. He noted that Cassidy had expressed great remorse regarding her role in Tabatha's death.

"She's at peace with the fact that she's going to have to do fifteen years," Lapine said. "She has cried in front of me about how she could've done this to Mrs. Bryant, who was really a friend of hers for some period of time, and she said that she'll regret it for the rest of her life."

Winslow added after the hearing, "I'm glad for the community's sake and the family's sake that this case is now coming to a conclusion and that there were convictions in the three parties who were responsible. I think it has ended with the best-case scenario. I think it's a win-win for Monroe County. I think in all three cases, we obtained the best results we could. It was a long road, but I think we've come to a good destination."

CHAPTER 79

Speranza Moves On

Speranza may have lost the Bryant case, but his next high-profile murder trial had, from his vantage point, a happier outcome. This case, which had obvious parallels to Tabatha's murder, also involved accusations that one spouse had paid to have the other murdered.

Speranza defended forty-year-old Kimberly L. Warner, an employee at a Gates Wal-Mart, who was accused of conspiring to have her husband murdered. If convicted, she could have been sentenced to twenty-five years to life in prison.

Warner and codefendants David Frazier, thirty-seven years old, and Derrick M. Peace, twenty-three years old, were charged with conspiring to kill Roy Warner after a man allegedly pointed a shotgun at him on July 18, 2004, and pulled the trigger in the driveway of his Scottsville Road home. According to police, the gun didn't fire because the safety was on.

On Friday, February 25, 2005, state supreme court jurors acquitted Kimberly of attempted first-degree murder and second-degree conspiracy. The jury con-

cluded that Warner's alleged five-page confession to
Monroe County sheriff's investigators was involuntar-
ily given.

"In my estimate, they found that her whole alleged
confession and everything about it was irregular,"
Speranza said.

Warner had testified that investigators accused her
of lying, then told her she could go home if she agreed
to incriminate a codefendant and testify against him.
She said the investigators wrote out her statement for
her and she signed it without reading it.

After her acquittal Kimberly said that she hoped to
return to work at Wal-Mart.

The criminal justice system had not been as kind to the
other two defendants in the case: the person who pulled
the trigger and the one who drove the getaway car.

In a separate trial in November, jurors convicted
Frazier of attempted first-degree murder, but acquitted him of conspiracy. They determined he was the
man who tried to shoot Roy Warner with a shotgun.
Frazier was ordered to prison for twenty years to life.

Peace pleaded guilty to third-degree criminal possession of a weapon and was sentenced to seven years in
prison. Peace testified that he drove Frazier to Roy
Warner's home after Frazier told him that Kimberly
Warner, who worked with Frazier, offered to pay $5,000
for Roy Warner's death.

CHAPTER 80

The Final Gavel

Judge Marks made her last appearance on the bench regarding Tabatha Bryant's murder on the afternoon of Wednesday, March 30, 2005. The occasion was the sentencing hearing for Cyril Winebrenner and Cassidy Green.

Sitting among the spectators, who filled the large courtroom, were members of the families of Kevin Bryant, Tabatha Bryant, Cyril Winebrenner, and Cassidy Green.

Also there was Richard Oliver, who had been Tabatha's boyfriend. The families tended to sit in the center section of the spectator area—which was cut into three parts by a pair of aisles—but Richard sat off to one side, away from the others. He was with a female companion.

Judge Marks announced that Virginia Winebrenner, the mother of both Tabatha Bryant and Cyril Winebrenner, had written a letter to her, asking that she show her son mercy. But the letter was not read, a fact that would always make Ginny angry.

Cyril and Tabatha's sister, Samantha, who had at-tended every day of Kevin Bryant's trial, as well as the subsequent hearings for sibling Cyril and Cassidy Green, read a statement. Samantha said, "'Honorable Patricia Marks, Tabatha Bryant was a fun loving, caring, won-derful person who wasn't given a chance to watch her boys grow up, graduate high school, get married or have children of their own. Her two boys will never remem-ber how much she loved them. (More than anything in the world!!) Their girlfriends will never have the joy of having an instant friend in Tabby. She could meet anyone anywhere and be their friend very quickly. I miss being able to have someone to call at eleven-thirty P.M. just to talk. She was always up and usually baking some-thing. She was a good chef. She loved to bake. Her son liked to stand on a stool and watch. "I want to help, Mommy!" When Cyril needed a place to stay, Tabby opened her home up to him and told him that he could stay as long as he needed to. Even though he is our half brother, we didn't know him very well. We had only met him a few times. But it didn't matter to her. She was like a guardian angel. She helped anyone who needed it. Even if what they needed wasn't very prac-tical for her. Because of Cyril I have had to tell every-one in my family that my only sister is gone. That someone broke into her home and attacked her while she slept. Isn't that our worst nightmare? That our own home isn't safe? I have now had to tell my mother twice that one of her children is gone. Chris, our brother, died in a car accident. Now Tabby. I really think that losing a child is the hardest thing to go through, but telling your mom that two are gone ranks right up there. Telling any parent. I also had to call my father and tell him. Cyril knew for a long time that Kevin wanted Tabby gone, he could have at any time went to the police and told them of the plan. So could a lot of other people. But for Cyril, this was his sister that he was planning to kill. Cyril has made a lot of lives nearly unbearable for a long, long time. After almost two years I am just starting to get back to my normal self. I still think of Tabby everyday. I still miss her everyday, but the pain of losing my only sister is almost bearable now. Cyril deserves to spend the rest of his life in jail for what he has done. If he is willing to kill his sister for a lousy five thousand dollars what else is he capable of doing? Please sentence him to life without parole. At least he will have his life. It is a lot more than he was willing to give Tabby. Thank you, Tabatha's sister, Samantha Bassett.'"

Tabatha's uncle the Reverend Terry Smith spoke, telling Judge Marks that in his opinion Cyril Winebrenner did not deserve to see the light of day ever again.

When asked if he had any last statements before his sentence was pronounced, Winebrenner said, "You're going to make the best choice you can, and I accept that." Those who were waiting for an apology from Cyril Winebrenner were disappointed.

Judge Marks began by saying that one of her toughest jobs as a judge was "to tell someone they won't leave jail until they die." She then sentenced twenty-four-year-old Winebrenner to life in prison without the possibility of parole, the same sentence as was received by Kevin Bryant.

Moments later, after a couple of interruptions involving noncustody matters, it was Cassidy Green's turn. Once again, Tabatha's sister Samantha read an impact statement to Judge Marks.

This time she said, "'Honorable Patricia Marks, Tabatha Bryant befriended Cassidy Green when she met Cyril and moved in with Tabby and Kevin and their two boys. Tabby helped Cassidy make a dinner for her parents. Tabby let Cassidy bring her dog even though Tabby preferred cats. She took Cassidy shopping, out to dinners, and on picnics with the family. Cassidy repaid that kindness by helping to kill Tabatha. Cassidy could have at any time went to the police and told of that plan. Cassidy took a very spirited, kind, wonderful person from all of her family. Numerous cousins, aunts, uncles, a nephew, a sister, grandmother, parents and two sons and many, many friends. Her boys won't remember Tabatha. They will only know her from pictures. Tabatha Bryant was a fun loving, caring, wonderful person who wasn't given a chance to watch her boys grow up, graduate high school, get married or have children of their own. Her two boys will never remember how much she loved them. More than anything in the world! I know Cassidy's sentence will be fifteen to twenty-five years for cooperation but my sister didn't get any time at all. Because Cassidy cooperated with Kevin and Cyril, Tabatha is gone. We will never see her bright smile again. No more phone calls to Grandma at eleven-thirty just to talk to her and see how her day was. While I am grateful to Cassidy for testifying against Kevin and being willing to against Cyril, I ask you to give Cassidy the maximum sentence of twenty-five years. Thank you, Samantha Bassett, Tabatha's sister.'"

Cassidy was then asked to give a final statement before her sentencing. Her attorney, Felix Lapine, read a long and emotional message to the court from Cassidy. In the written statement, Cassidy expressed great remorse over her part in Tabatha's death, and over the fact that even though she had had the chance, she had not told Tabatha that there was a plot afoot to kill her. She said that a day did not go by when she didn't think of Tabatha and the two little boys she left behind. She remembered how she and Tabatha had shared makeup and how Tabatha had allowed her to wear her clothes. She said that Tabatha had been a very good friend, a fact that she didn't realize until after Tabatha was gone. Her actual words were that Tabatha was "the truest friend I didn't know about."

"'My days are filled with the face of Tabatha and her legacy of children who are now left motherless and fatherless,'" Lapine read aloud. "'I hope someday they will be able to forgive me.'"

Prosecutor Joanne Winslow then spoke on Cassidy's behalf, describing how she had cooperated with the district attorney's office throughout the process and how, she believed, the prosecution might not have been able to secure a guilty verdict against Kevin Bryant if it had not been for Cassidy Green's testimony.

Tabby's uncle Terry Smith then read a message from Essie Bassett, the grandmother who had raised Tabatha. Essie recalled sitting at Tabatha's dinner table, playing cards and laughing with Cassidy Green. She also recalled the deep sense of betrayal she felt when she learned of the Bloomfield woman's role in her granddaughter's murder: "Cassidy Green is someone who would take from a person one week and take part in their murder the next week," Essie had written.

Judge Marks then imposed a fifteen-year sentence on Cassidy Green. Her sentence came with the condition that, after her sentence was completed, she would be on supervised release.

About forty-five minutes after court had been called to order, Judge Marks pounded her gavel one last time and court was then adjourned. Throughout the legal process, every time a court session ended, Kevin Bryant's family would flee the courthouse.

"It was as if they were afraid the press would chase them, although we never did," one reporter commented.

Tabatha and Cyril's family, on the other hand, seemed more secure, and although not overly friendly with the press, they didn't act afraid of them, either. They generally filed out of the courtroom and the courthouse at a normal pace. On this final day, that pattern continued. In the biggest hurry to leave were the parents of Kevin Bryant, both of whom were barely

five feet tall. They left the courthouse as if fleeing reporters who were in hot pursuit. When Kevin's
mother—who had been known to give reporters the
evil eye and occasionally made growling and other
unintelligible noises at the gathered members of the
media—found her path momentarily and inadver-
tently blocked by a newspaper reporter holding a
notebook, she tried to slap the notebook out of the reporter's hand before pushing past.

One other reporter from one of the local television
stations saw the incident and muttered, "Teach your son
not to murder people, why don't you?"

Outside the courtroom following the sentencing, DA
Michael Green was asked about Cyril Winebrenner's
statement to the court. The DA said, "The telling thing
is not one word of remorse. Never once up there did he
apologize. All he did was blame the prosecutors and
blame the system and I thought that spoke volumes."

One of Winebrenner's attorney's, Peter Pullano,
came to Cyril's defense when it came to his apparent
lack of remorse. "My client's comments were very
much in the moment. Apologies are really something
for another day," Pullano said.

ADA Winslow said, "This is the most vicious, cold-
blooded, and calculated murder I've seen in my eight-
een-year career. Winebrenner's actions were driven by
greed and selfishness. He could have spared the family
all of this pain by turning Kevin Bryant in to the authorities. Certainly the facts here are what movies are
made of. It's just unfathomable what occurred here."

About the letter Ginny Winebrenner had written to
Judge Marks, Cyril's attorney Don Thompson said,
"It's obviously a letter of someone who's terribly torn.
She certainly grieves the loss of a daughter, yet holds
out for the redemption of a son, and expressed that to
the court."

Green's attorney, Felix Lapine, told the press that

because of his client's sincere remorse regarding her part in Tabatha's murder, and her complete cooperation with the prosecution of Kevin and Cyril, the fifteen-year sentence she received was too harsh.

Speaking to another reporter, Cyril's attorney Peter Pullano said, "We spoke as advocates asking for a sentence that showed some hope, some hope for redemption, some hope for reconciliation. Certainly the prosecution had the position that there should be no such sentence."

There would be no hope for redemption for Cyril. During Cyril's last statement to the court, he seemed, as he had for most of the time since his arrest, resigned to his fate—but he had never seemed contrite.

About Cyril's lack of remorse, Winslow said, "Isn't it interesting how he deflects any responsibility from himself to anyone else in the courtroom? Saying that I have an emotional attachment, or in the end even saying to the judge, 'It'll be in your best judgment, whatever happens here.' The manner in which Tabatha was killed, the gun jamming, running to get a knife, stabbing her fourteen times, causing the injuries I described in there (court), it's unfathomable. It's nothing I've seen before. And did you ever hear him accept responsibility or say he was sorry? No. No, he didn't." And, because of that, no "hope for reconciliation" was warranted.

Samantha Bassett was relieved. Tabatha's older sister, who had turned thirty just ten days before, was still living in the Southern Tier of New York State. She had been at every day of Kevin's trial, every court hearing dealing with the murder of her sister.

"I sat with my uncles," Samantha said. "I knew Kevin was guilty. I knew. My uncles wanted to go to hear what was going on so they could be convinced, but I already knew. I think they thought he was guilty, but they wanted to know without a doubt, just because of the connection between the families. It's just not something that we ever thought he would do, you know?"

Although Samantha had her own place, she still frequently stayed with Essie, her grandmother, whom she called Gram. As the sentencing hearing was held, Sam was just finishing up one job as a deli clerk and cashier at a convenience store, and was searching for another—which would turn out to be as a teller at a credit union.

"The hearing was tough," Samantha said several days after that final hearing. "Not so much because of the public, but because of the situation. Asking for life for your own brother isn't fun. None of this has been fun, as I'm sure you can imagine to some extent. I'm glad that that whole court part is over."

If she had her druthers, what would she want her baby sister's legacy to be?

"She loved her boys and she would do anything for them," Samantha said.

Though Kevin's parents still had custody of the Bryant boys, Kevin and Tabby's sons were still allowed to spend a weekend regularly with their aunt and great-grandmother, Samantha and Essie.

Ginny Winebrenner, the woman who had to grieve both over a murdered daughter and a murderer son, said, "We are still having a hard time dealing. I love all my children and it's hard for a lot of people to understand that. Sometimes it's hard for me, too. But I'm a mom and can't forget that they all are mine—or stop loving them. There are days when I blame Cyril for all of this, sure. There are days when I want to walk right up to him and punch him. To say, 'What is *wrong* with you?' And then there are other times when I want to hold him and tell him, 'It's okay, honey, it'll be all right.'"

She says she still can't believe that Cyril was so heavily involved in drugs at the time of the murder: "That part came as a complete shock to me. That one threw me. I am a confirmed hater of drugs, and so is my husband. We would kick kids out of our house for carrying pot in. And they knew it," Ginny said.

During the last weeks of her life, Tabby told her mother on the phone that she was worried about Cyril.

"She wouldn't tell me why, she would just say that he was in over his head," Ginny recalled.

"I wanted to go to Kevin's trial. According to Sammy, it was a good thing I wasn't there, but I wanted to go. I wanted to be there for Tabby and I wanted to be there for Sammy and I wanted to be there for Cyril. I would have wanted to be there for all of my children, both the ones who were there and the ones who were gone. But my question is, if I had gone, where would I sit?"

Ginny had heard her court news secondhand—from daughter Sam, who told her that she had had a statement read in court, but she didn't give her mother details on what she said. Cyril was her mother's son, and Sam had said harsh things. The news that really angered Ginny, though, was that one of her cousins from Minnesota, she had a lot of them, had written a statement for the court that called for no mercy for Cyril.

"I was mad because she didn't know them. She never even met Tabby until Chris died and she met her at the funeral," Ginny said, clearly agitated at the memory. "I know that Sammy had an impact statement read at the sentencing. But I haven't seen it. Cyril said he didn't want me to see it, because he didn't want to cause problems between me and Sammy. That's not an issue. Sammy and I don't have a problem. We just won't discuss it. We're not going to let it tear us apart."

Because of her unique position in the case, Ginny had been left out of the loop systematically.

"The first time I talked to Cyril's lawyer was three days before Cyril's sentencing," Ginny said. "Somebody who had called me about Cyril had asked me if I was going to write an impact statement. I said that I hadn't been asked to. An impact statement would have been my statement about how all of this affected me. I wrote the statement sort of, but I don't know if it communicated how I feel. I can't explain to someone else how I feel when I don't know.

"No one ever talked to me. The only one I talked to was Donna, that was Cyril's lawyer's secretary. I would call to find out how Cyril was doing. And all she could tell me was, yeah, he was fine, he was okay. She couldn't tell me anything about the case. She couldn't tell me anything that hadn't already been put out in the newspaper.

"I couldn't get any information at all. The DA wouldn't answer my calls. Somebody told me to call Victim's Advocate to get a copy of the transcript of the trial. They told me they couldn't help me, because Cyril was my son. Even though Tabby was my daughter, they couldn't help me because Cyril was my son. The DA couldn't talk to me because Cyril is my son. Cyril's lawyer couldn't talk to me because Tabby's my daughter. I haven't seen a copy of the coroner's report. Cyril said he wasn't ready, and then when he was ready, he decided he wasn't ready for me to see it. The only person who talked to me was Cyril's counselor, who was named Noreen. She talked to me a couple of times and she came up here to visit. And Cyril's lawyer's investigator talked to me."

Ginny still held out hope for Cyril's innocence. She said, "There will be people who will wonder, how did I raise a murderer? And to them, I say, I didn't. Cyril was not a violent child, he had no criminal past. He was a computer geek.

"(Investigator) Siena told me that some of Kevin's clients were, and I quote, lawyers, drug dealers, white-collar criminals, higher-ups, and it would affect a lot of people and a lot of people would not be happy campers if that information came out.

"Cyril was apparently terrified that they were going to come after us. What it was all about or who it was, I don't know, but Cyril was really scared for us. I have no idea what actually went on because he *wouldn't* tell me, he *couldn't* tell me.

"Cyril told me once, sometime during the first year after he was arrested, that he could never tell me what had happened or why until he was out of prison. Until then, he said, he couldn't tell.

"He said he was going to admit to things he didn't do. He said he had to, to keep us safe. That was all he ever told me. That leaves a lot of open territory. Whether it was true, or if he just didn't want to admit it to me, I don't know," Ginny said.

How was Ginny's father taking the bad news? His dementia had grown worse, even since Chris's funeral.

"Well, my dad doesn't know about Tabby," Ginny said, speaking of her father, who needed to be hospitalized in the spring of 2005. "He wouldn't remember who she was anyway. He doesn't remember who I am, from week to week sometimes. We figured it was easier not to tell him. It was kind of a family decision."

Ginny still got to see her daughter-in-law and grandson regularly. "Patty and 'Little One' live here in Minnesota," Ginny said. "When we go down to visit my family, which is about two-and-a-half hours away, we stop in and see them."

About learning details of her daughter's violent death—Ginny was in no hurry to be informed.

"Cyril said he was going to send me the coroner's report," she related. "He didn't think I should see it, but I said I wanted to, and he's pretty good about getting me what I want. He just doesn't want me to read it right away. He said, 'Take your time, when you're ready.' And he's probably right because I'm still trying to deal."

Referring to her son, Ginny said, "I talked to him the other day. They are moving him, finally. From the Monroe County Jail to some transfer place where they go while they get them ready to go where they are going.

"Cyril is quite a character. It's very difficult to keep in one mind the thoughts of the child I raised. It's like two different people he has become. It amazes me. When I talk to him now (in jail), he is still the child I raised. He is the same. Don't worry about him. He'll be okay.

"A parent is supposed to be there to protect their kids and sometimes I feel like I've failed all the way around," Ginny said.

A common truth among murders: they terrify the survivors. Those who lived near the crime scene, who knew the victim, or the murderer, or even who passed by the place "where it happened" every day, they get scared. If the killer is on the loose, the terror is palpable. Trees on front lawns that might be potential hiding places for intruders are cut down. New locks are purchased, security systems installed. Even after the alleged perpetrators are apprehended, the fear does not go away completely, especially for those who were close to the victim or the murderer. If it happened once, it could happen again.

A certain power—almost magical, occasionally practical but swollen with hyperbole—is bestowed upon those convicted of murder. The terrified survivors—who could be termed victims of the crime, of a sort—feel that their lives are no longer as safe as they were before, because they have crossed paths with evil. The intimacy of those encounters, of course, widely vary. Despite the fact that that evil now squats in a cage, its power—or so the fearful would believe—emanates and affects those on the outside. Though it is hard to imagine Kevin Bryant as a Charlie Manson type—a man who has an army of ragtag believers on the outside who will continue committing violent crimes at his whim despite his absence— there is evidence that Kevin's method of operation was to recruit those who had little to lose to carry out his dirty work for him. Still, from the evidence we have, it is hard to think of any Kevin henchmen still free and active on the outside. Even if they did exist, it is hard to imagine them being an effective lot. Kevin does hold a certain amount of power over Tabby's family, however, because through his parents he maintains an element of control over his sons' lives. There are family members who don't want to talk about Kevin because they want to see the boys, and they are afraid he will take that privilege away if they do anything to upset him.

Uncle Terry, the minister who lived in Ohio and who had delivered Tabby's eulogy, noted that Tabatha's murder, the arrest of Cyril and Kevin, and the conviction of Kevin for first-degree murder have affected the families in ways that might not be immediately apparent to outsiders.

Terry said: "Tabatha's family and Kevin's family have been good friends for half a century, and Kevin's family remains convinced of his innocence. Because many in our family do not agree, this has caused difficulty and threatens to compromise our families' shared involvement with Tabatha's two little boys, whom Kevin's parents keep now, not to mention those old friendships."

William R. Shero, Kevin's lawyer buddy and former housemate who hadn't gotten along with Tabby, said, "I didn't know anything until I read in the paper what happened. His father called me. There were a few cases outstanding, a few cases we were still working on together. I couldn't deal with it, I really couldn't. I mean, I should have gone to see him in court. We were pretty close, but I just lost touch."

Shero said that he was cooperating with this book because he didn't want history to remember Kevin as just a murderer.

"I want the story to reflect the fact that Kevin was a good guy. I don't know what it is, but people do not want to acknowledge that men and women can be good and bad. There are good men and bad men. There are good women and bad women. Generally, society is quick to condemn the bad man and send him to jail. But the bitch, they don't want to know that. They don't want to know that a woman can cause misery, too. They kill men and they kill children. They kill their own children. It's bad. It's bad news. I don't understand. I guess it is because they are mothers. Mama, mama, mama. I don't understand why they can't just say, 'Well, the guy got screwed.' You know what I mean? I'm not saying that Kevin should have reacted in the way he did, but you react in proportion to the provocation. Kevin was a good guy, smiling, with the glasses on, like a kid—and then a serpent comes around. I want to make it clear that Kevin was a nice guy, but he was provoked to the point where he could not, he could not handle it. So he said, 'What the hell, I've got to get rid of her.' That wasn't the first case in history."

In April 2005, a few weeks after Cyril's sentencing, his aunt Becky—Rebecca Hentges, wife of Ginny Winebrenner's brother Jerry—wrote this author saying that she and Jerry had not known Tabby as a child, but had gotten to know her after she grew up. They knew Cyril better than they had Tabby, she explained. She then warned that there were members of Ginny's family who, although they didn't know Tabby or Cyril well, seemed eager to make their opinions known.

"Please don't let anyone convince you that Cyril is all bad," Becky wrote. "Believe it or not, he isn't. Jerry and I weren't sure what to believe. It's not something we've ever had to deal with, but we sure didn't feel we needed to add to Ginny's pain with words."

Later, Samantha gave her opinion as to what had occurred and why. "I think that Tabby knew enough about Kevin's lifestyle, stuff that his family didn't know, that he couldn't go through a divorce because all of that would come out in a custody battle. He told her that she wouldn't ever get the boys if they divorced and you can bet that she would have fought that with everything that she had. She loved those boys and would do anything to keep them. She didn't always make the best decisions, but I think that she did the best she could. She always felt abandoned by Mom and Dad and she wouldn't want her boys to feel that way. I don't think that her reaction was to boredom. She never stopped. She was always doing something. Baking at midnight, for example. She found some e-mails on Kevin's computer and found out that he had been cheating on her. I think that she lost all respect she had for him and wanted to pay him back. She wasn't happy in the marriage and, most of all, she wasn't loved. She turned to someone, anyone, who would love her. Even though that person may not have been the best at the time. It was an abusive relationship, but I think that the worst thing he could have done to her was to stop loving and respecting her. He demoralized her," Sam said.

Then she sang Judge Marks's praises: "Judge Marks did an awesome job. Everything was kept fair, as far as

I could see. She was real respectful to us. Everyone that we met that worked on the case was great."

Speaking of Judge Marks, in 2005, she found time, despite a full schedule of tough cases, to travel to Russia. "It was very exciting," Judge Marks said. "I was part of a Rule of Law group that did presentations and made exchanges. It was a lot of fun."

Today, Kevin C. Bryant is New York State Department of Correctional Services Dept. Identification Number (DIN) O4B3003. Beginning November 3, 2004, he was incarcerated in Elmira Correctional Facility.

In a letter dated February 22, 2005, Kevin's father acknowledged that Kevin had received this author's request for an interview and that Kevin was unable to respond personally because of illness. He explained that he believed his son to be innocent and would not be able to comment on anything until the conclusion of the appeal process.

"Thank you for your interest in this case. Sincerely yours, Vivian M. Bryant, Jr.", the letter concluded.

Kevin Bryant suffered a heart attack and a stroke after his conviction. He is currently serving his sentence in a prison hospital bed, paralyzed on one side.

Tabatha's friends at the M & T Bank in Perinton, New York, where she worked, have set up a fund to help the Bryants' children. Contributions are welcome.

Afterword

I became interested in crime in the mid-1960s when I was a kid and the teenage girl who lived two houses away was murdered, along with her friend who lived down the road a spell. I grew up in a rural section of Monroe County, south of Rochester, New York.

The girls were last seen on a hot June evening, the first Saturday of summer vacation, swimming in a creek near a trestle just beyond our back field. When the girls didn't come home, the assumption was that they had run away.

Not to be unkind, but these were not the two girls with the best reputations. When their bodies were found a month later, a mile or two down the road hidden in some bushes, victims of multiple stab wounds, the community was shocked, kids and their parents were terrified that the boogeyman had visited, but in the newspapers the story went away fairly quickly. It was assumed that the girls' lifestyle was a contributing factor to their demise.

Both law enforcement and the neighborhood came to the conclusion that a local man had committed the crime. When that man died soon thereafter in a car accident, many felt justice had been served. Today, many of the people who reside in that neighborhood have no idea that the murders occurred.

I grew up to be a book writer. Among others, I wrote a book about the assassination of President Kennedy, and another about the history of baseball parks dating back to the Civil War. It got to be the 1990s and I thought about writing a book about the murders that shook my world thirty years before. They had changed my life and the lives of others around me. Before the girls disappeared, the back fields were crisscrossed with paths made by barefoot kids playing games, taking shortcuts, building forts, etc. After the murders those paths grew over as kids were forced to stay closer to home.

I quickly learned that it is very difficult to investigate a crime that is technically open, and it is even harder to publish a book about such a crime. The police won't give out information if a case is not solved, and publishers, with rare exceptions, do not like to publish books about crimes unless the culprits are caught, convicted, and behind bars.

With the help of a few retired sheriff's deputies who had worked the case, I learned enough to realize that the local man probably had not committed the crimes. The murders were not just a matter of overkill—they were the work of a killer who had stabbed the teenagers playfully, getting his kicks. The killings were ritualistic, fetishistic, and very individual in their MO. The killer had left, with his method, a so-called signature. I came to the conclusion that they had been the work of someone who killed for fun, probably a serial killer, who had committed other similar crimes.

Were the murders the result of satanic activity? For a time I thought there might be significance in the fact that the crime took place in June 1966, which numerically abbreviated would be 6/66—Sign of the Beast.

I began to read every true crime I could get my hands on. I learned that Kenneth Bianchi, one of the "Hillside Stranglers," had lived in the town of Gates at the time of the 6/66 murders. However, he was probably too young at the time, and was a better suspect for Rochester's "Alphabet Murders," which occurred during the 1970s. I also learned that Bianchi and I had once attended the same school at the same time. He had been in fifth grade while I was in kindergarten at Holy Family School in the Dutchtown section of

Rochester. I hadn't known him, and though the info
gave me a quick chill, it didn't help my research.

After years of reading, I found my man, a convicted
serial killer. At the time of the crimes near my house,
he had been driving around upstate New York in a
pickup truck looking for places to fish.

In his later crimes, he had abducted his victims—
some children, some adults—near fishing spots. Following his arrest, he had described committing a crime
that greatly resembled the killing of the Monroe
County teenagers during the 1960s, but he changed the
time and location. In fact, those who had looked into
the details of his scenario had come to the conclusion
that it had never occurred. In some of his known
crimes, the signature was identical to the one I was looking for.

I contacted the Monroe County Sheriff's Office regarding my suspicion. A team of interrogators was
sent to the maximum-security prison where the man
was spending the rest of his life. Confronted with questions regarding the murder of my neighbor and her
friend, the killer neither confirmed nor denied his
guilt. He clenched his fists and placed his chin on his
chest. It was the same reaction, I was told, that the serial
killer had whenever interrogators mentioned his
mother. The question confronted the killer's delu-
sion that those crimes actually had occurred a year or
so later in his life, during the savagery of jungle war-
fare.

That was as far as it went. These weren't just cold
cases—they were icy cold cases, more than thirty years
old. Since there was no confession, and the man was
already in prison for the rest of his life, there was no
urgency to pursue the matter. The case remained
every bit as open as it had been when I first started looking into it.

Publishers were no more interested than they had

been before, but I was happy. I had, at least in my own mind, solved the mystery. But before I gave up the book deal, I had pestered many editors around New York's publishing community. Enough, apparently, to make an impression. Rochester. Murder. Michael Benson. When news of Tabatha Bryant's murder made the New York papers, I got a phone call.

Although both involved knifework, Tabatha's murder was dissimilar to the murders that had haunted me as a child. "The 6/66 Murders" (as my book also would have been called, had it been written) were cold-blooded, the result of an indifferent pervert at play. Tabby's killing was domestic, a crime of passion. It is doubtful that Kevin, Cyril, and Cassidy found anything about Tabatha's murder "fun."

The lone similarity was the attempt by some to relate the victim's reputation to her fate. And now, as then, I'm having none of it. Tabatha Bryant may not have been a perfect wife, but—as she slept or otherwise lay helpless on the living-room fold-out couch at 2 Pennicott Circle—she, all ninety-nine pounds of her, presented no immediate threat to the well-being of her killers.

She no more deserved what she got than she would have if her reputation were as pure as the driven snow, which, during the long winters, blows so plentifully across Penfield golf courses.